WITHDRAWN

THE ART OF THE *Lyrical Ballads*

THE ART OF THE
Lyrical Ballads

STEPHEN MAXFIELD PARRISH

Harvard University Press

Cambridge, Massachusetts

1973

Publication of this book has been aided by
a grant from the Hyder Edward Rollins Fund

Library of Congress Catalog Number 72–90646
SBN 674–04810–5

Printed in the United States of America

To Maddy and Anne

Preface

The two poets who inaugurated a poetic revolution in the *Lyrical Ballads* of 1798 and 1800 left differing accounts of their intentions. Wordsworth, who spoke first, announced the poems at their publication as "experiments" testing how well the "language of conversation" could serve as a language of poetry. Two years later he sharpened his terms somewhat and went on to state the purpose of the experiments in phrases that have echoed ever since: to trace in incidents of common life "the primary laws of our nature: chiefly as far as regards the manner in which we associate ideas in a state of excitement."

Coleridge never confirmed this focus on psychology. When he set down his own account he defined not a single but a dual purpose, growing out of "the two cardinal points of poetry" that he and Wordsworth had been talking about in 1797. There were to be two sorts of poems. His own were to feature "persons and characters supernatural, or at least romantic," and their aim (again in phrases that have scarcely ceased to echo) was "to transfer from our inward nature a human interest and a semblance of truth sufficient to procure for these shadows of imagination that willing suspension of disbelief for the moment, which constitutes poetic faith." Wordsworth's poems were to center on common life, "and to excite a feeling analogous to the supernatural, by awakening the mind's attention from the lethargy of custom, and directing it to the loveliness and the wonders of the world before us."

Wordsworth, for his part, never confirmed this dual purpose. Years afterward he spoke about the origins of "The Ancient Mariner," which he and Coleridge had undertaken to write together to be sold to a magazine. He added, in plain words that undercut his partner's eloquence, that the volume they subsequently planned was to be made up of "Poems chiefly on natural subjects taken from common life, but looked at, as much as might be, through an imaginative medium."

Both accounts made the *Lyrical Ballads* seem more planned, more formal in design and strategy, than they actually were. The truth is that they were rooted more in conflict than in harmony. The two poets shared many enthusiasms and dislikes, but their attempt at collaboration in 1797 brought out sharp differences of view between them. Out of these differences arose the experimental poems and the critical, sometimes polemical, essays that accompanied and followed them. Some of these poems appeared in the several editions of *Lyrical Ballads*, some did not. They cover a space of more than ten years, from "The Three Graves" of 1797 to "The White Doe" of 1807 and 1808 (roughly the span of Wordsworth's great decade). The critical disagreements that ran through these years reached a summing up in Coleridge's *Biographia Literaria* in 1817, where besides defining the dual purpose of the volumes, Coleridge pronounced Wordsworth's experiments—which "in a comparatively small number of poems he chose to try"—a failure.

I have not tried to give a full account of these years of partnership and controversy. I have wanted mainly to understand Wordsworth's share in them, because Wordsworth was from the start the major partner, the bolder and more interesting experimenter, the more formidable poet. No one could wish to reduce Coleridge's achievement in the *Biographia*, which contains some of the most brilliant criticism ever written. At the same time we have to place in context his appraisals of Wordsworth. One of the wisest of an older generation of Wordsworthians, George McLean Harper, put the matter pungently in 1916: "As between Wordsworth and Coleridge, it is important to note that the former, though a stiffer and more practical nature, was the innovator, the iconoclast, the radical, both in theory and in practice; while the latter, a dreamer, a person reckoned irresponsible, was full of hampering misgivings and retrospective qualifications. He stood aghast at Wordsworth's audacity, and thought him ruthless," (Harper's remark can be found in his biography, *William Wordsworth*, 2 vols. [New York: Charles Scribner's Sons, 1916], II, 46). Another older critic, his dogmatic wisdom now rather out of fashion, talked perceptively to the same point. Irving Babbitt used to declare that in the first volume of the *Biographia*, that is, in Chapters I to XIII, Coleridge showed himself, as he developed his theories of the imagination, to be a follower of Schelling. But in the second volume, which Coleridge later pronounced one of his best achievements, he was, Babbitt went on, "an enlightened Aristotelian, criticizing Wordsworth's theory and practice by reference to the universality demanded of art, and to the doctrines of decorum and probability" (Babbitt's unpublished remarks were quoted by Thomas M. Raysor in *Coleridge's Shakespearean Criticism*, 2 vols. [Cambridge, Mass.: Harvard University Press, 1930], II, 326n).

In freshly analyzing Wordsworth's poetic intentions, I have had to deal with the prevailing commonplaces about *Lyrical Ballads*. Some clearly deserve acceptance, others need to be qualified or refuted. Against the notion that *Lyrical Ballads* represented a triumph of Nature over Art, it seemed important to focus, first, on Wordsworth's conscious artistry, his tireless commitment to the poet's craft, and to emphasize that his poetic theory was not so much "expressive" as "rhetorical." Second, it seemed important to bring out the meaning and the consequences of his partnership with Coleridge, which looks in long perspective hardly more fruitful than destructive for them both.

The newest notion about *Lyrical Ballads* is one of the most challenging. It is the notion that these poems were not after all original, but simply developed poetic modes widely prevalent in the 1790's. This notion sets aside—or ignores—a number of contemporary opinions. Wordsworth himself seemed to think his poems original, both when he discriminated them from "the popular Poetry of the day" in 1800 and when he reflected in 1815 how much they had altered English poetry and English taste. Coleridge thought some of them rather too original. Reviewers complained of their differences from poems they had learned to like. De Quincey called their publication "the greatest event in the unfolding of my own mind," finding in them "an absolute revelation of untrodden worlds, teeming with power and beauty, as yet unsuspected among men." Hazlitt felt in them Wordsworth's characteristic "power and pathos" and got "the sense of a new style, and a new spirit in poetry," like "the turning up of the fresh soil, or the first welcome breath of spring."

Yet this notion has enough truth in it to require a special kind of refutation. I have tried to counter it by tracing the literary antecedents of Wordsworth's most experimental poems (mainly to Bürger in Germany, to Burns in Britain) and by showing how Wordsworth moved away from them in original directions. His intention was not simply to experiment with the language of poetry or the psychology of passion. It was, beyond this, to work in experimental forms that were distinctive in several important respects: some were marked by heightened metrical patterns, some by a jocular, mock-heroic, almost comic manner; some were innovations in dramatic method; some were Wordsworth's versions of pastoral; some were designed to reduce the role of story or event in narrative, in favor of passion or feeling—to internalize the action. Each of these distinctive experiments reveals a central intention of *Lyrical Ballads*.

Several essays in this book have appeared separately, and I am grateful for permission to print them here, revised, expanded, and reintegrated. Part of Chapter 1 was published as "Wordsworth and Coleridge on Meter," *JEGP*, 59 (January 1960) 41–49; reprinted by permission of the University of Illinois Press. Parts of Chapters 1 and 2 were read at a convention of the Modern Language Association of America in 1965 as "Poetry and Philosophy in Wordsworth." Part of Chapter 3 appeared as " 'The Thorn': Wordsworth's Dramatic Monologue," *ELH*, 24 (June 1957), 153–163; © The Johns Hopkins Press and reprinted by their permission. Part of Chapters 3 and 4 made up two articles in *PMLA*, "The Wordsworth-Coleridge Controversy," 73 (September 1958), 367–374, and "Dramatic

Technique in the *Lyrical Ballads*," 74 (March 1959), 85–97; reprinted by permission of the Modern Language Association of America. Part of Chapter 5 was read at the 1963 MLA convention and later printed as "*Michael* and the Pastoral Ballad," Chapter 4 in *Bicentenary Wordsworth Studies in Memory of John Alban Finch*, edited by Jonathan Wordsworth (Ithaca: Cornell University Press, 1970); copyright © 1970 by Cornell University and used by permission of Cornell University Press. Part of Chapter 6 appeared as my contribution to a debate with David Erdman, "Who Wrote *The Mad Monk?*" *BNYPL*, 64 (April 1960), 209–237, and is reprinted by permission of *BNYPL*.

Put together mainly in Paris and in London, this book owes much to the amenities of life in those cities with their splendid libraries, but even more to the agencies that permitted me to work there on leave from teaching: the John Simon Guggenheim Memorial Foundation, and Cornell University through its Humanities Council and its sabbatical leave program. I am deeply grateful to the Trustees of Dove Cottage for the privilege of working in the Wordsworth Library in Grasmere and for permission to consult and quote from manuscripts in their keeping. I also owe an immeasurable debt to the communities of Wordsworthians gathered at Cornell and at Grasmere over the past decade. Friends and colleagues, my mentors and my students, they have unfailingly shared their knowledge and their enthusiasm, and strengthened my own.

S. M. Parrish
Ithaca, 1972

Contents

Abbreviations

BL   Coleridge, *Biographia Literaria*, ed. J. Shawcross, 2 vols.
          (Oxford: Oxford University Press, 1907)

BNYPL   *Bulletin of the New York Public Library*

BWS   *Bicentenary Wordsworth Studies in Memory of John Alban
          Finch*, ed. Jonathan Wordsworth (Ithaca: Cornell University
          Press, 1970)

Chronology Mark L. Reed, *Wordsworth: The Chronology of the Early
          Years: 1770–1799* (Cambridge, Mass.: Harvard University
          Press, 1967)

DC MS.   Dove Cottage Manuscript

E in C   *Essays in Criticism*

EY   *The Letters of William and Dorothy Wordsworth: The Early
          Years 1787–1805*, ed. Ernest de Selincourt; 2nd ed., rev.
          Chester L. Shaver (Oxford: Oxford University Press, Clar-
          endon Press, 1967)

Grosart   *The Prose Works of William Wordsworth*, ed. Alexander
          B. Grosart, 3 vols. (London, 1876)

HCR   *Henry Crabb Robinson on Books and Their Writers*, ed.
          Edith J. Morley, 3 vols. (London: J. M. Dent and Sons, 1938)

JEGP   *Journal of English and Germanic Philology*

LY   *The Letters of William and Dorothy Wordsworth: The
          Later Years*, ed. Ernest de Selincourt, 3 vols. (Oxford:
          Oxford University Press, Clarendon Press, 1939)

MLN   *Modern Language Notes*

MLR   *Modern Language Review*

Moorman   Mary Moorman, *William Wordsworth: A Biography*:
          I. *The Early Years: 1770–1803* (Oxford: Oxford University
          Press, Clarendon Press, 1957);
          II. *The Later Years: 1803–1850* (Oxford: Oxford University
          Press, Clarendon Press, 1965)

MY   *The Letters of William and Dorothy Wordsworth: The
          Middle Years*, ed. Ernest de Selincourt, 2nd ed.:

Part I: 1806–1811, rev. Mary Moorman (Oxford: Oxford University Press, Clarendon Press, 1969)

Part II: 1812–1820, rev. Mary Moorman and Alan G. Hill (Oxford: Oxford University Press, Clarendon Press, 1970)

N&Q	*Notes and Queries*
Owen	*Wordsworth and Coleridge: Lyrical Ballads 1798*, ed. W. J. B. Owen, 2nd ed. (Oxford: Oxford University Press, 1969)
PBSA	*Papers of the Bibliographical Society of America*
Prelude	Wordsworth, *The Prelude*, ed. Ernest de Selincourt; 2nd ed., rev. Helen Darbishire (Oxford: Oxford University Press, Clarendon Press, 1959); the 1805 text is cited unless the 1850 text is specified
PW	*The Poetical Works of William Wordsworth*, 5 vols., ed. Ernest de Selincourt and Helen Darbishire (Oxford: Oxford University Press, Clarendon Press, 1940–1958), Vol. I, 1940, rev. 1952; Vol. II, 1944, rev. 1952; Vol. III, 1946; Vol. IV, 1947, rev. 1958; Vol. V, 1949
RES	*Review of English Studies*
SB	*Studies in Bibliography*
SP	*Studies in Philology*
STCL	*Collected Letters of Samuel Taylor Coleridge*, ed. Earl Leslie Griggs, 6 vols. (Oxford: Oxford University Press, Clarendon Press, 1956–1971)
STCNB	*The Notebooks of Samuel Taylor Coleridge*, ed. Kathleen Coburn: *Vol. I: 1794–1804* (New York: Pantheon Books, 1957); *Vol. II: 1804–1808* (New York: Pantheon Books, 1961)
STCPW	*The Complete Poetical Works of Samuel Taylor Coleridge*, ed. Ernest Hartley Coleridge, 2 vols. (Oxford: Oxford University Press, Clarendon Press, 1912)
TLS	London *Times Literary Supplement*
UTQ	*The University of Toronto Quarterly*

A Note on the Dove Cottage Manuscripts

The manuscript notebooks and papers deposited at Dove Cottage by Gordon Wordsworth were sorted out and serially numbered by Ernest de Selincourt and Helen Darbishire in the 1930's. Over the past decade scholars working with them have made fresh discoveries about their contents, their provenance, and their relationships; some notebooks have been redated, and some have been shown to be parts of a single original. In 1972 a new numbering scheme was adopted whereby each manuscript, prose or verse, is placed according to the date of its earliest use by Wordsworth for broadly creative purposes. For convenience of reference to the old numbers (which were widely cited) I provide below a table of equivalents, showing the manuscripts I quote or mention.

new DC number	old DC number
MS. 2	MS. Verse 4
MS. 11	MS. Verse 12
MS. 14	MS. Verse 19
MS. 15	MS. Verse 18
MS. 16	MS. Verse 18A
MS. 18	MS. Verse 34
MS. 26	MS. Prose 31
MS. 29	MS. Verse 37A
MS. 33	MS. Verse 36
MS. 41	Uncatalogued
MS. 56	MS. Verse 52
MS. 59	MS. Verse 39
MS. 60	MS. Verse 35
MS. 61	MS. Verse 53
MS. 80	MS. Verse 62A

MS. 41, a volume known as "Sara Hutchinson's Poets," was acquired by Dove Cottage after the original series of numbers had been assigned.

THE ART OF THE *Lyrical Ballads*

CHAPTER 1

The Poet's Art

Matthew Arnold's cool assertions that Wordsworth "has no style," that Nature seems "to take the pen out of his hand, and to write for him with her own bare, sheer, penetrating power,"[1] have helped to obscure important tendencies of Wordsworth's poetic theory. As he made the assertions Arnold lifted Wordsworth to a rank a little below Shakespeare and Milton in the English heirarchy of genius, and he could scarcely have believed that an artless submission to the power of Nature was enough to lodge any poet that high, but the elegant force of his pronouncements gave currency to a notion already widely circulating. Readers of *Lyrical Ballads* from Coleridge on down had complained that Wordsworth's adoption of the language of conversation instead of the language of poetry turned the creative artist into a recorder or at best imitator of nature's sounds and sights. The Lake School, for example, wrote Hazlitt, was "founded . . . on a principle of sheer humanity, on pure nature void of art."[2] In our day it became conventional to say not just that Wordsworth took the side of Nature against Art (in terms of the old antithesis) but even that the revolt he inaugurated was a revolt against literature, or against language, or against

1. Preface to his "Golden Treasury" selection of Wordsworth's *Poems* (London, 1879), pp. xxii, xxiv. These two separate assertions were first put together by John Jones, who called them "a graceful evasion; but not on that account to be ignored"; *The Egotistical Sublime* (London: Chatto and Windus, 1954), p. 3.

2. "Lectures on the English Poets" in *The Complete Works*, ed. P. P. Howe, 21 vols. (London and Toronto: J. M. Dent and Sons, 1930–1934), V, 162.

the literary element of poetry—in short, a revolt against art.[3]

Now it must be granted that the roots of these notions lie deeper than Arnold; they lie in Wordsworth's own pronouncements about the processes of literature. "I vindicate the rights and dignity of Nature," he proclaimed at the opening of his third essay upon epitaphs, "Celebrated Epitaphs Considered." This vindication had to be made, he went on to explain, not because Nature is weak, but "because the adversary of Nature (call that adversary Art or by what name you will) is *comparatively* strong" (Grosart, II, 60, 64). Throughout his poetry Wordsworth used the terms of this opposition in a wholly conventional way ("tones of Nature smoothed by learned Art," "simple Nature trained by careful Art," "All growth of nature and all frame of Art,"[4] and so forth). Sometimes he kept the terms in balance; more often, and especially in the early years, he seemed to take the side of Nature, as, for example, in his contemptuous challenge to the so-called "Poet" who had "put his heart to school" (*PW*, III, 52):

> Thy Art be Nature; the live current quaff,
> And let the groveller sip his stagnant pool.

Yet we need to remember that Wordsworth was not a conventional (or indeed a systematic) thinker, and that if he used conventional terms it was usually to modify them to his distinctive concepts. The term "Nature" in the old antithesis enjoyed so many meanings that it would be hard to single out even one or two that might be called conventional, and like everyone else Wordsworth used the term in several ways. But he more often used it to mean "simple," for instance, than "wild," and when he talked about poetic creation or about the poetic response—that is, when he gave the term a psychological application, which is what matters here—he used it with a fairly

3. See, for example, Thomas Raysor, "Coleridge's Criticism of Wordsworth," *PMLA*, 54 (June 1939), 496–510 (esp. 503); Helen Darbishire, *The Poet Wordsworth* (Oxford: Oxford University Press, Clarendon Press, 1950), p. 35; and Roger Sharrock, "Wordsworth's Revolt Against Literature," *E in C*, 3 (October 1953), 396–412.

4. *Prelude* (1850), VI, 674; "Valedictory Sonnet," *PW*, III, 59; "The Tuft of Primroses," *PW*, V, 354.

limited range of meanings, to denote what he called in the essays "Upon Epitaphs" "those primary sensations of the human heart, which are the vital springs of sublime and pathetic composition" (Grosart, II, 48). In the third of those essays he gave examples of the "universal feelings and simple movements of mind" that he associated with Nature: "Energy, stillness, grandeur, tenderness, those feelings which are the pure emanations of Nature, those thoughts which have the infinitude of truth" (Grosart, II, 60, 64). Elsewhere, as in the Preface to *Lyrical Ballads* (Owen, 156), we have his suggestive statements about our "elementary feelings," "the essential passions of the heart," the passions which "are incorporated with the beautiful and permanent forms of nature."

More troublesome is the other term of the antithesis. Perhaps because it seems less fresh, less attention had been paid to what Wordsworth said about Art than to what he said about Nature, though the former was no less copious or important. His reluctance to call Nature's adversary "Art" is significant, because "Art" was a term he almost always used with approbation. The Preface to *Lyrical Ballads* is more a vindication of "the Poet's art"[5] than a vindication of Nature. "I yield to none," Wordsworth later trumpeted, "*in love for my art*," and he once explained that he "used the word *art*, from a conviction . . . that poetry is infinitely more of an art than the world is disposed to believe."[6] The word that Wordsworth liked to use for Nature's adversary was "artifice," or something like it. In the essays "Upon Epitaphs" the weakening of Nature by its adversary was symbolized by the "artifices" that had overrun English verse since the days of Dryden and Pope. Speaking to Isabella Fenwick about his sonnet on the "Poet" who had put his heart to school (*PW*, III, 436), Wordsworth said he had been impelled to write it by the "disgusting frequency" with which the German term "*artistical*" was being used, and he urged that the meaning of that term could be brought out by substituting "artificial."

The struggle against artificiality in verse was one of Wordsworth's major concerns as a critic and as a poet. As we recognize,

5. The term appears in the Preface of 1802; Owen, 167.
6. To Sir William Gomm, 16 April 1834; *LY*, II, 700.

he called consistently for naturalness and "sincerity" in the expression of feeling; for a union of feeling and thought, passion and reason; for language that was not the dress or the ornament but the incarnation of ideas. Whenever the poet spoke insincerely, or allowed artifice to dictate the terms of his expression, or submitted to the common taste for extravagance, or to any prevailing decorum, he stifled the power of nature to reach and move "the human heart, by which we live."

It has commonly seemed that the primary doctrine by which Wordsworth asserted the power of nature over art was the most famous of his statements about the origins of poetry. No remark in the 1800 Preface to *Lyrical Ballads* or in any other critical text of Wordsworth's has taken on the historical significance of the one which describes good poetry as "the spontaneous overflow of powerful feelings." In the focus here upon the poet's own passions, in the image of the mind as a fountain, in the idea that creation is natural, artless, even involuntary, we find the central premises of Romantic criticism. But I should like to suggest that Wordsworth's remark is not by any means central to his own critical theory. There are two important points about it that have to be recognized before its force can be rightly understood. The first of them concerns the origin of poetry, which is the subject of the remark itself; the second concerns the function of poetry, which is the subject of the context in which the remark falls.

To assert, first of all, that poetry is the spontaneous overflow of feeling is to assert that poetic creation is automatic; the poet need only obey "blindly and mechanically the impulses" (Owen, 158) of certain habits. But here lies a peculiar ambivalence. For Wordsworth says in the same breath that the habits which lie at the root of the process are not themselves automatic or natural; they are built up and cultivated artfully by long-continued practice. A like ambivalence appears in the discussion of poetic language inserted into the Preface of 1802. Here Nature and Art alternate as though contesting for control of the creative process. No artificial distinction of language is ever required in poetry, Wordsworth declares, "for, if the Poet's subject be judiciously chosen [Art], it will naturally, and upon fit occasion [Nature], lead him to passions the language of which, if selected truly and judiciously [Art], must necessarily [Nature] be dignified and variegated, and alive with metaphors and figures" (Owen, 164).

These ambivalences are never cleanly resolved, although Dorothy probably indicated the kind of compromise her brother would accept when she reported in 1798 (*EY*, 200) that William now "composes with much more facility than he did, as to the *mechanism* of poetry, and his ideas flow faster than he can express them." Wordsworth does, however, bend consistently one way and on the whole treats the creative process as though it were a matter of conscious artistry. In a revealing passage of blank verse possibly written as early as 1798 but never taken into the *Prelude* or the *Excursion*, he appears to suggest the inadequacy of a spontaneous overflow of feeling:

> oftentimes I had burst forth
> In verse which with a strong and random light
> Touching an object in its prominent parts
> Created a memorial which to me
> Was all sufficient and to my own mind
> Recalling the whole picture seemed to speak
> An universal language: Scattering thus
> In passion many a desultory sound
> I deemed that I had adequately cloathed
> Meanings at which I hardly hinted thoughts
> And forms of which I scarcely had produced
> A monument and arbitrary sign.

De Selincourt, who printed these lines for the first time in 1950,[7] conjectured, rightly I think, that at this point (a space in the manuscript) the argument required the speaker to admit the inadequacy of this "random and desultory" verse and to recognize that the artist reveals his true power only in the way the succeeding lines describe:

> In that considerate and laborious work
> That patience which admitting no neglect
> By slow creation doth impart to speach
> Outline and substance even till it has given
> A function kindred to organic power
> The vital spirit of a perfect form.

7. *Prelude*, ed. de Selincourt, p. lvi. The lines appear in DC MS. 59.

All in all, one suspects that in another critical climate the remark about "the spontaneous overflow of powerful feelings" might have rung out less memorably; it takes on meaning both from the contrasting Augustan standards that lay behind it and from Coleridge's genetic theories that lay ahead. Certainly Wordsworth never again suggested that good writing was automatic or unpremeditated, governed by Nature rather than by Art. He characteristically distinguished between "compositions" and "effusions"[8] and once even disparaged the latter by scornfully echoing his most famous critical metaphor: sending Coleridge a copy of his ballad on George and Sarah Green in 1808 (*MY*, I, 219), he called it "effused" rather than "*composed*"—"for it is the mere pouring out of my own feeling." Some years later he assailed Milton for using the same metaphor. For Milton to talk of "pouring easy his unpremeditated verse" was misleading and false, Wordsworth argued (*LY*, II, 586), for like all great poets Milton was a conscious craftsman, obligated to the labor of composing and revising. "Again and again I must repeat," Wordsworth insisted in language he used a number of times, "that the composition of verse is infinitely more of an art than men are prepared to believe."[9] Though he spoke to this subject intermittently all his life, his views are summed up in a representative way in a letter of 1816 to R. P. Gillies (*MY*, II, 301). Criticizing an essay by Sir Egerton Brydges, Wordsworth attacks the notion that poetic fire may be extinguished by artifice.

Sir E. is quite correct in stating that no Poetry can be good without animation. But when he adds, "that the position will almost exclude whatever is very highly and artificially laboured, for great artifice must destroy animation," he thinks laxly, and uses words inconsiderately.—Substitute for the word "artificially" the word "artfully," and you will see at once that nothing can be more erroneous than the assertion. The word "artificially" begs the question, because that word is always employed in an unfavourable sense.

8. As, for example, writing to John Scott, 11 March 1816 (*My*, II, 284).

9. De Selincourt speaks perceptively about some of these matters in his Introduction to the *Prelude*, pp. lv–lvi.

After a brief discussion of Gray's failure as a poet, which he attributed not to his having extinguished his poetic fire by taking too many pains, but only to the wrong sort of pains applied to insufficient fire, Wordsworth concluded the subject: "Do not let any Body persuade you that any quantity of good verses can ever be produced by mere felicity; or that an immortal *style* can be the growth of mere Genius."

Poeta fit, non nascitur; and if this doctrine seems jarring or inconsistent we might remind ourselves that it is foreshadowed in the splendid delineation of the poet inserted in the Preface of 1802. Though the notion of poetry suggested there is, we may agree, "sublime," the poet himself is only "a man speaking to men," who writes with the desire of giving them pleasure. The faculties with which he is "endued" are those that any man might have; he simply has them in an uncommon degree. From them in part but also "from practice, he has acquired a greater readiness and power in expressing what he thinks and feels." Wordsworth goes on to explain that "however exalted a notion we would wish to cherish of the character of a Poet," his descriptions remain "mechanical" compared with the reality he imitates, so that he finds it necessary to adopt the tactics of self-projection, sympathetic identification, and the like (Owen, 165–166). These are, of course, the tactics of Art, and they show the limits of Nature's role in the creative process. If Wordsworth could hope, in the speaking voice of the *Prelude* (XII, 309–312)

> that a work of mine
> Proceeding from the depth of untaught things,
> Enduring and creative, might become
> A power like one of Nature's,

if "the great Nature that exists in works / Of mighty Poets" can take the form of a "Visionary Power . . . embodied in the mystery of words," (*Prelude*, V, 618–621), these high aims can be achieved only by means of "the pains and anxiety of original composition"[10] as he explicated it in his letters and critical prose.

The second important point about Wordsworth's famous re-

10. Appendix on Poetic Diction (1802); *PW*, II, 409n.

mark "all good poetry is the spontaneous overflow of powerful feelings" concerns its context. The fact has been overlooked, I think, that the remark falls rather casually in a passage of the Preface which treats of the aims of poetry, announcing a specific *"purpose"* in each of Wordsworth's poems. When it recurs in Wordsworth's "general summary," it is subordinated to a statement of his reasons for writing in verse instead of prose that consists chiefly of an analysis of meter as a stimulant of esthetic pleasure. In the first passage Wordsworth does describe the process of poetic creation, but in the course of the discussion he executes a tactic that was characteristic of his critical discourse. Desiring to connect the poet's feelings and mental activities with the reader's "understanding" and "affections," he moves away from the poet and toward the reader—through the manner in which the poet "communicates" his feelings toward the effect these feelings have on the reader's sensibilities.

This concern with the reader's response, and hence with the artful means by which the poet plays upon it, was, I suggest, Wordsworth's central concern through all his critical writing, altering little throughout his career. After his critical (and social) attitudes began to harden and his creative powers to atrophy, he put an emphasis upon art and labor that sounds unlike the implications that can be read into the earlier prefaces. But the originator of a new mode of verse who seeks to win public acceptance describes his purposes in public statements in such a way as to heighten the differences between his mode and prevailing modes; the established poet looking back to the hard but successful beginnings of his career speaks privately and casually of the pains of composition and outlines the poetic strategy by which his victories were won.

Moreover, the rhetorical bias shows up in Wordsworth's earliest statements about his art, where he emphasized (as any Augustan poet might) the purpose of the poems he had written or planned to write, and talked of writing as though it were a craft to be learned, not a spontaneous or artless activity. "Fluency in writing," he assured William Mathews in 1792 (*EY*, 76), "will tread fast upon the heels of practice, and elegance and strength will not be far behind." In 1794, after a recital of his political and social views (*EY*, 124–125), he cited the duties of every writer like himself "who has the welfare of mankind at heart," adding: "I would put into each man's hand a lantern to guide him." The lantern he had in mind was "Salisbury Plain," whose "object," he told Francis Wrangham the following year (*EY*, 159), was "partly to expose the vices of the penal law and the calamities of war as they affect individuals." And it should be remembered that like other poems of the early years the great *Recluse,* in which Wordsworth hoped to convey most of the knowledge of which he was possessed, was conceived with a didactic object.

Wordsworth's earliest formal statement about poetry, the Advertisement to the 1798 *Lyrical Ballads*, brief as it is, exhibits the same rhetorical bias. There is nothing here about the poet, but a good deal about the reader. The central statement is a statement of purpose: these poems were "written chiefly with a view to ascertain how far the language of conversation in the middle and lower classes of society is adapted to the purposes of poetic pleasure." Lest readers should allow their habits of response to obstruct the pleasure available to them, they are invited to ask simply whether the poems contain "natural" (as opposed to gaudy or artificial) portrayals of human beings, and to form a judgment independent of convention or rules of decorum. Apart from specific notes on five poems, the Advertisement ends with a statement about the cultivation of taste.

It was, he said, the prior obligation of surveying "the present state of the public taste" that kept Wordsworth from undertaking any theoretical statement about the *Lyrical Ballads* in the Preface of 1800, and obliged him to be content with "a few words of introduction" to these experimental poems. But before he wrote the Preface Wordsworth had had a chance to read his reviews, and he was able to judge what sort of objections his poems were meeting. Hence despite his apparent diffidence and his later disclaimers of any interest in theory, he took elaborate pains in this essay to reason out the principles of poetic art on which his shorter pieces were written. The Preface has never been admired for its lucidity or even its insight,[11] and Coleridge's ingenious rebuttals in *Biographia Literaria* have sometimes made it seem confused and shallow. In recent years sources have been found for some of its major ideas, hitherto believed to be original. But it remains a remarkably literate, coherent, and rich analysis of what Wordsworth felt throughout his career to be the central topics of criticism. As Wordsworth summed them up in 1800, these topics were the "subjects," the "aims," and the "style" of poetry; in 1802 the delineation of "the Poet" was added. Within, or beneath, these topics lie several pervasive ideas which illustrate Wordsworth's devotion to "the Poet's art," and which deserve, I think, fresh elucidation.

The underlying rhetorical tendency of the Preface is apparent even in its earliest form, where remarks emphasizing the didactic purpose of literature balance or half-submerge the scattered remarks that seem to point another way. We have already seen how the notion of "spontaneous overflow of powerful feelings" becomes adulterated by rhetorical concerns. The same balance of concerns can be found in the passage which develops the distinctions between the lyrical ballads and "the popular Poetry of the day" (Owen, 157–159). Each lyrical ballad has a purpose, but besides that, "the feeling therein developed gives importance to the action and situation and not the action and situation to the feeling." Wordsworth goes on to reveal what this feeling is, and where it exists. It proves to be excitement generated without "gross and violent stimulants," and it exists in the mind of the reader; "to produce or enlarge" the power of entertaining this feeling is one of the noblest aims any writer can aspire to, and the aim to which these volumes are dedicated. In "Simon Lee," to take a single example, Wordsworth explained (rather heavily) that

11. Northrop Frye, in his *Anatomy of Criticism* (Princeton: Princeton University Press, 1957), p. 5, pronounced it "a remarkable document," but thought that "as a piece of Wordsworthian criticism nobody would give it more than about a B plus." F. R. Leavis recently called its arguments "confused and ineffective, though not essentially unintelligent." See his essay "Wordsworth: The Creative Conditions," in *Twentieth-Century Literature in Retrospect*, ed. Reuben A. Brower (Cambridge, Mass.: Harvard University Press, 1971), p. 334.

he had carried out his object, which was to follow the "fluxes and refluxes" of the agitated mind "by placing my Reader in the way of receiving from ordinary moral sensations another and more salutary impression than we are accustomed to receive from them."

Rhetorical statements of this sort inevitably emphasize Art over Nature, but hardly more than other remarks in the Preface of an entirely different sort. A number of statements, for example, touch on the mimetic function of poetry. Some of these are simply statements about language. Where Wordsworth had proposed in 1798 to adopt "the language of conversation in the middle and lower classes" (Owen, 3), by 1800 he prudently allowed only "a selection of the real language of men" (Owen, 153), and went on to explain that (presumably in the process of selection) this language would be "purified" (Owen, 156) of inappropriate elements. Although the shift between 1798 and 1800 accompanied a shift away from dramatic form in the poems (and this important matter will require separate discussion), it probably represents only a more careful statement of what Wordsworth intended from the beginning. For in 1802 he added an even flatter mimetic statement, putting it as his purpose "to imitate, and, as far as is possible, to adopt the very language of men" (Owen, 161). This statement was again related to dramatic technique, and nothing shows its limits better than the way in which Wordsworth at the same time redefined the process of "selection": "this selection, wherever it is made with true taste and feeling, will . . . entirely separate the composition from the vulgarity and meanness of ordinary life" (Owen, 164). However his practice in the plainer ballads may have struck his readers, here is a clear, and typical, rejection of phonographic realism in favor of selective imitation, controlled by the poet's taste and by his desire to achieve psychological realism. For this purpose the language of Nature provides no more than the raw material of Art.

Other mimetic statements in the Preface go deeper than language, to Wordsworth's underlying concern with truth as the "object"—later, indeed, "the soul and essence"—of poetry

(Grosart, III, 488). "I have at all times endeavoured to look steadily at my subject," he declared in 1800, as if to underline the realism of his portrayals of "incidents of common life." (Similarly, "I have wished to keep my Reader in the company of flesh and blood," Owen, 161.) But Wordsworth found it necessary to amplify this notion, and in 1802 he inserted a fuller statement of his intentions. It was his design, he said, to "throw over" these incidents "a certain colouring of imagination" in order to freshen the significance of "ordinary things" (Owen, 156).

Taken all together, these statements correspond very closely to Coleridge's later account of the purposes of *Lyrical Ballads*, couched in terms of "the two cardinal points of poetry, the power of exciting the sympathy of the reader by a faithful adherence to the truth of nature, and the power of giving the interest of novelty by the modifying colors of imagination" (*BL*, II, 5). Whether or not Coleridge was only echoing Wordsworth's language, or his own (or even Schiller's), we ought to notice that on these theoretical principles the partners in *Lyrical Ballads* were less divided than might be supposed from Coleridge's accompanying remarks. In the Preface Wordsworth spoke rather darkly of the "triviality and meanness" (Owen, 157) he found in some of his contemporaries' verse. Later, but still some years before Coleridge published his misgivings about his partner's "matter-of-factness," Wordsworth expressed the very same misgivings about Crabbe, and from them we can sense his concern for the imaginative perspective contributed by the poet to any recital of common events. Writing to Samuel Rogers on 29 September 1808 (*MY*, I, 268), Wordsworth condemned Crabbe's "verses"—"for *poetry* in no sense can they be called"—singling out a portrait from *The Village:* "After all, if the Picture were true to nature, what claim would it have to be called Poetry? At the best, it is the meanest kind of satire, except the merely personal. The sum of all is, that nineteen out of 20 of Crabbe's Pictures are mere matters of fact; with which the Muses have just about as much to do as they have with a Collection of medical reports, or of Law cases." By 1815, Wordsworth was able to sum these principles up in positive terms: the business of poetry, he insisted, "her privilege and her *duty*, is to treat of things not as they *are*, but as they *appear*; not as they exist in themselves, but as they *seem* to exist to the *senses*, and to the *passions*."[12]

Years later, in order to contrast "the imaginative influences which I have endeavoured to throw over common life with Crabbe's matter of fact style of treating subjects of the same kind," Wordsworth called attention to "Lucy Gray," written in 1799, inviting the reader to notice "the way in which the incident was treated and the spiritualizing of the character."[13] He probably had in mind the frame of the incident, three prefatory and two concluding stanzas. In these stanzas Lucy's solitude is emphasized ("the solitary Child," "no Mate, no comrade," "the lonesome Wild," "a solitary song"), she is compared to creatures who live in Nature (the fawn, the hare), and most important of all she is presented as living on in local memories and in the imagination of the poet who three times calls her "sweet" and who "chanc'd to see" her once just as she appeared to popular belief:

> O'er rough and smooth she trips along,
> And never looks behind;
> And sings a solitary song
> That whistles in the wind.

Thus Lucy's character was spiritualized, in part by throwing over the bare incident of her death "a certain colouring of imagination." But a corollary power invoked and controlled by the poet's art contributed equally to this end; this was simply what Wordsworth later called "the tranquillizing power of time" (*Excursion*, IV, 547). In the 1800 Preface, of course, this power is summed up in the genetic analysis of the poet's feeling developed from the famous phrase, "emotion recollected in tranquillity." The phrase may have been Coleridge's (in 1800 Coleridge jotted down a note, possibly for the Preface, about "recalling of passion in tranquillity"; *STCNB*, entry 787); but the idea is quintessentially Wordsworthian.

12. Essay, Supplementary to the Preface; *PW*, II, 410.
13. Fenwick note; *PW*, I, 360.

"Not used to make / A present joy the matter of my song" (*Prelude*, I, 55–56), he consistently built his narrative and lyrical poems on recollection. Like Wordsworth's other recitals of distress, the incident of "Lucy Gray" is set back in time, and both the incident itself and the feelings it generated are recalled by the poet, first tranquilly, one supposes, then with rising though simulated emotion, and always with "enjoyment."

The artistic function of memory was thus to impose on experience the control of art: to distance both poet and reader from reality in such a way as to transfigure painful or shocking events and heighten their meaning. Fittingly enough, literary art itself could serve the same function in a special way, as Wordsworth seemed to show in the episode of the drowned man in the *Prelude* (V, 450–481). The watching boy felt no "vulgar fear" at the ghastly sight of the recovered corpse because reading about similar things in story books "hallowed" the spectacle for him. But more important are some other devices of poetic art that carried out the same function. In tracing them, as in appraising any critical statement by one partner in *Lyrical Ballads*, it will be illuminating to contrast parallel statements by the other partner. Though Wordsworth and Coleridge talked their way into accord on a number of critical premises, the roots of their profound disagreements run back to the earliest days of their alliance. Thus one device available to provide esthetic distance—"to throw a sort of half consciousness of unsubstantial existence over the whole composition," as Wordsworth put it in 1802 (Owen, 172)—was the supernatural, accepted by Coleridge and rejected by Wordsworth. Another was the introduction of a dramatic dimension, like the dimension of time provided by memory, adopted by Wordsworth and vigorously argued down by Coleridge. A third was meter, employed of course by both partners but on theoretical grounds that were entirely different.

No statement in the Preface to *Lyrical Ballads* provoked Coleridge so sharply as Wordsworth's claim that "there neither is, nor can be, any *essential* difference between the language of prose and metrical composition." Quoting the claim in Chapter XVIII of *Biographia Literaria,* Coleridge called it "the most important" of the points he desired to refute, "its examination having been, indeed, my chief inducement for the preceding inquisition" (by which he seems to have meant Chapter XVII). The refutation he arrived at (*BL,* II, 57) could hardly have been blunter: "there may be, is, and ought to be an *essential* difference between the language of prose and of metrical composition." In the course of his argument Coleridge was driven to a close analysis of meter. Wordsworth, having ruled out all other candidates, had left meter, so Coleridge reasoned, as "the sole acknowledged difference" (*BL,* II, 62) between verse and prose, and that a relatively slight one. Coleridge, therefore, bent on asserting a deep and essential difference, seemed to elevate meter to high importance, setting it in intimate union with other discriminants of verse—language, style, passion. Where Wordsworth, in short, disparaged meter as ornamental, "adventitious to composition," no more than a "superadded charm," Coleridge defended meter as organic, essential to composition, uniquely valuable in stimulating the reader to keener esthetic perception.

Or so convention has had it.[14] But I should like to suggest that convention errs; that this view, however widely held, is misleading, even inaccurate. It seems hardly too bold to assert that Wordsworth, far from disparaging meter, gave it the highest possible importance, while Coleridge made it a relatively insignificant feature of poetry. Wordsworth's ideas in particular seem to me to have been misunderstood. A fresh reading of them may put his treatment of meter and Coleridge's into truer perspective.

Wordsworth's concern with meter runs through the Preface to *Lyrical Ballads,* but centers in six paragraphs of the 1800 text, expanded and multiplied by generous additions in 1802. Let us review, to begin with, the scattered "disparaging" re-

14. These views are well summarized in René Wellek's *History of Modern Criticism,* Vol. II: *The Romantic Age* (New Haven: Yale University Press, 1955), pp. 169–170: "Coleridge . . . writes an excellent defense of meter against Wordsworth's comparative disparagement of it as a mere 'superadded charm.'" The last phrase, incidentally, though much quoted, does not appear in Wordsworth.

marks about meter found in these paragraphs. They grow out of Wordsworth's insistence (in paragraph one; Owen, 163–164) on "the affinity betwixt metrical and prose composition . . . both speak by and to the same organs; the bodies in which both of them are clothed may be said to be of the same substance, their affections are kindred, and almost identical." Against this testimony, the features that discriminate poetry from prose can hardly seem very important. Yet Wordsworth's concern here is specifically with language, as he goes on to show. Meter remains, after all, "the only strict antithesis to Prose," and Wordsworth's purpose is not to disparage but to isolate it. What he attacks, in the second of his six paragraphs, is the notion that the "distinction" of rhyme and meter "paves the way for other distinctions" between poetry and prose. As he proceeds to discriminate among distinctions, in a passage that later attracted Coleridge's scornful censure (*BL*, II, 63–65), Wordsworth in fact gives meter a peculiar integrity. "The distinction of rhyme and metre [so 1800; "metre" only in 1802] is regular and uniform," while that of diction is "arbitrary, and subject to infinite caprices" (Owen, 164, 170). Diction, that is, is controlled by the poet, but the poet must obey the laws of meter.

The Appendix to the Preface (1802) takes as its text a phrase from this paragraph. As he develops there his opposition to "what is usually called Poetic Diction," Wordsworth may seem again to disparage meter. But again his real concern is with language. Tracing the growth of an artificial poetic diction, he observes (*PW*, II, 406) that meter "was the great temptation to all the corruptions which have followed." For meter became, unfortunately, a "symbol or promise" of a special language, so that whoever wrote in verse was likely to adopt what he conceived to be the language of verse. But if the languages of prose and verse are identical, it would follow that meter, a property of verse, has no connection with language: it is "superadded" thereto, hence "adventitious to composition" (the last phrase was not added to the Appendix until 1836). These arguments, which have failed to move most critics, are of course related to Wordsworth's adoption for poetry of a prose language—"the language of conversation," the "language really spoken by men." Whatever their merits, whatever their apparent implications, their purpose was, again, not to disparage meter but to separate it from other features commonly, and in Wordsworth's view mistakenly, associated with poetry. The result is once more to give meter unique prominence, as the single discriminant of verse.

To return to the Preface, one other remark is often cited as a disparagement of meter. Wordsworth sets out in 1800, in the third of his six paragraphs on meter, to explain why, if verse and prose share a common language, he has chosen to write in verse; there he takes up some hypothetical objections, meeting them with hypothetical replies. Trying to make his choice seem wholly natural and innocuous, he pointedly understates his argument. Assuming "for a moment" that prose might have served as well as verse, why should he be "condemned," he asks innocently (Owen, 170), for attempting "to superadd the charm which by the consent of all nations is acknowledged to exist in metrical language?" Critics examining this remark seem to have taken it to mean that meter yields nothing more than superficial charm. It surely means only that "charm," being the least controversial of meter's gifts, may be aptly cited as the minimum justification of verse. One critic has even gone on to misread the next sentence of the Preface, attributing to Wordsworth a view he is controverting,[15] that only "a very small part of the pleasure given by poetry depends upon the meter." Here Wordsworth's reply is simple and clear: those who would advance this view "greatly under-rate the power of metre in itself."

The reply leads Wordsworth to a closely reasoned appraisal of meter's power. "I might point out various causes why, when the style is manly, and the subject of some importance," Wordsworth declared at the opening of his fourth paragraph on meter, "words metrically arranged will long continue to impart such a pleasure to mankind as he who is sensible of the extent of that pleasure will be desirous to impart. The end of

15. Herbert Read, *The True Voice of Feeling* (London: Faber and Faber, 1953), p. 39.

Poetry is to produce excitement in coexistence with an over-balance of pleasure." But excitement itself may become unpleasant: either distressing images or the sheer power of language may arouse painful feelings in the reader. Meter, being regular and familiar, helps to temper or restrain these feelings. The specific virtue of meter, Wordsworth explained in an 1802 insertion (Owen, 172), was its tendency "to divest language in a certain degree of its reality, and thus to throw a sort of half consciousness of unsubstantial existence over the whole composition."

It is worth observing that for Wordsworth meter worked in roughly the same way as the supernatural might have worked, each helping to make painful events seem partly unreal. This fact may remind us of one of the large disagreements between the partners in *Lyrical Ballads:* Coleridge, Wordsworth later charged, having suffered too much himself, hence being unable "to dwell on or sanctify natural woes . . . took to the supernatural."[16] Wordsworth took instead to meter. For him, any description "either of passions, manners, or characters"—and poetry has no business describing anything else—was likely to be at once more enduring and more endurable in verse than in prose.

This analysis of the power of meter has been widely commented on. H. W. Garrod, for example, cited it when he called the whole Preface "quite as much a defence of the employment of metre in poetry as a protest against the use of 'poetic diction.' "[17] But those who find disparagement of meter in the Preface may perhaps remain unsatisfied. For Wordsworth's analysis may appear to endow meter with an essentially negative virtue. Though meter does produce a "complex feeling of delight," it serves mainly as "a device for sparing the reader pain, an anodyne, a soothing syrup," as Herbert Read has put it[18]—pain being an accompaniment of passionate ex-

16. Quoted by Ernest de Selincourt, *The Early Wordsworth* (n.p.: The English Association, 1936), p. 28n, from Barron Field's unpublished "Memoirs" of Wordsworth in the British Museum.

17. *Wordsworth: Lectures and Essays*, 2nd ed. (Oxford: Oxford University Press, 1927), p. 156.

18. *True Voice of Feeling*, p. 40; see also p. 44.

perience. Against this objection, however serious it may be, one need only cite the conclusion of Wordsworth's discussion, too often overlooked. Meter may sometimes spare the reader pain, he says at the close of paragraph four (Owen, 171–173), but what will happen "much more frequently," in poems where the words are "incommensurate with the passion, and inadequate to raise the Reader to a height of desirable excitement," is that meter itself will help "to impart passion to the words, and to effect the complex end which the Poet proposes to himself."

This virtue of meter provided something more than a means of strengthening weak or dull poetry. It provided, in fact, one of the distinctive features of a "lyrical ballad." For having chosen in his experiments to imitate the language of men in humble and rustic life, Wordsworth faced the problem, as he explained in his 1800 note to "The Thorn" (*PW*, II, 512–513) of ensuring "that words, which in their minds are impregnated with passion, should likewise convey passion to Readers who are not accustomed to sympathize with men feeling in that manner or using such language." The solution he hit upon was a simple one. "It seemed to me that this might be done by calling in the assistance of Lyrical and rapid Metre." Similarly, having observed that Pope "by the power of verse alone, has contrived to render the plainest common sense interesting, and even frequently to invest it with the appearance of passion," Wordsworth, as he says in the 1800 Preface (Owen, 174–175), "related in metre the Tale of Goody Blake and Harry Gill," one of the "rudest" of his collection. As a result, he had the satisfaction of knowing, the important truth illustrated by the tale was communicated to people who would not have heard of it "had it not been narrated as a Ballad, and in a more impressive metre than is usual in Ballads."[19]

Finally, this positive virtue of meter, essential to the principles on which the *Lyrical Ballads* were written, merges into a larger virtue, visible, I think, in a wider perspective of Wordsworth's critical theory. Evidence of it arises from Wordsworth's

19. This passage, which stood at the close of the sixth and last paragraph on meter, was dropped from the Preface after 1836.

use of the crucially important term "pleasure." The purpose of *Lyrical Ballads*, set forth at the very opening of the Preface, was "to ascertain, how far, by fitting to metrical arrangement a selection of the real language of men in a state of vivid sensation, that sort of pleasure and that quantity of pleasure may be imparted, which a Poet may rationally endeavour to impart." Farther along in the Preface, as already observed, Wordsworth cited ways in which "words metrically arranged" could impart "pleasure": meter could serve as a tempering agent or as a stimulant of passion. But after presenting these notions Wordsworth shied away from the problems they raised. "If I had undertaken a systematic defense of the theory" here maintained, he says apologetically—and here we reach paragraph five of the passage on meter (Owen, 173)—"it would have been my duty to develope the various causes upon which the pleasure received from metrical language depends." But he is content to mention one principle, namely, "the pleasure which the mind derives from the perception of similitude in dissimilitude," the principle that underlies sexual appetite, taste, and moral judgment. "It would not have been a useless employment," he concludes, "to have applied this principle to the consideration of metre, and to have shewn that metre is hence enabled to afford much pleasure, and to have pointed out in what manner that pleasure is produced." Useful or not, it is no part of Wordsworth's present task, and he proceeds to his "general summary," paragraph six.

Wordsworth never followed up this inquiry, but two years later when he revised the Preface he took some pains to define and explore the meaning of pleasure. Into the second paragraph of the passage on meter he inserted a lengthy addition, which ran to some nine paragraphs of the 1802 text. It contains his lofty portrait of the poet and his eloquent appraisal of poetry, both centered around a definition of "pleasure." To give pleasure, Wordsworth declared, is the immediate end of poetry. But pleasure meant something more than idle amusement. It performed, in fact, a vital function. As he launched his characterization of "the Poet," Wordsworth, citing Aristotle but going beyond him, described that function (Owen, 166–167), linking pleasure—the immediate end—with truth—the ultimate end—of poetry.

Nor let this necessity of producing immediate pleasure be considered as a degradation of the Poet's art. It is far otherwise. It is an acknowledgement of the beauty of the universe, an acknowledgement the more sincere, because it is not formal, but indirect; it is a task light and easy to him who looks at the world in a spirit of love: further, it is a homage paid to the native and naked dignity of man, to the grand elementary principle of pleasure, by which he knows, and feels, and lives, and moves. We have no sympathy but what is propagated by pleasure: I would not be misunderstood; but wherever we sympathize with pain, it will be found that the sympathy is produced and carried on by subtle combinations with pleasure. We have no knowledge, that is, no general principles drawn from the contemplation of particular facts, but what has been built up by pleasure, and exists in us by pleasure alone.

Pleasure, it is clear, lay at the heart of the "sublime notion of Poetry" that Wordsworth was endeavoring to present. At once a psychological, esthetic, almost an epistemological term, pleasure was the "grand elementary principle" of man's nature, the distinctive achievement of poetic art, and something like an instrument of truth. And a main source of pleasure in poetic art was meter, as Wordsworth had already made clear in his "general summary" of 1800 (Owen, 173–175). Meter seemed to work in two ways. First, it evoked "a complex feeling of delight, which is of the utmost use in tempering the painful feeling which will always be found intermingled with powerful descriptions of the deeper passions"—this especially in "pathetic and impassioned poetry." Second, in "lighter compositions," it became itself "a principal source of the gratification of the Reader."

If Wordsworth left these processes vague, he did make abundantly clear his belief in the importance of meter as an ingredient of poetry. Far from leading a "revolt against literature" or against the literary element in poetry, Wordsworth offers in his theory of meter a defense of literary art. For meter becomes an important means by which art controls nature. At the creative level the natural language of real life is modified and made pleasing by meter, allowing the reader to form "an indistinct perception . . . of language closely resembling that of real life, and yet, in the circumstance of metre, differing from it so widely."[20] Or, from another point of view, the spontaneous overflow of powerful feeling is regulated by meter. At the level of esthetic response, the reader's passion and excitement are subdued or heightened, as necessary, and made to serve the ends of poetry.

When Coleridge came to deal with Wordsworth's theory of meter, he advanced some curiously mixed opinions. Part of the theory he seemed to approve (*BL*, II, 51): "the discussion on the powers of metre in the preface is highly ingenious and touches at all points on truth." Yet in his own summary of the powers of meter, Coleridge seemed to contradict his partner. Where Wordsworth had seen meter partly as a sedative, subduing excitement in the mind, Coleridge saw it only as a stimulant, tending "to increase the vivacity and susceptibility both of the general feelings and of the attention." Moreover, though Wordsworth had tried at some length to describe the effects of meter "in itself," Coleridge professed to be unable to find in the Preface "any statement of its powers considered abstractly and separately": "Mr. Wordsworth seems always to estimate metre by the powers, which it exerts during (and, as I think, in *consequence of*) its combination with other elements of poetry." Coleridge's own effort to define meter (*BL*, II, 52) led him to compare it, in a characteristically organic image, to yeast, "worthless or disagreeable by itself, but giving vivacity and spirit to the liquor with which it is proportionally combined."

But what Coleridge objected to at bottom was, of course, Wordsworth's view that meter had no necessary connection with language. He assailed Wordsworth, that is, first for combining meter with language in considering its powers, second for separating meter from language in considering its origin. The latter offense was much the greater. For Coleridge, meter arose from "the balance in the mind effected by that spontaneous effort which strives to hold in check the workings of

20. This is an addition of 1802; Owen, 174.

passion" (*BL*, II, 49). "*Metre itself* implies a *passion*," he had put it years earlier in a letter to William Sotheby of 13 July 1802—the very letter in which he had first confided his suspicion that between Wordsworth and himself there lay "a *radical* Difference" of opinion about poetry (*STCL*, II, 812). Where meter is used, therefore, it must be accompanied by the language of passion, which is the language of poetry.

What Coleridge was appealing to, of course, was his own criterion of wholeness. A "*legitimate* poem" he defined as that species of composition "the parts of which mutually support and explain each other; all in their proportion harmonizing with, and supporting the purpose and known influences of metrical arrangement" (*BL*, II, 10). To isolate meter as Wordsworth did and to regard the poet as subject to its laws was to risk turning poetry into a mechanical art, and thus recreating the very coldness and artifice which Wordsworth was trying to eliminate (see *BL*, II, 64–65).

Yet the criterion of wholeness is not an entirely accurate means of contrasting Wordsworth and Coleridge on meter, for Coleridge did not blend meter organically into the creative process. Though he traced meter to a "spontaneous effort" of the mind, he went on at once (*BL*, II, 50) to make clear that its elements, whatever their source, were "formed into metre *artificially*, by a *voluntary* act"—and he talked of meter as "superadded" no less freely than did Wordsworth (*BL*, II, 9, 53, 55). Meter, in fact, was for Coleridge a matter of "superficial *form*," and his definition of a "*legitimate* poem" involved the premise that "if metre be superadded, all other parts must be made consonant with it."

Perhaps the most accurate, then, and the simplest, way of pointing up the contrast here is to compare the replies Wordsworth and Coleridge made to the question set by Wordsworth: why do I write in verse? (Owen, 170). Wordsworth's reply, part of which had been delivered before he asked the question, is essentially that meter, the distinctive feature of verse, is a prime source of pleasure, which is in turn both the immediate end of art and the agent by which the ultimate end is achieved. He writes in verse, therefore, because verse has meter, and meter is valuable in itself. Toward these notions, Coleridge was wholly unsympathetic. Several of his partner's poems, he countered, would have been "more delightful" in prose (*BL*, II, 53). For not only may prose have as its immediate end "the communication of pleasure," as he had earlier declared, but "poetry of the highest kind may exist without metre" (*BL*, II, 9, 11). Pleasure, Coleridge later showed himself ready to agree, is always the "*immediate* object" of poetry, and "the communication of pleasure is the introductory means by which alone the poet must expect to moralize his readers" (*BL*, II, 104–105). But as for the pleasure supposedly afforded by meter in itself, that is entirely "*conditional*, and dependent on the appropriateness of the thoughts and expressions, to which the metrical form is superadded" (*BL*, II, 53). It was not meter (which "in itself is simply a stimulant of the attention") but language that Coleridge made the essential discriminant of verse. "I write in metre," he concluded flatly, "because I am about to use a language different from that of prose." Meter is therefore of value to Coleridge only as a symbol or promise of a special language—precisely the notion that Wordsworth had set out to attack in his Preface.

It will, I hope, be clear from this analysis who disparaged and who defended meter. In the end it is probably fair to say that however unequal the results each poet did define the virtue of meter in his own way, Wordsworth by showing its importance in the esthetic response, Coleridge, its place in the creative process. It may be half-right to look upon Wordsworth's consequent isolation of meter in his rhetorical theory as a gesture of disparagement, and upon Coleridge's integration of it in his genetic theory as a gesture of defense. But to allow these gestures to overweigh both poets' explicit statements on the function and powers of meter is to distort a highly important element of Wordsworth's poetic theory and to miss the blunt sense of Coleridge's critique.

Wordsworth's treatment of meter reinforces the strong affective and rhetorical tendency of his criticism. Especially toward the autumn of his career didactic pronouncements fell

from him like leaves from a tree, but some of the most eloquent were made before his great decade was over. In 1802
Wordsworth acknowledged John Wilson's praise "for having
reflected faithfully in my poems the feelings of human nature"
(*EY*, 355), then went on: "But a great Poet ought to do more
than this he ought to a certain degree to rectify men's feelings,
to give them new compositions of feeling, to render their feelings more sane pure and permanent, in short, more consonant to
nature, that is, to eternal nature, and the great moving spirit
of things." Writing to Beaumont, 17 October 1805 (*EY*, 627),
Wordsworth reinforced this principle by defining the object
of art: "to move the affections under the controul of good
sense." To this might be added the lofty statement of purpose
of the 1807 volumes that he communicated to Lady Beaumont:
"to console the afflicted, to add sunshine to daylight by making
the happy happier, to teach the young and gracious of every
age, to see, to think and feel, and therefore to become more
actively and securely virtuous."[21]

The accomplishment of these high aims, and more than that,
the very notion that literature was capable of enlarging and refining the reader's sensibilities, rested upon a philosophy of
literature that Wordsworth probably developed early in his
career but left to De Quincey to enunciate. The celebrated
distinction that De Quincey drew between the literature of
knowledge (which instructs) and the literature of power (which
moves)—particularly what De Quincey called the rhetorical
use of the word "power"—was taken, he said, from conversations with Wordsworth.[22] The roots of this distinction lie in
two interesting paragraphs of the "Essay Supplementary to
the Preface" of 1815 (*PW*, II, 427–428), where the word
"power" takes on thematic importance. Having surveyed some
fickle and irrational turns of literary popularity, Wordsworth
concludes by citing a remark of Coleridge's, that every great

21. 21 May 1807; *MY*, I, 146.
22. De Selincourt (*Prelude*, p. 541) called attention to this debt and
quoted briefly from De Quincey's "Essay on Pope" and his "Letters to a
Young Man" in *Collected Writings*, ed. David Masson, 14 vols. (London,
1896–1897), XI, 55, and X, 48n.

and truly original writer "has had the task of *creating* the taste by which he is to be enjoyed." How then is this taste to be created, Wordsworth inquires, and what difficulties stand in the way? The answers are complex, but they follow from two clear alternatives: either the poet forms taste by "the mere communication of *knowledge*" or he "has to call forth and to communicate *power*" (both italics are Wordsworth's). The second alternative is the only reasonable one: "to create taste," Wordsworth concludes, "is to call forth and bestow power, of which knowledge is the effect." Taste, Wordsworth explains, is an awkward and inexact metaphor. It appears to denote only a passive faculty, but "the profound and the exquisite," "the lofty and universal," and in plainer prose "the pathetic and the sublime," if they are to be communicated as the poet feels them, all require "the exertion of a co-operating *power* in the mind of the Reader." The ability to evoke this power is the highest creative endowment; or, as Wordsworth put it in terms that again reveal his rhetorical and didactic bias, "of genius, in the fine arts, the only infallible sign is the widening the sphere of human sensibility for the delight, honour, and benefit of human nature." It was on these terms that, in the end, he desired his poems to be judged—not, that is, for their moral qualities, but for the "powers of the mind" they called forth and excited in the reader.[23]

Whether Wordsworth always succeeded in calling forth in the reader the powers or passions that had stirred his own mind to poetic utterance is often disputed. One tends to think that the poet's intentions sometimes outran his achievement, that some of the early experimental poems fall short of Wordsworth's hopes for them. Yet his intentions are important, for when we can know them they reveal with unique authority the tactics by which the poet sought to achieve the perfection of his art, the vital spirit of a perfect form. More revealing, that is, than Wordsworth's endless, meticulous, sometimes controversial revisions are his deliberate statements of intent, some of which develop into formal explications of his own poems.

23. See the entry for 31 May 1812 in *HCR*, I, 89.

The Fenwick notes were dictated by an old man looking backward as far as fifty years, and though frequently illuminating they are likely to dwell on personal memories related to the poems rather than on the poems themselves ("This dog I knew well"). Much more illuminating are the earlier scattered statements, mostly in conversation or letters, made in defense of poems that had puzzled or displeased Wordsworth's friends. Uncommonly literal, sometimes pompous and insensitive, but always opening out the poet's intention with rare precision, these statements deserve close reading.

One of the earliest is a notebook entry of 1801 or 1802 concerning "To Joanna," one of the "Poems on the Naming of Places" that Wordsworth wrote to fill out the second volume of the 1800 *Lyrical Ballads*. The entry may have been written down to put into a letter, but it has not survived in any other form and it remained unpublished until 1944. "To Joanna," a blank-verse poem of 85 lines, commemorates a rock in the Vale of Grasmere on which Wordsworth had inscribed Joanna Hutchinson's name. Cast in the form of a verse epistle, the poem tells of an encounter at the rock "some ten days past" with the Grasmere Vicar who "with grave looks demanded" why the poet

> like a Runic priest, in characters
> Of formidable size, had chisel'd out
> Some uncouth name.

To introduce his answer, which occupies the remaining half of the poem, the poet rather cryptically reports (to Joanna) that

> by those dear immunities of heart
> Engender'd betwixt malice and true love,
> I was not loth to be so catechiz'd.

To the Vicar he then recounts an incident. In the course of a summer morning's stroll, he had become entranced with the beauty of the tall rock grown over with shrubs and flowers, and had stopped to gaze upon it. Joanna, seeing his "ravishment," had laughed aloud, whereupon

> The rock, like something starting from a sleep
> Took up the Lady's voice, and laugh'd again:
> That ancient Woman seated on Helm-crag
> Was ready with her cavern.

The laugh thus echoed through the rocks and hills and beyond, tossed back and forth from Helm-crag, to Hammar-scar, to Silver-How, Loughrigg, Fairfield, mounting even to Helvellyn and Skiddaw, Glaramara and Kirkstone.

> Now whether, (said I to our cordial Friend,
> Who in the hey-day of astonishment
> Smil'd in my face) this were in simple truth
> A work accomplish'd by the brotherhood
> Of ancient mountains, or my ear was touch'd
> With dreams and visionary impulses,
> Is not for me to tell; but sure I am
> That there was a loud uproar in the hills.
> And while we both were listening, to my side
> The fair Joanna drew, as if she wish'd
> To shelter from some object of her fear.

Hence it was that "long afterwards" the poet, happening to walk by the rock in the calm of an early morning, sat down and "in memory of affections old and true" chiseled out Joanna's name.

We may wonder whether the Vicar's smiling astonishment could have been more intense than any reader's upon learning that in 1801 Wordsworth told his sister and brother that "Joanna" along with "Nutting" showed "the greatest genious of any poems in the 2^d Vol" of *Lyrical Ballads*.[24] The best blank verse in the poem, and the strongest feeling, seem to belong to the opening paragraph, but Wordsworth's explication, which is worth reproducing in full, makes it clear that the part he valued was his discourse to the Vicar.

The poem supposes that at the Rock something had taken place in my mind either then; or afterwards in thinking upon what then took

---

24. John Wordsworth, writing to Mary Hutchinson, 27 February 1801, quotes a letter from Dorothy reporting William's opinion; *Letters of John Wordsworth*, ed. Carl Ketcham (Ithaca: Cornell University Press, 1969), p. 96.

place which if related will cause the Vicar to smile. For something like this you are prepared by the phrase "Now by those dear immunities" &c. I begin to relate the story, meaning in a certain degree to divert or partly play upon the Vicar. I begin,—my mind partly forgets its purpose, being softened by the images of beauty in the description of the rock, & the delicious morning & when I come to the 2 lines, "the Rock like something" &c I am caught in the trap of my own imagination. I entirely lose sight of my first purpose. I take fire in the lines "that ancient Woman". I go on in that strain of fancy "Old Skiddaw" & terminate the description in tumult "And Kirkstone" *etc* describing what for a moment I believed either actually took place at the time, or when I have been reflecting on what did take place I have had a temporary belief, in some fit of imagination, did really or might have taken place. When the description is closed, or perhaps partly before I waken from the dream & see that the Vicar thinks I have been extravagating, as I intended he should. I then tell the story as it happened really; & as the recollection of it exists permanently & regularly in my mind, mingling allusions suffused with humour, partly to the trance in which I have been, & partly to the trick I have been playing upon the Vicar. The poem then concludes in a strain of deep tenderness.[25]

The heart of this remarkable explication lies in the statement "I am caught in the trap of my own imagination." For the poem turns out to be not a poem about Joanna, or a poem about the rock or about an incident there, or even a poem about Nature, but rather a dramatic self-portrait, a poem about the contest between the poet's imagination and his sense of reality. Released by a playful impulse, his imagination rises to a wild excitation in which his sense of reality is momentarily overwhelmed, then sinks once more under rational control, leaving a current of warm emotion as the poet looks tranquilly back through the filter of memory. And here, it should now be perceived, lie the affinities between this poem and "Nutting." For "Nutting," too, is a dramatic poem, a poem about a contest that rages within the poet's sensibilities. After the passionate indulgence of destructive joy, the contest ends in mingled pain and exultation, and the tenderness that survives in the poet's heart is best pointed toward a moral summing-up in the closing lines of an early draft:

25. The explication is quoted from DC MS. 33; see *PW*, II, 487.

> Then dearest maiden if I have not now
> The skill to teach thee think I pray of him
> The ragged boy & let his parting look
> Instruct thee how to move along these shades
> In gentleness of heart.—With gentle hand
> Touch, for there is a spirit in the woods.[26]

Wordsworth's explication of "To Joanna" points to what he felt to be the real center of his poem, where his "genius" displayed itself, and after reading it one sees why he complained so often that his poems had not been understood. Despite the realism of the echo (and it was this that Coleridge, for example, emphasized when he assured Richard Warner that "tho' purposely beyond Nature," it was yet "only an *exaggeration* of what really would happen"[27]), the center of the poem lies in the power of the poet's "dreams and visionary impulses" to transport him out of reality into a state of mind absolutely beyond anything that would or might happen—to catch the poet in the trap of his own imagination.

Another revealing explication analyzes an unpretentious sonnet published in the volumes of 1807:

> With Ships the sea was sprinkled far and nigh,
> Like stars in heaven, and joyously it showed;
> Some lying fast at anchor in the road,
> Some veering up and down, one knew not why.
> A goodly Vessel did I then espy
> Come like a Giant from a haven broad;
> And lustily along the Bay she strode,
> Her tackling rich, and of apparel high.
> This ship was nought to me, nor I to her,
> Yet I pursued her with a Lover's look;
> This Ship to all the rest did I prefer:
> When will she turn, and whither? She will brook
> No tarrying; where she comes the winds must stir:
> On went She, and due north her journey took.

Writing to Lady Beaumont a few weeks after the publication of these volumes, Wordsworth declared that virtually all his poems focused upon some law of the mind's operation (*MY*,

---

26. In DC MS. 15.
27. As reported on 27 July 1802 to Sara Hutchinson; *STCL*, II, 827.

I, 145–151). As for the sonnet in question, which had been criticized by a friend of Lady Beaumont's, the law illustrated was simply that the mind is distracted and made restless by any "multitude of objects" presented to it and tends to fix upon a single object to which the others can be subordinated. Thus Milton, describing the heavens aglow with stars, had fixed upon "Hesperus, that *led* / The starry host"[28]—at least until the moon rose and dominated the scene. Wordsworth then moved into his detailed explication, again worth quoting in full:

Having laid this down as a general principle, take the case before us. I am represented in the Sonnet as casting my eyes over the sea, sprinkled with a multitude of Ships, like the heavens with stars, my mind may be supposed to float up and down among them in a kind of dreamy indifference with respect either to this one or that one, only in a pleasurable state of feeling with respect to the whole prospect. "Joyously it showed," this continued till that feeling may be supposed to have passed away, and a kind of comparative list-lessness or apathy to have succeeded, as at this line, "Some veering up and down, one knew not why." All at once, while I am in this state, comes forth an object, an individual, and my mind, sleepy and unfixed, is awakened and fastened in a moment. "Hesperus, that *led* The starry host," is a poetical object, because the glory of his own Nature gives him the pre-eminence the moment he appears; he calls forth the poetic faculty, receiving its exertions as a tribute; but this Ship in the Sonnet may, in a manner still more appropriate, be said to come upon a mission of the poetic Spirit, because in its own appearance and attributes it is barely sufficiently distinguish[ed] to rouse the creative faculty of the human mind; to exertions at all times welcome, but doubly so when they come upon us when in a state of remissness. The mind being at once fixed and rouzed, all the rest comes from itself; it is merely a lordly Ship, nothing more:
    This ship was nought to me, nor I to her,
    Yet I pursued her with a lover's look.
My mind wantons with grateful joy in the exercise of its own powers, and, loving its own creation,
    This ship to all the rest did I prefer,
making her a sovereign or a regent, and thus giving body and life to all the rest; mingling up this idea with fondness and praise—
    where she comes the winds must stir;
and concluding the whole with

28. *Paradise Lost*, IV, 695–696.

On went She, and due north her journey took.

Thus taking up again the Reader with whom I began, letting him know how long I must have watched this favorite Vessel, and inviting him to rest his mind as mine is resting.

Again this explication shows, as no outsider's analysis possibly could, the intricate artistic design that controlled the diction, the movement, and the order of a simple poem. Whether the poem entirely succeeds is likely to be disputed, for again the poet's understatement makes his intention hard to grasp: without the explication we could hardly sense the passion that floods the simple line "This ship to all the rest did I prefer." But the success or failure of the poem matters less than its intention. The center of the extraordinary explication is a summary remark very much like the remark that applied to the poem "To Joanna." There Wordsworth had declared, "My mind is caught in the trap of her own imagination"; here, "my mind wantons with grateful joy in the exercise of its own powers." The remark helps to bring into focus the point which the careful reader of Wordsworth will have looked for at the poem's center—the dramatic tension between two states of the speaker's mind, the one "sleepy and unfixed," the other "fixed and rouzed." As this tension moves to its inevitable resolution, leaving the mind tranquil, the reader follows the ebb and flow, the fluxes and refluxes, of the poet's imagination.

But the reader is always more than a passive observer. Wordsworth's poetic tactics and his critical pronouncements taken together make it clear that poet and reader are joint participants in the experience of literature. The purpose of the poet's creative activity is not to give his feelings expression under the dictates of Nature, but to shape them under the control of Art so as to evoke responsive feelings in the reader. One of the strongest statements of this central purpose lies in the very essays in which Wordsworth had set out to vindicate the rights and privileges of Nature, the essays "Upon Epitaphs." The artist speaks out of "those primary sensations of the human heart, which are the vital springs of sublime and pathetic composition," but unless "correspondent ones [sensations] listen promptly and submissively in the inner cell of the mind to whom it is addressed, the voice cannot be heard; its highest powers are wasted." Only when poet and reader participate equally is literature able to inculcate virtue by exploiting "the grand elementary principle of pleasure," or to "call forth and bestow power, of which knowledge is the effect."

CHAPTER 2

Partnership

When Wordsworth composed the splendid tribute to Coleridge in Book VI of the *Prelude* (265–269),

> Twins almost in genius and in mind!
> . . . we were framed
> To bend at last to the same discipline,
> Predestin'd, if two Beings ever were,
> To seek the same delights, and have one health,
> One happiness,

he would have been looking back to the extraordinary creative partnership in which the two poets had lived at Stowey and Alfoxden.[1] For by 1804 when these lines were written, Coleridge's search for health had driven him to Malta, and his chances of happiness, as Wordsworth knew, were gravely threatened by incompatability with one Sara and hopeless passion for another. Moreover, it had become clear that the partners were not bent to the same discipline at all. Wordsworth was now engaged on the vast design which Coleridge had first set for himself, then urged upon his partner, the composition of a great philosophical poem; but the poet in Coleridge was virtually dead, and his unfocused energies and talents were playing weakly over diverse subliterary activities. "I abandon Poetry altogether," Coleridge had declared in 1800, while he was struggling to finish "Christabel." "I leave the higher & deeper Kinds to Wordsworth, the delightful, popular & simply dignified to Southey; & reserve for myself the honourable

---

1. "For more than one whole year I was with Wordsworth almost daily —& frequently for weeks together," Coleridge wrote Southey on 8 August 1799 (*STCL*, I, 525).

attempt to make others feel and understand their writings"
(*STCL*, I, 623). Seven months later he wrote mournfully to
Godwin: "If I die, and the Booksellers will give you any thing
for my life, be sure to say—'Wordsworth descended on him,
like the Γνῶθι σεαυτόν from Heaven; by shewing to him what
true Poetry was, he made him know, that he himself was no
Poet' " (*STCL*, II, 714).

The extinguishing of one creative talent betrays some of the
tensions that must have strained the two poets' regard for each
other almost from their earliest days together. Most accounts
of this relationship have idealized it, playing up the partners'
compatibility and playing down their discords.[2] Yet, looking
back to the *annus mirabilis* and beyond, the differences that
separated Wordsworth and Coleridge—differences of personality, of taste, of ambition, of poetic philosophy—seem so wide
and various that one can reasonably wonder what mutual at-
traction they could have felt. While some of the differences
may at first, to be sure, have stimulated the poets' interest in
each other, they must swiftly have grown exacerbating. Coleridge's acute, pitiless self-analyses reveal a nature easier to
admire from a distance than to live with. "My thoughts," he
once wrote, "bustle along like a Surinam toad, with little toads
sprouting out of back, side and belly, vegetating while it
crawls."[3] Afflicted with what he dispassionately called "the
thinking disease" ("in which the feelings, instead of embody-
ing themselves in *acts*, ascend and become materials of general
reasoning and intellectual pride"),[4] and driven by his hideous
distresses, Coleridge persistently sublimated his creative energies into talk and speculation ("you spawn plans like a her-
ring," Southey scolded;[5] "half his time was passed in dreams,"

2. Truer accounts may be found in A. M. Buchan's discriminating
article, "The Influence of Wordsworth on Coleridge," *UTQ*, 20 (July
1963), 346–365, and more recently in William Heath's *Wordsworth and
Coleridge* (Oxford: Oxford University Press, 1970).

3. H. Crabb Robinson quotes, 24 May 1843, an old letter of Coleridge's
to Mrs. Clarkson; *HCR*, II, 632. See also *STCL*, III, 94–95.

4. *Anima Poetae*, ed. E. H. Coleridge (London, 1895), p. 169.

5. 4 August 1802; Charles Cuthbert Southey, *The Life and Correspondence of the Late Robert Southey*, 6 vols. (London, 1850), II, 190.

Wordsworth ungenerously remarked forty years later).[6] As a consequence, Coleridge himself knew, he dropped away from the sunlit fields of poetry into the "unwholesome quick-silver mines of abstruse Metaphysics."[7] To Godwin he lamented his incapacity to act: "In plain & natural English, I am a dreaming & therefore an indolent man—. I am a Starling, self-incaged, & always in the Moult, & my whole Note is, Tomorrow, & to-morrow, & tomorrow" (22 January 1802; *STCL*, II, 782). It was a note his publishers came to know well. "He never could write a thing that was immediately required of him," Daniel Stuart testified; "the thought of compulsion disarmed him."[8] Coleridge himself put it to Joseph Cottle more poetically, in another ornithological image: "I cannot, as is feigned of the Nightingale, sing with my Breast against a Thorn" (11 March 1815; *STCL*, IV, 552).

For his incapacities Coleridge devised infinitely complex excuses; his letters are a fascinating, melancholy record of them. As disarming as any was the one he offered Southey in 1795. Southey had complained of being cheated in their literary partnership. Though their output may have been unequal, Coleridge innocently responded, their industry was about the same: "—You sate down and wrote—I used to saunter about and think what I should write." The measure, he explained, ought to be "the number of Thoughts collected," not "the number of Lines, thro' which these Thoughts are diffused" (*STCL*, I, 172).

Wordsworth, on the other hand, though he liked to represent himself as

> forlorn dejected weary slow
> A pilgrim wandering round the world of woe,[9]

or as

6. To H. Crabb Robinson, 10 March 1840; *The Correspondence of Henry Crabb Robinson with the Wordsworth Circle*, ed. Edith J. Morley, 2 vols. (Oxford: Oxford University Press, 1927), I, 402.

7. To Daniel Stuart, 22 August 1806; *STCL*, II, 1178.

8. *Gentleman's Magazine*, n.s. 9 (May 1838), 487.

9. From lines written into a copy of *Descriptive Sketches*; *PW*, I, 83.

> an idler in the land;
> Contented if he might enjoy
> The things which others understand,[10]

had a practical sagacity that attached him to the real world. Less bedeviled than Coleridge by social and family obligations, sterner in his self-discipline, he achieved a kind of serenity that lay beyond his partner's reach. Beneath an exterior that has sometimes been thought somber, he became, he testified to H. Crabb Robinson, "one of the happiest of men"—and only a happy man, he added, could truly understand his best poems (*HCR*, I, 73). Moreover, joy had literary consequences. Being "A Happy man, and therefore bold to look / On painful things" (*Prelude*, X, 871–872), Wordsworth believed "poor dear Coleridge's constant infelicity" to have been a severe handicap to him as a poet, for it prevented him from treating one of the great themes of poetry, "the sorrows of mankind."[11]

The earliest of Wordsworth's several verse-portraits of Coleridge, "A Character, in the Antithetical Manner," probably finished in October 1800, is hardly less patronizing than affectionate. Having remarked on the mixture of alertness and vacuity in his partner's face ("a face divine, of heaven-born ideotcy," it became in a later portrait),[12] he went on with what now seems prophetic irony to report not only weakness but

> strength both redundant and vain
> Such strength, as if ever affliction and pain
> Could pierce through his temper as soft as a fleece,
> Would surely be fortitude sister of peace.[13]

It was in fact the total absence of such strength that caused Wordsworth to look on his partner with increasing annoyance

10. "A Poet's Epitaph"; *PW*, IV, 67.

11. Reported by Barron Field, unpublished "Memoirs," and quoted by de Selincourt, *The Early Wordsworth* (n.p.: The English Association, 1936), p. 28n.

12. "Stanzas Written in My Pocket-Copy of Thompson's 'Castle of Indolence,' " 1802; *PW*, II, 26 (Wordsworth did not print this line).

13. *PW*, IV, 59 (the readings are from DC MS. 16). Robert Woof has lately challenged the identification of Coleridge with "A Character" (*Ariel*, 2 [April 1971]), but the case for identification summarized by Mark Reed (*Chronology*, p. 323 and *Ariel*, 3 [April 1972], 70–79) remains a very strong one.

and lessening sympathy, and at last to give up hopes of him. Wordsworth does not show at his best as a prophet or a friend in the measured, cold letter he wrote to Thomas Poole in 1809, upon the imminent collapse of the *Friend:* "I give it to you as my deliberate opinion, formed upon proofs which have been strengthening for years, that he [Coleridge] neither can nor will execute anything of important benefit either to himself his family or mankind. Neither his talents nor his genius mighty as they are nor his vast information will avail him anything; they are all frustrated by a derangement in his intellectual and moral constitution" (*MY*, I, 352). Wordsworth's tone seems brutally unsympathetic, but the vacillations and the failures, the complaints and the demands that provoked it are abundantly and movingly revealed in Coleridge's own writings.

Wordsworth's annoyance, as one sometimes forgets, would have been the sharper because of his own afflictions, which he had repeatedly to surmount. Subject for some years to nervous headaches and a consequent mental confusion, which he described in a letter of 1794 (*EY*, 138), he had begun shortly after leaving Alfoxden to complain of ailments that beset him when he tried to compose. Although one marvels, along with Coleridge and some of Wordsworth's other acquaintances, at the host of compliant women who did his writing for him, one sometimes overlooks the distress that drove Wordsworth to their constant use. In Germany he complained to Coleridge that he would have written five times as much, had he not been "prevented by an uneasiness at my stomach and side, with a dull pain about my heart" (*EY*, 336). These symptoms grew more intense, and Dorothy was for a time in 1801 obliged to keep all manuscript poems out of her brother's reach, as she reported to Coleridge, having agreed to deny them to him even if he should forget himself and ask for them (*EY*, 335).

By 1803 Wordsworth had declared his "aversion from writing little less than madness." For three years, he told Beaumont, "I have never had a pen in my hand for five minutes, [b]efore my whole frame becomes one bundle of uneasiness, [a] perspiration starts out all over me, and my chest is [o]ppressed in a manner which I can not describe" (*EY*, 407). Coleridge, whose afflictions, whatever their origins, were more dramatic and certainly more real (swollen knees, swollen eyelids, ulcerated scrotum, boils behind the ears, facial spasms, diarrhea, insomnia, abscessed teeth, erysipelas, and the rest), attributed his partner's symptoms in a letter to Humphry Davy to "a particular pain, probably in the right hypochondrium" (16 July 1800; *STCL*, I, 606). With the wisdom of suffering he once presciently analyzed for Thomas Poole their respective afflictions: "My many weaknesses are of some advantage to me; they unite me more with the great mass of my fellow-beings —but dear Wordsworth appears to me to have hurtfully segregated & isolated his Being / Doubtless his delights are more deep and sublime; / but he has likewise more hours, that prey on his flesh and blood" (6 May 1799; *STCL*, I, 491).

In short, the two poets' afflictions drove them apart instead of drawing them together, and their dyspathy widened in proportion to their suffering. The briefest and truest expressions of their opinions were provoked by a single event, the quarrel at the commencement of their Scottish tour in 1803. They parted after some few days on the road, Wordsworth, according to Coleridge, "a brooder over his painful hypochondriacal Sensations" and Coleridge, according to Wordsworth, "too much in love with his own dejection."[14]

The catalogue of temperamental and psychological differences could be extended, to range from superficial attitudes (Wordsworth, we remember, liked to compose while pacing regularly along a path, Coleridge while scrambling over uneven ground; in later years Coleridge's enjoyment of music was "lively & openly expressed," while Wordsworth showed his by sitting silent and alone, "with his face covered")[15] to matters of the deepest conviction. Though most of these differences have long been in view, it has not always been recognized how wide and diverse they were or—what is more important

14. Coleridge made his remark to Poole 3 October 1803 (*STCL*, II, 1010), Wordsworth his to Miss Fenwick in 1843 (*PW*, III, 439).

15. *Blake, Coleridge, Wordsworth, Lamb . . . being Selections from the Remains of H. C. Robinson*, ed. Edith J. Morley (Manchester and London: Longmans, Green, 1922), p. 79 (hereafter cited as *Remains*). Robinson made these observations at a musical evening in London, 5 April 1823.

—how deeply they affected the two poets' literary philoso-
phies. On so fundamental an issue, for instance, as the relation
of Nature to Art, Coleridge reached a stand quite contrary to
Wordsworth's. Holding Art to be "the mediatress, the recon-
ciliator of Man and Nature,"[16] he consistently refuted (as M.
H. Abrams has shown) the old antithesis between Nature and
Art, which he thought more rhetorical than philosophical.[17]

On the central dogmas of their poetic revolution Coleridge
was rarely in full agreement with Wordsworth. Their early
guarded statements of accord were mainly public and had special motives. To the publisher of *Lyrical Ballads* Coleridge had
promised in 1798 that the volume would be *"one work, in
kind tho' not in degree,* as an Ode is one work," but this only,
one gathers, after the publisher, Cottle, had expressed fear
that the contents of the volume would not be homogeneous
(*STCL,* I, 412). In the volumes themselves from 1800 to 1805
Wordsworth assured readers that the poems of his friend
"would in a great measure have the same tendency as my own,
and that, though there would be found a difference, there
would be found no discordance in the colours of our style; as
our opinions on the subject of poetry do almost entirely coincide" (Owen, 153–154). But the bipartite program of *Lyrical
Ballads* reveals the kind of discordance that would have been
hard to reconcile, and in later years Coleridge was more candid. Despite a certain "congeniality of Taste," he reported in
1817, he had always been far more sensitive than Wordsworth's
critics to his "faults and defects . . . even from the first publication of the Lyrical Ballads—tho' for a long course of years my
opinions were sacred to his own ear" (*STCL,* IV, 780).

Actually, about the time Wordsworth finished and sent to
the printer his Preface for the 1800 *Lyrical Ballads,* Coleridge confided to Humphry Davy his strong desire to write
his own "Essay on the Elements of Poetry" (*STCL,* I, 632).
When he spoke to William Sotheby in 1802 of "a *radical* Dif-

16. "Poesy or Art," *Coleridge's Miscellaneous Criticism,* ed. T. M.
Raysor (London: Constable and Co., 1936), p. 205.
17. See *The Mirror and the Lamp* (New York: Oxford University
Press, 1953), pp. 111 and 122.

ference" between his theoretical opinions and Wordsworth's, he confessed that "we have had lately some little controversy on this subject" (*STCL*, II, 812). Even during the *annus mira-bilis*, by Hazlitt's testimony, some roots of this difference had come into sight. We all remember Coleridge's complaint "that Wordsworth was not prone enough to believe in the traditional superstitions" of Alfoxden, and that there was, in his "descriptive pieces," not in his "philosophical poetry," "a some-thing corporeal, a *matter-of-fact-ness*, a clinging to the palpa-ble, or often to the petty."[18] Wordsworth in his turn found in Coleridge "a sort of dreaminess which would not let him see things as they were" (*HCR*, II, 487); he believed that Cole-ridge was "not under the influence of external objects," but that he relied instead on his "extraordinary powers of summoning up an image or series of images in his own mind."[19] One might see it as a natural consequence of these opinions that where Coleridge thought Wordsworth endowed with a rich imagina-tion but "a sterile fancy," Wordsworth thought Coleridge a poet of some genius, but still more "talent."[20]

Though limited and somewhat hard, these judgments are illuminating. As the poets' own critical statements emphasize, poetry took its origin for the one in memory, for the other in fantasy or dream. But Coleridge's judgment had a narrower application than Wordsworth's (for Wordsworth, after all, had inventive powers that were sufficiently extraordinary), and his remarks should not be allowed to obscure more subtle and important differences between the partners' ways of treat-ing the objects of poetry. Nor should the rather silly example that used to be cited to support a conventional view: Coleridge's comment on the "Blind Highland Boy," in which he would have substituted a huge turtle-shell (as more harmonious with "the image and tone of romantic uncommonness") for Words-

18. "My First Acquaintance with Poets," *The Complete Works of William Hazlitt*, ed. P. P. Howe, 21 vols. (London and Toronto: J. M. Dent and Sons, 1930–1934), XVII, 117.

19. Christopher Wordsworth, *Memoirs of William Wordsworth*, 2 vols. (London, 1851), II, 444.

20. Both opinions were confided to H. Crabb Robinson, Coleridge's on 24 November 1811, Wordsworth's on 8 May 1812; *HCR*, I, 52 and 76.

worth's simple washing-tub (*Animae Poetae*, pp. 207–208). Plenty of better illustrations can be found. One of the best was pointed up by David Ferry in his book on Wordsworth's attitudes toward Nature and Eternity.[21] When Coleridge enumerated his partner's defects in *Biographia Literaria*, he illustrated one of them—"*mental* bombast," "thoughts and images too great for the subject" (*BL*, II, 109)—with Wordsworth's poem "Gipsies." Composed and published in 1807, the poem describes a simple sight, a band of idle Gipsies camped all day by their fire.

> Yet are they here?—the same unbroken knot
> Of human Beings, in the self-same spot!
> . . .
> —Twelve hours, twelve bounteous hours, are gone while I
> Have been a Traveller under open sky,
>   Much witnessing of change and chear,
>   Yet as I left I find them here!

Abruptly the poet is stirred to cosmic comparisons:

> The weary Sun betook himself to rest.
> Then issued Vesper from the fulgent West,
>   Outshining like a visible God
>   The glorious path in which he trod.

After invoking the "mighty Moon" as witness of the gypsies' idleness, the poem ends (in 1807) with a jocular soft reproach:

> The silent Heavens have goings on;
> The stars have tasks—but these have none.[22]

For Wordsworth, the poem, like the other "Moods of My Own Mind" of 1807, centered on a subject he thought "emimently poetical"—"the interest which objects in Nature derive from the predominance of certain affections . . . in the mind of the being contemplating these objects."[23] But for Coleridge, these affections were extravagant. For the poet here to invoke

21. *The Limits of Mortality* (Middletown, Conn.: Wesleyan University Press, 1959).
22. *PW*, II, 226–227; readings are from the 1807 volumes.
23. As he told Lady Beaumont 21 May 1807; *MY*, I, 147.

sun, moon, and stars violated important principles of realism and decorum. Invocations so inflated, Coleridge went on rather acidly *(BL,* II, 110–111), might even seem excessive "had they been applied to the immense empire of China improgressive for thirty centuries." In short, what Ferry calls "the common-sense foundation" of Coleridge's criticism (pp. 6–7) clashes with the "sublime egotism" of Wordsworth's fantasy; "where Coleridge asserts that the poet has obligations to the actual circumstances and conditions of what he sees . . . Wordsworth asserts an extraordinary freedom for the poet from such obli-gations," and moves to a characteristically personal realm of vision. Wordsworth himself put the same matter in slightly different terms when, speaking to Miss Fenwick about *An Evening Walk,* he described his own "unwillingness to submit the poetic spirit to the chains of fact and real circumstance" *(PW,* I, 319).

Another brief and simple illustration touches the same point. One favorite spot in the hills above Alfoxden, formed by a brook running through a shaded ravine, was commemo-rated by both poets in typically contrasting ways.[24] Words-worth's description of it long afterward, in a Fenwick note *(PW,* IV, 411–412), though it may owe something to Cole-ridge, is probably the best neutral account.

The brook fell down a sloping rock so as to make a waterfall con-siderable for that country, and across the pool below had fallen a tree, an ash, if I rightly remember, from which rose perpendicularly boughs in search of the light intercepted by the deep shade above. The boughs bore leaves of green that for want of sunshine had faded into almost lily-white; and from the underside of this natural sylvan bridge depended long and beautiful tresses of ivy which waved gently in the breeze that might poetically speaking be called the breath of the waterfall.

When Coleridge described the spot in "This Lime-Tree Bower my Prison" *(STCPW,* I, 178–181)—it is the first of the scenes to which he imaginatively accompanies the friends who

24. Identification of this spot, "The Mare's Pool," was made by W. L. Nichols; see *The Quantocks and their Associations,* 2nd ed. (London, 1891), pp. 23–24.

have had to leave him behind, "lam'd by the scathe of fire, lonely & faint"[25]—he kept a number of these details close to actuality. His first version, in a draft he sent to Southey, spoke of the "rifted Dell,"

> where many an Ash
> Twists it's wild limbs beside the ferny rock,
> Whose plumy ferns forever nod and drip
> Spray'd by the waterfall.

The finished version, published in 1800 in Southey's *Annual Anthology*, describes "the roaring dell,"

> o'erwooded, narrow, deep,
> And only speckled by the mid-day sun;
> Where its slim trunk the Ash from rock to rock
> Flings arching like a bridge; that branchless Ash
> Unsunn'd and damp, whose few poor yellow leaves
> Ne'er tremble in the gale, yet tremble still
> Fann'd by the water-fall! and there my friends,
> Behold the dark-green file of long lank weeds,
> That all at once (a most fantastic sight!)
> Still nod and drip beneath the dripping edge
> Of the dim clay-stone.

It is not surprising that Coleridge should have made the sight "fantastic," or have described as "long lank weeds" what Wordsworth remembered as "beautiful tresses of ivy." Coleridge's version could be thought to foreshadow the tactics of his share of *Lyrical Ballads*—tending as it does toward "giving the interest of novelty by the modifying colors of imagination" (*BL*, II, 5)—were it not that his language echoes some lines in Wordsworth's "Ruined Cottage" which Coleridge may have just heard read, describing "the cheerless spot" where Margaret's cottage stood:

> The goose-berry trees that shot in long lank slips,
> Or currants hanging from their leafless stems
> In scanty strings . . .

25. The line occurs in the draft Coleridge sent to Southey about 17 July 1797 (*STCPW*, I, 334).

... two tall hedgerows of thick alder boughs
Joined in a damp cold nook.[26]

What is important, however, are the contrasting colors of Wordsworth's imagination, roused by the same stimulus. Coleridge's roaring dell was the "grove" in which Wordsworth "sate reclined" in "Lines Written in Early Spring,"

In that sweet mood when pleasant thoughts
Bring sad thoughts to the mind.

What Wordsworth saw about him "in that sweet bower," from the periwinkle that "trail'd its wreathes" to the "budding twigs" on the ash that "spread out their fan, / To catch the breezy air," was simply the "fair works" of Nature, and evidence of her "plan" (in 1820 "Nature's holy plan" was added; see *PW*, IV, 58).

Despite the inevitable differences between a short lyric and a blank-verse meditation, these two poems have enough in common to make comparison interesting. Both assert the spiritual power of Nature—Wordsworth's by positing a "plan," Coleridge by concluding that "Nature ne'er deserts the wise and pure"—and both move to a moral speculation. But Coleridge traces the surfaces of Nature with close attention to realistic detail, only unobtrusively committing the pathetic fallacy, while Wordsworth glances at but moves beyond the surfaces, boldly investing Nature with life and feeling, then turns from Nature to man. In the end, Coleridge's poem is more an outright celebration of nature than Wordsworth's, and closer to the matter-of-fact world of eye and ear.

Wordsworth's poem illustrates what he finally identified as the feature of his poetry he most valued, "the spirituality with which I have endeavored to invest the material Universe, and the moral relation under which I have wished to exhibit its most ordinary appearances."[27] It was this feature, this en-

26. Lines 57–62 of MS. D, printed by Jonathan Wordsworth in *The Music of Humanity* (London: Thomas Nelson and Sons, 1969), p. 123. It is impossible to tell whose lines were earlier since the version of the "Ruined Cottage" Coleridge heard does not survive.

27. Letter to Henry Reed, 1 July 1845, printed by Leslie Broughton, *Wordsworth and Reed* (Ithaca: Cornell University Press, 1933), p. 144.

deavor—Wordsworth's reading of a "holy plan" behind the surfaces of nature—that troubled Coleridge as much as any other practice of his partner's. In his earliest recorded reference to Wordsworth, 15 May 1796, Coleridge, himself a little unorthodox but a convinced believer, pronounced his new friend to be "at least a *Semi*-atheist" (*STCL*, I, 216). On this point of difference, as on others, Coleridge kept silent for a time, but as early as 1803 he reported in his journals "a most unpleasant Dispute" with Wordsworth and Hazlitt, who had spoken irreverently, even "malignantly," of "the Divine Wisdom" (*STCNB*, entry 1616). After cautioning "dear William" against pedantry, Coleridge went on to talk about the dangers of nature-worship: "Surely always to look at the superficies of Objects for the purpose of taking Delight in their Beauty, & sympathy with their real or imagined Life, is as deleterious to the Health & manhood of Intellect, as always to be peering & unravelling Contrivances may be to the simplicity of the affections, the grandeur & unity of the Imagination." Whether Coleridge was thinking of poems like "Lines Written in Early Spring," or others less daring, his reproach is strengthened by his parallel allusion to his own unwholesome habits. Much later, in a letter to Thomas Allsop, he gave full voice to his strong distaste for "the vague misty, rather than mystic, confusion of God with the World & the accompanying Nature-worship" which he found the trait in Wordsworth's poetry he was most inclined to "dislike, as unhealthful, & denounce as contagious" (8 August 1820; *STCL*, V, 95).

Whether or not Coleridge correctly evaluated Wordsworth's nature poetry, one must marvel that an intimate and fruitful literary partnership could ever have formed across differences as wide and deep as this and the others here enumerated. Yet the explanation of the partnership is pretty obvious: while it strained some basic attitudes in each poet, it also satisfied some compelling needs. Wordsworth's needs evolved rather strangely from his egotism, which, sublime or not, was a central principle of his nature. Though solitary and self-isolated, he was rarely self-sufficient; both his literary taste and his self-confidence were nourished by drawing compulsively upon the energies and talents of other people, notably his sister and Coleridge. As this process continued, what had begun as a normal dependence on the literary advice of friends became an immoderate need for praise. As a young poet Wordsworth showed an average anxiety: "praise," he later confessed, "was prodigiously acceptable to me and censure most distasteful, nay, even painful" (*MY*, II, 345). Both the reception of his two earliest volumes and his own appraisal of their merits led him to regret not having submitted them to the judgment of a friendly reader (as Dorothy revealed, 16 February 1793; *EY*, 89); some twenty-five years later, following the publication of *Biographia Literaria*, H. Crabb Robinson was able to recollect hearing Hazlitt say that "Wordsworth would not forgive a single censure mingled with however great a mass of eulogy" (*HCR*, I, 213).

The effects of censure, even of constructive advice, could be paralyzing. The third sustained piece of writing Wordsworth finished, "A Night on Salisbury Plain," was ready for the press by May 1794, but instead of sending it off he held it for another revision, perhaps because the views it expressed were changing, perhaps out of insecurity. Early in 1796 he resolved to publish a revision of the poem, and asked Coleridge, whom he had recently met, to look it over for him before he sent it to the publisher. Coleridge was enthusiastic about the poem and urged that it be circulated through distributors of the *Watchman*. But, ominously, to express his enthusiasm Coleridge interleaved his copy with sheets of white paper, and when Wordsworth got it back with Coleridge's comments written on the sheets he again decided not to publish it.[28] He later explained that the poem's dénouement seemed too stark, too tragic, but his own appraisal of it must have been altered by Coleridge's notes. In 1797 and 1798 he talked of publishing the poem with the "Ruined Cottage" (another poem Coleridge admired, not published until 1814) or with *Peter Bell* (Coleridge admired this one less, and Wordsworth worked over it and held it for twenty years), but *Lyrical Ballads*, containing

28. The story is summarized by E. L. Griggs, *STCL*, I, 216n.

a fragment of "Salisbury Plain," was published instead, and Coleridge's insistent pressure on behalf of the *Recluse* commenced. It was in fact more than forty years before Wordsworth ventured to publish the first of the poems he had let Coleridge appraise.

This fact may suggest the mixed nature of Wordsworth's dependence on Coleridge. Generally stimulated to write by his partner's conversation—although it is worth remarking that in the first half of the *annus mirabilis* Wordsworth wrote virtually no new poetry—he must often have been dissuaded from publishing by Coleridge's critical remarks. From 1799 onward these remarks were closely linked with another powerful dissuasion, Coleridge's support of the *Recluse* at the expense of the shorter poems which, he came to feel, were wasteful, even destructive, of Wordsworth's talent. "William & I have atchieved one good Thing," Coleridge confided happily to Dorothy on 10 November 1799; "he has solemnly promised not to publish on his own account" (*STCL*, I, 543).

Though Wordsworth went through with several editions of *Lyrical Ballads*, he appears to have bent to Coleridge's desire and formed his literary plans around three large works: the poem on his own early life, his great "Philosophical Poem," and a blank-verse epic of the "narrative" kind[29] (this last still teases our imaginations; it may have been one of the designs listed in *Prelude*, I, 177–219). But his anxious demands for Coleridge's help went largely unanswered. By 1803 the critic as well as the poet in Coleridge seemed to be dying. Though he struggled to write to Wordsworth on the immense poetic subject he had persuaded his partner to undertake, Coleridge had to confess: "I could not command my recollections. It seemed a Dream, that I had ever *thought* on Poetry—or had ever written it—so remote were my Trains of Ideas from Composition, or Criticism on Composition" (*STCL*, II, 950). Shocked by alarming news of Coleridge's health, Wordsworth began to fear that his partner might expire before composing the long-awaited notes for the *Recluse*, and he begged for

29. Wordsworth cited these plans to Wrangham, January or February 1804; *EY*, 436.

them with fresh urgency in 1804: "I cannot say how much importance I attach to this, if it should please God that I survive you, I should reproach myself forever in writing the work if I had neglected to procure this help" *(EY,* 452). On the journey to Malta Coleridge tried to read the five books of the *Prelude* Wordsworth had given him, but confided to his notebooks: "I have not been able to deliver myself up to it" *(STCNB,* entry 2092).

In the absence of the notes, or of any help from Coleridge, Wordsworth brought the *Prelude* to a conclusion about the middle of 1805. Although he must have looked upon this trial of his powers as reasonably successful, it failed to give him much assurance, and he continued to hunger for Coleridge's advice. On Christmas day 1805, Dorothy reported her brother "reading for the nourishment of his mind" in preparation for beginning on the *Recluse* but doubted that he would be able to accomplish much until he heard from Coleridge *(EY,* 664). William had been talking of publishing "a few of the longest" of his shorter poems, but his feeling of responsibility about the *Recluse* still prevented him *(EY,* 636). Again in 1806 Wordsworth wistfully declared his need of "some conversation" with Coleridge to advance the *Recluse;* with it, he believed, he "should go on swimmingly" *(MY,* I, 64).

When Coleridge came back from Malta profoundly changed, a different being from the one the Wordsworths had known, the old need abated. Wordsworth's poem "A Complaint" records the sense of loss he felt in images that echo a tender sonnet of Coleridge's, "To Asra" of 1801, and the closing lines of his "Pains of Sleep" of 1803 (see Moorman, II, 94):

> There is a change—and I am poor;
> Your Love hath been, nor long ago,
> A fountain at my fond Heart's door,
> Whose only business was to flow;
> And flow it did; not taking heed
> Of its own bounty, or my need.
>
> What happy moments did I count!
> Bless'd was I then all bliss above!
> Now, for this consecrated Fount

Of murmuring, sparkling, living love,
What have I? Shall I dare to tell?
A comfortless and hidden WELL.

Unsure now of his ability to get on with the *Recluse*, Wordsworth put together the *Poems in Two Volumes* of 1807. Although he accepted some alterations that Coleridge wrote into
the margins of Book VI of the *Prelude*, he finished the *Excursion* without showing Coleridge any significant portion of it,
as Coleridge's later surprise reveals. The long letter of 1814
in which Coleridge expressed his disappointment undoubtedly
helped to keep Wordsworth from returning to the grand design, and two other occasions on which Wordsworth submitted
pieces of his work to Coleridge's review ended in the same
way. In 1808 Coleridge stopped publication of the "White
Doe," though only for six years, and in 1824 he killed altogether Wordsworth's translation of Virgil.

If Wordsworth's needs, first for critical advice then for
praise, kept him dependent upon Coleridge, what needs of
Coleridge's, one may wonder, drove him to play his secondary,
sometimes ignominious role? Here the best answer can again
be found in Coleridge's sardonic self-analyses. Writing to
John Thelwall in 1796, Coleridge described his own worst vice
as "a precipitance in praise" (*STCL*, I, 221). Although he was
alluding to his too-hasty admiration of Godwin and others,
his early commitment to Wordsworth was no less remarkable.
By May 1796 Wordsworth was "the best poet of the age"
(*STCL*, I, 215), and by 1798 "The Giant Wordsworth—God
love him!" had obliterated all other idols in Coleridge's mind
(*STCL*, I, 391). This precipitance in praise grew out of an insecurity as intense as Wordsworth's, but in some respects its
converse. "I own myself no self-subsisting Mind," Coleridge
confessed in 1804 (*STCL*, II, 1054–1055). "I know, I feel, that
I am weak—apt to faint away inwardly, self-deserted & bereft
of the confidence in my own powers—and that the approbation
& Sympathy of good & intelligent men is my Sea-breeze,
without which I should languish from Morn to evening." To
earn approbation and sympathy Coleridge was compelled—
"so far dog-like" were his instincts, as he put it (*Anima Poetae*,

p. 159)—to attach himself to beings whom he believed better, wiser, or more gifted. As he recognized after the break with Wordsworth, his devotion took a quasi-masochistic turn: "voluntary self-abasement . . . habitual abasement of myself and talents."[30]

Wordsworth, of course, was for about twelve years the prime object of this compulsion, enjoying what Coleridge regretfully came to see as "religious, almost superstitious Idolatry & Self-sacrifice" *(STCL, III, 437)*. Long before the break with Wordsworth, Southey had seen the unwholesome nature of the partnership, and recognized that its benefits ran all one way.[31] Though Coleridge's slavish idolatry disgusted him, he turned his main attack on Wordsworth for humoring and coddling his partner. When Coleridge "complained of the itch," Wordsworth and Dorothy "helped him to scratch, instead of covering him with brimstone ointment, & shutting him up by himself."

Wordsworth and his sister who pride themselves on having no selfishness, are of all human beings whom I have ever known the most intensely selfish. The one thing to which W. would sacrifice all others is his own reputation, concerning which his anxiety is perfectly childish—like a woman of her beauty: & so he can get Coleridge to talk his own writings over with him, & criticize them & (without amending them) teach him how to do it,—to be in fact the very rain & air & sunshine of his intellect, he thinks C. is very well employed, & this arrangement a very good one.

Whatever moral strength and material aid Wordsworth may have furnished from time to time, he appears to have given little return for Coleridge's adulation but the graciousness of accepting it. There is hardly a record of his having bestowed on Coleridge's poetry anything but reserved approval (and Wordsworth's careful praise could no doubt be chilling), and his published critique of the "Ancient Mariner" in the 1800 *Lyrical Ballads* ("the Poem of my Friend has indeed great defects") would have stung. Moreover, he disapproved of the

30. From a notebook entry of 3 November 1810 quoted by T. M. Raysor, "Coleridge and 'Asra,' " *SP*, 26 (July 1929), 305–324.

31. Southey's letter to John Rickman, April 1807, is quoted by Griggs, *STCL*, III, 4n.

critical and speculative inquiry to which Coleridge turned upon
the ebbing of his creative powers, partly because he understood its consequences as well as Coleridge did.[32] He published no other criticisms of his partner's poetry, but after his
death pronounced a revealingly patronizing epitaph. Coleridge
would have been "the greatest, the most abiding poet of his
age" had he not succumbed to German metaphysics: "his very
faults would have made him popular" (Grosart, III, 440–441).

Well before the break with Wordsworth, Coleridge betrayed
his awareness that his own energies had been made use of, his
genius checked, his incapacities given cold sympathy by those
he might have expected more tolerance from. We have hardly
dared to put the obvious interpretation upon the astonishing
epigram that he published in the *Morning Post* the month that
Wordsworth was married (*STCPW*, II, 969):

> SPOTS IN THE SUN
> My father confessor is strict and holy,
> *Mi Fili,* still he cries, *peccare noli.*
> And yet how oft I find the pious man
> At Annette's door, the lovely courtesan!
> Her soul's deformity the good man wins
> And not her charms! he comes to hear her sins!
> Good father! I would fain not do thee wrong;
> But ah! I fear that they who oft and long
> Stand gazing at the sun, to count each spot,
> *Must* sometimes find the sun itself too hot.

Whatever the intention of these lines, Wordsworth's with-
drawal into isolation after his marriage caused Coleridge particular pain, and it was not long before he expressed something
like resentment. Writing to Poole on 14 October 1803, he said
that he now saw little of Wordsworth; his own bad health and
Wordsworth's "Indolence, &c" kept them apart. Were he less
tolerant, he went on mildly, he could feel some injury at
Wordsworth's continued failure to visit him—"me, who had

---

32. Coleridge told Poole, 16 March 1801 (*STCL*, II, 707), that at Wordsworth's "fervent entreaty" he had "intermitted" a vast study of "Time,
and Space," to have been followed by a theoretical derivation of the
five senses from one single sense.

ever payed such unremitting attentions to him." Coddled and sustained as he was by his sister, his wife, and her female relatives, "more and more benetted in hypochondriacal Fancies," Wordsworth would have to take special care "lest a Film should rise, and thicken on his moral eye" *(STCL,* II, 1012–1013).

In the same letter Coleridge spoke of himself, in another connection, with mournful regret: "I lay too many Eggs in the hot Sands with Ostrich Carelessness & Ostrich oblivion— And tho' many are luckily trod on & smashed; as many crawl forth into Life, some to furnish Feathers for the Caps of Others and more alas! to plume the Shafts in the Quivers of my Enemies."[33] At about the same time Coleridge confided to his notebooks a pointed little disquisition on envy (entry 1606, October 1803):

A. thought himself unkindly used by B.—he had exerted himself for B. with what warmth! honouring, praising B. beyond himself.—&c &c—B. selfish—feeling all Fire respecting every trifle of his own— quite backward to poor A.— . . . Soon after this A. felt distinctly little ugly touchlets of Pain & little Shrinkings Back at the Heart at the report that B. had written a new Poem / an excellent one! & he saw the faults of B & all that belonged to B. & detested himself dwelling upon them.

Now "what was all this," A (that is, Coleridge) asks, and proceeds to analyze his feelings about B (Wordsworth). To be sure, B "is not so zealous as he might be, in some things—& overzealous for himself." But what is he in larger perspective, and compared with the rest of mankind? Sobered by the implied answer, A reminds himself that he must struggle to understand "the whole complex mixed character of our Friend," despite A's "having been himself deeply wounded by B.'s selfishness," and, moreover, "long, long idle owing perhaps in part to his Idolatry of B." In the end Coleridge suspected the feeling experienced by A to have been not envy but "mere Resentment."

Years later, Coleridge could be less generous. After his

33. Coleridge was echoing an entry in his notebooks, no. 1248, September–October 1802.

break with Wordsworth he gave bitter expression to what he
had felt about the slights and the coldness that had sapped the
"prime manhood" of his intellect. Hostile critics and reviewers,
he declared, had hurt him little.

But I have loved with enthusiastic self-oblivion those who have been
so well pleased that I should, year and year, flow with a hundred
nameless Rills into *their* Main Stream, that they could find nothing
but cold praise and effective discouragement of every attempt of
mine to roll onward in a distinct current of my own—who *admitted*
that the Ancient Mariner, the Christabel, the Remorse, and *some*
pages of the Friend were not without merit, but were abundantly
anxious to acquit their judgements of any blindness to the very numerous defects.[34]

The thread of self-pity that runs through some of these
remarks is the psychological counterpart of Coleridge's impulse toward self-abasement. Any reader of Coleridge's letters
will have recognized it, and most will have been moved by the
appealing form it often takes. Who, for example, can resist
the symbolic design Coleridge drew up in 1808 for his personal seal *(STCL, III, 101)*:

In the centre (as a coat-of-arms), a rose or myrtle in blossom, on the
right hand, a genius (or genie) holding in the right hand two torches
inverted, and one at least recently extinguished; on the other side, a
Love with a flaring torch and head averted, the torch in the direction
of the head, as one gazing after something going away. In the corner
of the left part of the composition a large butterfly flying off; the
motto under it, Che sarà sarà—What will be, will be.

And who can resist the moving letter Coleridge wrote to
Byron in Easter week 1815 *(STCL, IV, 599–560)*, in an effort
to secure Byron's support for the *Remorse?* Striking a properly
deferential tone, Coleridge ventured to observe that he had
had the pleasure, as it were, of working in the same vineyard
as Byron, "tho' your Lordship's ampler Lot is on the sunny
side, while mine has lain upon the North, my *growing* Vines
gnawed down by Asses, and my richest and raciest clusters
carried off and spoilt by the plundering Fox."

34. To Thomas Allsop, 2 December 1818; *STCL*, IV, 888. See also
Coleridge to Hugh Rose, 17 September 1816; *STCL*, IV, 669.

Wordsworth was no fox, or even an ass, but neither was he a very sympathetic or cooperative fellow-vintner. In the end it is unsure whether his uneven, sometimes intense, often strained partnership with Coleridge was altogether more fruitful than destructive. To it we may owe the brilliant handful of Coleridge's supernatural poems, and some of the fresh maturity found in Coleridge's verse from 1797 onwards. But some of its other effects on Coleridge have already been reviewed. Upon his arrival at Alfoxden in June 1797 Dorothy had found him radiant and appealing, "a wonderful man . . . so benevolent, so good-tempered and cheerful" *(EY,* 188–189). But in three and a half short years, from July 1797, when Coleridge declared Wordsworth to be "the only man, to whom *at all times* & in *all modes of excellence* I feel myself inferior" *(STCL,* I, 334) to the winter of 1800, when Coleridge somberly pronounced Wordsworth "a great, a true Poet" and himself "only a kind of a Metaphysician" *(STCL,* I, 658), his relations with Wordsworth served to play up his worst psychological disabilities and perhaps (as I. A. Richards has suggested) "to maim the poet" in him.[35] Even worse, it is not inconceivable that they helped him slide into the debilitating addictions that seem to have taken deep root in the winter of 1800–01, about the time he uttered one of his most wretched cries of despair: he was overwhelmed by "an extreme Disgust," he told Longman, 27 March 1801 *(STCL,* II, 715), whenever he read over his own poems, "which makes it exceedingly painful to me not only to revise them, but I may truly add, even to look on the Paper, on which they are written."

But what of Wordsworth? Suppose, as H. M. Margoliouth once wistfully conjectured, that John Thelwall had not visited Coleridge in 1797, that the owners of Alfoxden house had not become suspicious of Wordsworth and had consented to renew his lease, and that instead of going to Germany and then wandering to the north of England Wordsworth and Coleridge had stayed on at Alfoxden and Stowey? Or that they had found another refuge—in Malta, the Azores, or America—

35. "Coleridge: The Vulnerable Poet," *Yale Review,* 48 (June 1959), 491–500.

where the intimacy of the *annus mirabilis* could be prolonged, so that we would have had, as Margoliouth put it, "for another thirty years that imaginative cross-breeding of great but diverse minds"?[36] What then would have been the consequences for Wordsworth's poetry, and for the revolution in taste he helped to inaugurate?

Answers to these interesting questions emerge as we review the cross-breeding that did take place. One proposition may be boldly ventured: if the relationship had continued, the results could only have been damaging. We need not minimize the immense debts to Coleridge of which Wordsworth himself was conscious. It was not simply that he owed to Coleridge and to Dorothy a revitalization of his powers; in later years he dated from the *annus mirabilis* the only significant change that had ever taken place in his poetic manner.[37] If he meant his adoption of a fresh language, it is uncertain, to be sure, how much Coleridge helped. If he meant his turn to philosophical poetry—the grand design of the *Recluse* and the mode of utterance it represented—Coleridge's influence is incontestable. Coleridge's plan for his unwritten poem, "The Brook," taken over in part in the *Prelude*, where the metaphors of the stream of life and "the river of my mind" persist, is less important than his fundamental strategy of wedding poetry to philosophy. But the question to be answered is whether this strategy was a good thing or a bad—whether Wordsworth's debt was one he should have been grateful to incur.

The fanatical ardor with which Coleridge pressed the strategy upon Wordsworth evidently sprang from his own sense of incapacity. As early as 1796 Coleridge had rested all his hopes for fame and distinction on his "Religious Musings" (*STCL*, I, 203), the first of his poems which he showed to Wordsworth. It was the style of philosophic verse embodied in this poem that Coleridge evidently desired to develop in "The Brook," which he said later was to "give equal room and freedom for description, incident and impassioned reflections

36. *Wordsworth and Coleridge, 1795–1834* (Oxford: Oxford University Press, Clarendon Press, 1953), p. 42.
37. Writing to an unknown correspondent, 1 April 1843 (*LY*, III, 1159).

on men, nature, and society" (*BL*, II, 129). When he transferred this charge to Wordsworth, who, as "the first & greatest philosophical Poet—the only man who has effected a compleat and constant synthesis of Thought & Feeling and combined them with Poetic Forms"—was to write the "first and finest philosophical Poem" (*STCL*, II, 1034), he helped to bring the *Prelude* and *Excursion* into being. Whatever doubts Wordsworth might have had about the synthesis he was endeavoring to make would have been dispelled, for a time at least, by Coleridge's absolute faith in its viability. For Coleridge, Wordsworth perfectly illustrated the "diversity in identity" between the philosopher and the poet.[38] To Lady Beaumont, who found Wordsworth more philosopher than poet, Coleridge once gently explained, as he later told Wordsworth, "that you were a great Poet by inspirations, & in the Moments of revelation, but that you were a thinking feeling Philosopher habitually— that your Poetry was your Philosophy under the action of strong winds of Feeling—a sea rolling high" (23 July 1803; *STCL*, II, 957).

The artful metaphor conceals a paradox. For wedding poetry to philosophy, at least in the way Coleridge envisioned, was something no mortal could have managed. We need only look at the prescriptions Coleridge laid down, occasionally echoed by Wordsworth in his letters or notes. When Coleridge planned himself to undertake a similarly vast design, before his intimacy with Wordsworth, he had counted on putting no less than twenty years into it, ten to collect materials and "warm my mind with universal science" (as he put it to Cottle in April 1797; *STCL*, I, 320), ten to compose and revise. He could dream as grandly for his partner as for himself. Consider the fantastic letter he wrote Wordsworth to express the disappointment he felt at reading the *Excursion* through in 1815. He had expected to find, he said, "the Colours, Music, imaginative Life, and Passion of *Poetry*; but the matter and arrangement of *Philosophy*," that is, "Facts elevated into Theory—Theory into Laws—& Laws into living & intelligent

38. A phrase Coleridge used in talking of Milton, as H. Crabb Robinson reported, 12 January 1812; *Remains*, ed. Morley, p. 129.

Powers—true Idealism necessarily perfecting itself in Realism, & Realism refining itself into Idealism" *(STCL,* IV, 174–175).

If these remarks reflect the counsel Coleridge was giving Wordsworth in earlier years, one need hardly wonder at the foundering of the *Recluse.* But what is important here is not simply that the *Recluse* failed—for the *Recluse* may well have been Coleridge's idea in the first place, both in its lineaments and in its epic scale. ("My object is to give pictures of Nature, Man, and Society," Wordsworth declared enthusiastically at its inception; "indeed, I know not any thing which will not come within the scope of my plan"; *EY,* 212.) Equally important is the fact that the failure was in part of Coleridge's making. Coleridge always thought the story of Margaret one of Wordsworth's greatest achievements. If it had been published separately, he once regretfully remarked, it would have made "one of the most beautiful poems in the language."[39] But he went on to talk about Wordsworth's grand design without appearing to recognize that it was in the later books of the *Excursion,* not the first one, that Wordsworth attempted to achieve that design.

There is, here, an even greater irony, and a more fateful one. It is that Wordsworth's efforts to write the first and finest philosophical poem to his partner's formula encouraged the egotism and the remoteness that marked his poetic decline. The formula worked brilliantly for a time, but at its Coleridgean center lay the seeds of its failure. For Coleridge insisted from the beginning that his partner's work be both elevated and personal, a "Faithful Transcript of his own most august and innocent Life, of his own Habitual Feelings & Modes of seeing and hearing" *(STCL,* II, 1034). The two poets used different images to represent the undertaking, and both drew upon worlds they knew little about, the one nautical, the other architectural. Coleridge liked to think of the great work as his partner's "natural Element," in which he could sail in "an open Ocean & a steady Wind; unfretted by short tacks, reefing, & hawling & disentangling the ropes—great

39. 21 July 1832; *Table Talk and Omnia of Samuel Taylor Coleridge* (London: Oxford University Press, 1917), p. 188.

work necessarily comprehending his attention & Feelings within the circle of great objects, & elevated Conceptions" *(STCL,* II, 1013). Wordsworth later pictured it as a Gothic church to which all his smaller pieces stood in the relation of "little cells, oratories, and sepulchral recesses" *(PW,* V, 2). But both images suggest a damaging elevation, a lofty abstract grandeur, a fatal remoteness from the sources of Wordsworth's inspiration.

Quite simply, Wordsworth's prolonged effort to realize Coleridge's idea of philosophical poetry, though it helped to produce the *Prelude,* drew him away at last from the modes of lyrical, narrative, and dramatic utterance in which some of his most brilliant verse was cast and brought him to an end like Coleridge's, mired not in abstruse metaphysics but in moral and social philosophy.

Another measure of Coleridge's influence may be taken from a slightly different angle. Wordsworth's critical writing is commonly cited as an important by-product of his partnership. Wordsworth himself admitted in 1845 that the Preface of 1800 had been written at Coleridge's prompting—indeed "solely to gratify Coleridge," Wordsworth himself being "quite against anything of the kind"[40]—and we have sometimes regretted that the *Friend* did not last long enough to draw more theoretical essays out of him. Actually, Wordsworth testified in his marginal notes to Field's "Memoirs" that he was ready to write essays for the *Friend* but that Coleridge, far from encouraging him, put him off by urging him to wait until Coleridge's own principles had been set down. In any case, while Wordsworth's prefaces are a valuable component of his total achievement, they are correctly looked upon as symptomatic of certain attitudes, and as the product of certain tensions. As in the case of Coleridge, the growth of the critic in Wordsworth ran along with a corresponding diminution of the poet.

40. Wordsworth made remarks to this effect to several people, among them Moxon (10 April 1845; *LY,* III, 1248–1249), John Heraud (23 November 1830; *LY,* II, 537), and William Rowan Hamilton (4 January 1838; *LY,* II, 910), and he inserted a note to the same effect in the margin of Barron Field's "Memoirs."

But the problem was more complicated than that. Coleridge put his finger on it when (in 1803) he rejoiced that his partner had at last "bidden farewell to all small poems" and embarked on his great work. "In those little poems," Coleridge explained, "his own corrections coming of necessity so often—at the end of every fourteen or twenty lines, or whatever the poem might chance to be—wore him out; difference of opinion with his best friends irritated him, and he wrote, at times, too much with a sectarian spirit, in a sort of bravado" (*Anima Poetae*, p. 30). It was precisely this sectarian spirit, this bravado, that the partnership with Coleridge provoked. Whether or not we can go all the way with George Whalley, who has suggested that "Wordsworth's theory may have been made as a reaction *away from* Coleridge," and even further that as early as 1802 Coleridge thought of Wordsworth as his "antagonist,"[41] we ought to perceive that the critical discussions, of which we have a glimpse in the surviving letters that Wordsworth and Coleridge exchanged, stimulated and hardened their doctrinaire views. To present his side of the arguments Wordsworth wrote, almost in Coleridge's presence, poems like "The Idiot Boy," "The Thorn," *Peter Bell*, and some of the other frankly experimental pieces of 1798; it is not hard to believe that the same motives inspired the preface of 1800, which Coleridge reported arose from their mutual conversation and which was written when Wordsworth and Coleridge were intermittently together. For it was these particular works to which Coleridge most bluntly proclaimed his "hostility," first in letters of 1802, then in the *Biographia Literaria*, and later.

It is, in short, one of the largest ironies of this strange partnership that Coleridge should have been in part responsible for the faults he criticized so pointedly in Wordsworth. "With many parts of this [1800] preface . . . " he summed it up in Chapter XIV (*BL*, II, 7–8), "I never concurred; but on the contrary objected to them as erroneous in principle, and as contradictory (in appearance at least) both to other parts of the same preface and to the author's own practice in the greater

---

41. George Whalley, "Preface to *Lyrical Ballads*: A Portent," *UTQ*, 25 (July 1956), 467–483; and see "The Integrity of *Biographia Literaria*," *Essays and Studies: 1953*, n.s. 6, pp. 87–101.

number of the poems themselves." Only a few poems, he explained in Chapter XXII *(BL,* II, 95–96), were involved—those in which Wordsworth "chose to try an experiment; and this experiment we will suppose to have failed." At the very time that he attacked the poems Wordsworth had written to the program of *Lyrical Ballads,* Coleridge singled out for praise poems Wordsworth had written later, with his sister along the Wye or in Goslar, or at Grasmere, when he was separated from his partner and freed from the theoretical disputations concerning the language and the very nature of poetry that Coleridge so relished. It is in these poems that generations of later readers, along with Coleridge, have heard the true ring of Wordsworth's major voices.

Despite their differences—and at the beginning perhaps because of them—Wordsworth and Coleridge moved steadily together following their meeting in Bristol in August 1795. Although the close partnership of *Lyrical Ballads* took nearly two years to form, they soon began to write along parallel paths, working from the same ideas, on the same topics, even on the same poems. Their collaboration, that is, if it may be loosely called that, was of several kinds. In one they tried parallel but independent treatments of a single theme or subject; in another they undertook joint composition; in a third Coleridge simply touched up or padded out pieces Wordsworth had written and then set aside. Growing out of shared tastes and enthusiasms, all these efforts reveal important, sometimes irreconcilable, differences of poetic philosophy.

The first sort of collaboration was a wholly natural one. As the two poets shared and exchanged ideas they first imitated then competed with each other, touching the same themes or experimenting with the same modes of utterance. The little translations they contributed to Francis Wrangham's *Poems* (dated 1795, but issued later) might have represented a friendly competition. Their tragedies, *The Borderers* and *Osorio,* both completed in 1797, were finished in a kind of rivalry, and a number of other pieces, some of them portions of larger works, followed.

The second sort of collaboration, though it might appear

unworkable, must also have come quite naturally. Before they came together both Wordsworth and Coleridge had tried writing poems jointly with friends. Wordsworth had collaborated with Wrangham on an ambitious "imitation" of Juvenal in modern dress and circumstances; they first composed "jointly" then endeavored to go on separately. The collaboration was an informal one—Wordsworth even used a couple of lines supplied by Southey, whom he identified to Wrangham in November 1795 as "a friend of Coleridge" *(EY, 158)*—and it broke down after several dozen lines. Coleridge had meanwhile undertaken various sorts of collaboration with Southey; he contributed, for example, more than 200 lines to *Joan of Arc*, and Southey contributed five stanzas to Coleridge's "Devil's Thoughts."[42] While Coleridge compared this partnership to "a sort of familiar conversation between two clever men"[43] and once blandly observed that he contributed the ideas, Southey the execution, it satisfied Southey less well (though as late as 1800 Coleridge and Southey thought of composing a joint poem on Mohammed, to be divided up between them by books, and contemplated writing a novel together). In any case, the kind of collaboration that Wordsworth and Coleridge essayed when they started to compose "The Ancient Mariner" together, during the latter months of 1797, was one they might have hoped to find familiar and congenial.

The third kind of collaboration was forced upon Coleridge by his commitments and his incapacities. As early as 1796 he began contributing to London reviews and newspapers, and late in 1797 he contracted to furnish poems and notes to the *Morning Post* for a guinea a week. It was a task he soon found suffocating—"the worst occupation for a man who would wish to preserve any delicacy of moral feeling." Always "something must be written & written immediately," he lamented in 1798 *(STCL, I, 365)*. If anything good occurred to him he hated to send it "garbled to a newspaper"; if anything cheap or ludicrous, he hated to reject it, "because *some-*

42. See Coleridge's note of 1829; *STCPW*, I, 321n.
43. Quoted by Thomas Allsop, *Letters, Conversations, and Recollections of S. T. Coleridge*, 3rd ed. (London, 1864), p. 51.

thing must be written." Finding his promises impossible to keep, Coleridge occasionally sent in scraps of Wordsworth's verse, sometimes taken from notebooks he was allowed to look over, sometimes apparently taken from letters. He may have been following easy habits he had formed when he was publishing *The Watchman.* In most cases he altered Wordsworth's drafts, sometimes adding a distinctive flavor which has helped to confuse later readers. A number of these pieces, like "Lewti" and "Alcaeus to Sappho"—in its original form probably one of Wordsworth's Lucy poems—were included in posthumous collections of Coleridge's poems, and their histories have only recently been straightened out.

The earliest instance of any kind of "collaboration" between Wordsworth and Coleridge took place before the *annus mirabilis* opened. Following their meeting in Bristol late in 1795, along with their exchange of manuscripts the two poets paid each other public notice and the compliment of imitation. In a footnote to a poem published in his 1796 volume Coleridge acknowledged indebtedness to Wordsworth for the phrase "green radiance" (taken from *An Evening Walk*), and went on to declare him "unrivalled" among modern poets for two or three particular qualities. But he moderated his praise in terms which Wordsworth must have found unacceptable: Wordsworth was, it seemed, "a Poet whose versification is occasionally harsh and his diction too frequently obscure." This measured allotment of praise and criticism may have helped provoke Wordsworth's ambivalent note on "The Ancient Mariner" in 1800, commonly thought gratuitous. But Wordsworth made an earlier reply in the form of an imitation of Ossian parallel to one of Coleridge's. In November 1796 he published in a provincial journal, the *Sherburne Weekly Entertainer*, a poem entitled "Address to the Ocean," the first line of which, he observed in a note, was borrowed "from Mr. Coleridge" (whose Ossianic poem, "Complaint of Ninathoma," was published in 1796). J. R. MacGillivray, who noticed the parallel in 1954, showed that Coleridge stayed relatively close to the Ossianic original, while Wordsworth, who seemed to be inviting comparison, "turns from the supernatural to the natural, from the mythical to the ordinary."[44] A further important difference might be mentioned. Although both lyrics are "complaints" (Coleridge also called his an "effusion"), written in identical meters, Coleridge's is restrained, decorous, and conventional, while Wordsworth's reveals intense and swiftly-moving feeling on the part of the speaker:

> Oh! where are thy beauties, my lover?
> And where is thy dark flowing hair?
> Oh God! that this storm would uncover
> Thy body that once was so fair![45]

Another possible case can be found in 1796. Much taken by Wordsworth's "Salisbury Plain," in particular by the portion later published in *Lyrical Ballads* as "The Female Vagrant," Coleridge developed a similar scene in similar language in blank-verse lines he wrote in 1796 to be called "Visions of the

44. "An Early Poem and Letter by Wordsworth," *RES*, n.s. 5 (January 1954), 62–66.

45. It has been suggested that another poem in the same journal published four months later (March 1797) was from the pen of Wordsworth or Coleridge, or both. Signed teasingly "W. C." with a note attached, "Read at a Literary Club," the poem was attributed to Wordsworth by Helen Darbishire, who printed it in the 2nd edition of *PW*, II (533–534). Miss Darbishire argued from the signature that Coleridge may also have had a hand in it ("An Approach to Wordsworth's Genius," *English Studies Today*, ed. C. L. Wrenn and G. Bullough [Oxford: Oxford University Press, 1952] pp. 141–157). She rested her attribution partly on internal evidence—one phrase, "Our noisy years," later appeared in the "Intimations" ode—and partly on the poem's appearance in a notebook of Wordworth's over the initials "W W"; she also cited an entry in the diary of a Racedown servant, Joseph Gill. But Miss Darbishire's case has been convincingly refuted by F. W. Bateson in *Wordsworth: A Reinterpretation* (London: Longmans, Green, 1956), pp. 136–137, and by R. S. Woof, "A Misreading," *TLS*, 6 July 1962, p. 493. The notebook version of "Address to Silence" is not a draft in Wordsworth's hand but an incomplete fair copy in Dorothy's, and it bears a superscription identifying its source: "Passages taken from an address to Silence published in the *Weekly Entertainer*" (only 16 of the poem's 67 lines are copied); the intials "W W" disappear upon close examination, for they show up not once but several times, along with some solitary "W" 's scattered over the page and the page facing (it looks as though before Dorothy used this page Wordsworth began using it with the notebook reversed, and as he did so tested his pen with a series of sweeping strokes roughly resembling the letters "M M"); Joseph Gill's diary entry was incorrectly transcribed.

maid of Orleans."[46] Emile Legouis was the first to assert the parallel;[47] if less than entirely convincing, it seems possible. Coleridge's maid is witness to a spectacle of horror laced with grotesque: a stricken team, a dead horse, a family—mother and children—extinguished by "Fright and Cold and Hunger," the husband only surviving briefly, "hopeless, strengthless, sick for lack of food." Before he dies he tells the maid the story of their demise. Their village having been overwhelmed by war and set afire, they had fled and wandered the frosty roads until they collapsed. The same sort of tragedy had overtaken the family of Wordsworth's "Female Vagrant." In the "Western Worlds" where they had taken refuge from other perils,

> "The pains and plagues that on our heads came down,
> Disease and Famine, Agony and Fear,
> In wood or wilderness, in camp or town,
> It would thy brain unsettle even to hear.
> All perished, all in one remorseless year,
> Husband and children one by one, by sword
> And scourge of fiery fever . . .[48]

The woman alone had survived to reach England, where she had languished, sick, hungry, helpless.

Though the "artless story" she tells resembles the "simple tale" of Coleridge's victim, both in some of its details and in its occasional Gothic extravagance, the fundamental difference is that hers is spoken in direct utterance, while Coleridge's is reported in the words of the poet. Whether or not the passages are related, Wordsworth's selection of a dramatic form and his consequent use of the language of suffering—if not quite yet the language of real life—as against Coleridge's preference for the poet's own voice and his consequent control of language and point of view foreshadowed a division that was shortly to open between the two poets' theoretical opinions as well as their poetic practice.

In this connection *The Borderers* and *Osorio* take on special

46. Included in "The Destiny of Nations," *STCPW*, I, 139–140. See Coleridge's letter to Thelwall, 17 December 1796 (*STCL*, I, 285).
47. *The Early Life of William Wordsworth*, trans. J. W. Matthews (London: J. M. Dent; New York: E. P. Dutton, 1921), pp. 342–343.
48. Lines 316–322 of the earliest version; see *BWS*, p. 161.

interest, but before turning to them another possible collaboration of 1797 ought to be looked at, for it reaches into the
earliest close exchange of ideas between the two poets. Readers
of Wordsworth and Coleridge have long been teased by verbal echoes between a 1797 poem of Wordsworth's, "Lines
left upon a Seat in a Yew-tree" (*PW*, I, 92–94), and various
letters and poems of Coleridge's dating from 1796 to 1798.
The "Yew-tree poem" was one of the pieces talked about and
admired during the first days of Coleridge's memorable visit
to Racedown in June 1797. About a year later it appeared in
Lyrical Ballads (1798), standing third in the volume, between
two pieces of Coleridge's. The lines follow a conventional
pattern. Addressed to the passing "Traveller" or "Stranger,"
they describe the man who built the rustic seat, which became
first "an emblem of his own unfruitful life," then "his only
monument." A man of exceptional gifts who had met neglect
in the world, he had withdrawn, turned inward, and sustained
himself on pride and sentimental self-pity. The final paragraph points a moral:

> If thou be one whose heart the holy forms
> Of young imagination have kept pure,
> Stranger! henceforth be warned; and know that pride,
> Howe'er disguised in its own majesty,
> Is littleness; that he, who feels contempt
> For any living thing, hath faculties
> Which he has never used; that thought with him
> Is in its infancy. The man, whose eye
> Is ever on himself, doth look on one,
> The least of nature's works, one who might move
> The wise man to that scorn which wisdom holds
> Unlawful, ever. O, be wiser thou!
> Instructed that true knowledge leads to love,
> True dignity abides with him alone
> Who, in the silent hour of inward thought,
> Can still suspect, and still revere himself,
> In lowliness of heart.

This final paragraph in particular has been thought to develop a distinctively Wordsworthian theme: "revulsion," as
Ernest de Selincourt put it, "from the intellectual arrogance
and self-sufficiency of Godwinism" (*PW*, I, 329). The theme

is Wordsworthian, though it is hardly less Coleridgean, and some questions have been raised about it. Recently, Jonathan Wordsworth, after perceptively exploring connections between the Yew-tree poem and some of Coleridge's language and philosophy, cited "the enigmatic reference to Imagination" in the final paragraph, speculating that it may have been a late insertion made in the summer of 1798 when *Lyrical Ballads* was being readied for the press.[49]

The speculation is both ingenious and astute, and a further possibility is raised by some penciled notes in one of the three known copies of *Lyrical Ballads*, Volume I (1800), which contain the uncanceled preface leaf alluding to "Christabel."[50] These notes, in an unknown, apparently nineteenth-century, hand, attribute to "Coleridge" or "S T Coleridge" not only each of the five Coleridge poems in the volume but also, evidently, the final paragraph of the Yew-tree poem. Is it conceivable that an early owner of the volume, knowing the identity of its contributors, knew that Coleridge wrote part of this poem? The suspicion deserves to be entertained for a moment, for certain small details appear to support it.

In 1843 Wordsworth told Miss Fenwick that the poem had been "composed in part at school at Hawkshead" (*PW*, I, 329), but the only notebook in which any lines of the poem survive is DC MS. 11, in use at Racedown in 1797 (for his 1815 collection Wordsworth dated the poem 1795). The notebook has draftings toward most of the final paragraph apparently in Wordsworth's hand, but some of them differ from the published text, and the published text contains two distinctive passages nowhere found in the MS drafts (though, as Mark Reed notes, *Chronology*, p. 192n, four leaves have been cut out of the book at this place). One passage is the opening of the final paragraph, with its abrupt imperative address:

> If thou be one whose heart the holy forms
> Of young imagination have kept pure,
> Stranger! henceforth be warned . . . .

49. *The Music of Humanity*, p. 206n.
50. No. 6 in George Harris Healey's catalogue, *The Cornell Wordsworth Collection* (Ithaca: Cornell University Press, 1957).

The other is the closely specified, complex, rather awkward sentence:

> The man, whose eye
> Is ever on himself, doth look on one,
> The least of nature's works, one who might move
> The wise man to that scorn which wisdom holds
> Unlawful, ever.

It is at least possible that the notebook drafts represent Wordsworth's effort, unsuccessful and abandoned, to write a conclusion to his poem. If that effort was taken up by Coleridge, one striking fact of the poem's textual history might be explained: Wordsworth retouched the poem for every edition from 1800 to 1836, revising freely through the first forty-odd lines, but he left the final paragraph unaltered.

The verbal echoes that everyone has noticed are inconclusive. Most of them can be dated later than the time at which Coleridge would have heard the Yew-tree poem, or its first paragraphs, read. In the title character of *Osorio* Coleridge tried, as he explained, "to represent a man, who, from his childhood had mistaken constitutional abstinence from vices, for strength of character—thro' his pride duped into guilt, and then endeavouring to shield himself from the reproaches of his own mind by misanthropy" (*STCPW*, II, 519). Osorio's self-reproaches and self-analyses, in Acts IV and V, occasionally echo language of the Yew-tree poem. "He was a man," he says of himself, "different from other men, / And he despised them, yet revered himself" (Act IV, 83–84)—a man who looked on "all things with a quiet scorn" (IV, 116). Other reproaches in the drama ring even more strikingly, like Alhadra's of herself (V, 47–48), which Coleridge quoted in a letter of 14 October 1797 (*STCL*, I, 350)—"I need the sympathy of human faces / To beat away this deep contempt for all things"—or Albert's of Osorio (V, 187–190):

> Thou blind self-worshipper! thy pride, thy cunning,
> Thy faith in universal villainy,
> Thy shallow sophisms, thy pretended scorn
> For all thy human brethren.

But it is not only in *Osorio* that Coleridge used language

closely paralleling that of the Yew-tree poem's final paragraph. "I am as much a Pangloss as ever," he wrote about 17 July 1797 to Southey, "—Only less *contemptuous,* than I used to be, when I argue how unwise it is to feel contempt for any thing—" (*STCL,* I, 332–337). Coleridge went on to praise Wordsworth, then to quote a portion of the "Lime-Tree Bower" in which occur the phrases "a living Thing" and "Each faculty of sense." Another letter points even more suggestively to Coleridge's participation in the Yew-tree poem's final paragraph. Written before Coleridge could have seen Wordsworth's poem, even before he had set to work on his own tragedy, or had projected "a book of Morals in answer to Godwin" (*STCL,* I, 320), the letter parallels both the language and the sense of the paragraph. To Thelwall on 17 December 1796 Coleridge declared:

Contempt is Hatred without fear—Anger Hatred accompanied with apprehension. But because Hatred is always evil, Contempt must always be evil—& a good man ought to speak *contemptuously* of nothing. I am sure a wise man will not of opinions which have been held by men, in *other* respects at least, confessedly of more powerful Intellect than himself. 'Tis an assumption of *infallibility;* for if a man were wakefully mindful that what he now thinks foolish, he may himself hereafter think wise, it is not in nature, that he should *despise* those who now believe what it is possible he may himself hereafter believe . . . (*STLC,* I, 280)

The freedom with which Wordsworth and Coleridge echoed each other undercuts evidence of this sort, and for the same reason vocabulary tests of the Yew-tree poem itself are unhelpful. What does stand out is the word "imagination," used by Wordsworth at this period "rarely, scrupulously," as Jonathan Wordsworth has pointed out (*Music of Humanity,* p. 204). Markham Peacock cites no occurrence earlier than 1800,[51] where imagination shows up in the note to "The Thorn" as "the faculty which produces impressive effects out of simple elements" (as discriminated from the fancy, "the power by which pleasure and surprise are excited by sudden

51. Markham Peacock, *The Critical Opinions of William Wordsworth* (Baltimore: Johns Hopkins Press, 1950).

varieties of situation and by accumulated imagery"). In the 1800 Preface to *Lyrical Ballads* "imagination" is found once only, as the faculty whose "power" is illustrated in "Goody Blake and Harry Gill." It occurs once in the discarded draft conclusion of the "Ruined Cottage," MS. B., line 108 (see Appendix 2 of *The Music of Humanity*), probably composed in 1798, and once in the preface to *The Borderers*, of uncertain date but now thought to be as late as 1800. If Coleridge contributed anything to the Yew-tree poem, this term, which he used freely and rather loosely in the late 1790's, was probably his.

The pieces read aloud during the early days of Coleridge's visit to Racedown, June 1797, included not only the Yew-tree poem and the "Ruined Cottage," but about half of Coleridge's *Osorio* and all or most of Wordsworth's *Borderers*. Partly because neither play was published by its author in its original form—Coleridge rewrote *Osorio* as *Remorse* for stage presentation in 1813; Wordsworth thoroughly revised *The Borderers* for publication in 1842—we have sometimes lost sight of their historical, if not their literary, importance. Yet they were written when the two poets were approaching the height of their powers, and both poets testified to the significance of the plays as documents of their intellectual histories. On his, Coleridge said soon afterward, he "employed and strained all my thoughts and faculties for six or seven months: Wordsworth consumed far more time, and far more thought, and far more genius" (*STCL*, I, 402). Late in his life Wordsworth linked some of his knowledge of the "secrets of human nature" with his early "turn for dramatic writing" (*LY*, III, 1118).

Not only do the plays, moreover, contain elements of some of the principal "lyrical ballads"—"The Ancient Mariner," "The Idiot Boy," "The Thorn," "Ruth," and some others have been traced to them—but they were once intended to mark the joint appearance of Wordsworth and Coleridge before the British public. About 13 March 1798 Coleridge proposed to Cottle that the two tragedies be published in a single volume, "with small prefaces containing an analysis of our principal characters" (*STCL*, I, 400). One wonders what the Romantic

Revival might have looked like if this volume, the plays redo-
lent of Schiller and Shakespeare, the prefaces intense and con-
voluted studies in the psychology of guilt, had served to
inaugurate it. Perhaps we should all long ago have agreed with
Yeats that it was in fact Blake who opened the long-sealed
well of Romantic poetry. In any case, five days later Coleridge
withdrew the offer (the plays were to be held back for the
stage) and within a month the plan of *Lyrical Ballads* had been
formed. But as they stand, *Osorio* and *The Borderers* afford
us a chance to follow Wordsworth and Coleridge in the early
days of their acquaintanceship working in the dramatic form
on the same themes, with similar approaches, in something
like a friendly rivalry.

One common source of the two plays appears to be *Die
Raüber* of Schiller,[52] though one or two other German dramas
show up in the background, together with assorted books of
travel and novels of Mrs. Radcliffe and of Godwin. It was
almost certainly Coleridge who hit upon Schiller. In his university days he had read the *Robbers* and found its power
overwhelming; early in 1796 he proposed to translate it. He
told of this early enthusiasm in a note to his "Effusion" to
Schiller in the *Poems* of 1796, adding: "Schiller introduces no
supernatural beings; yet his human beings agitate and astonish
me more than all the *goblin* rout—even of Shakespeare."[53]
Sometime during the same year Coleridge listed among his
own unwritten works "A Tragedy" (*STCNB*, entry 161 G
156). When Wordsworth began writing *The Borderers* in the
autumn of 1796 he would have known something of these
matters, and if he visited Coleridge in March or April of 1797,
having mostly completed his play, he would have communicated something of his own designs.

For Coleridge had been invited by Sheridan at the beginning
of February 1797 to write a tragedy himself, "on some popular subject" (*STCL*, I, 304). His first response had been diffi-

52. A very good appraisal of this debt was made in 1916 by Margaret
Cooke, "Schiller's 'Robbers' in England," *MLR*, 11 (April), 156–175.

53. *STCPW*, I, 73. Coleridge had begun *The Robbers* the night of 3
November 1794, and at once expressed to Southey his terror and delight
(*STCL*, I, 122).

dent: "I have conceived so high an idea of what a Tragedy ought to be, that I am certain I shall myself be dissatisfied with my production." Furthermore, he was unsure just what a "popular subject" meant. On 10 March he told Cottle of the invitation but confessed that he had "no genius" for the drama (*STCL*, I, 313). At about the same time he told Bowles that the plan he had sketched out for his tragedy, "romantic & wild & somewhat terrible," was still "too chaotic" to be summed up but that he would send it as soon as he understood it himself (*STCL*, I, 318). Not until early April was he "roused" by conversations with Wordsworth to move forward in earnest. By early June he was able to read two and one half acts of his play, receive Wordsworth's praise, then hear Wordsworth read *The Borderers*, evidently just finished.

It was this experience that opened the full flood of Coleridge's admiration for Wordsworth. *The Borderers* he found "absolutely wonderful," he reported at once to Cottle, containing "those *profound* touches of the human heart, which I find three or four times in 'The Robbers' of Schiller, & often in Shakespeare—but in Wordsworth there are no *inequalities*." "I feel myself a *little man by his side*" (*STCL*, I, 325). As the summer and fall wore on, Coleridge finished his play and Wordsworth seems to have worked his down into an acting version for Sheridan. Wordsworth's task must have been trying, for he was contemptuous of purely "*theatric* merit," as Coleridge later revealed in a comment on a popular play of "Monk" Lewis's (January 1798; *STCL*, I, 379). By December both pieces had been rejected, and the newly-formed partnership had begun work in other genres.

The two plays sound almost identical in their intentions. Coleridge wanted to present in Osorio a man "seduced into pride and the love of power, by these into misanthropism, or rather a contempt of mankind, and from thence . . . into a most atrocious guilt" (*STCPW*, II, 1114). Wordsworth, who actually wrote his preface but left it unpublished,[54] wanted to

54. De Selincourt printed it in *PW*, I, 345–349. To make reference easier quotations from *The Borderers* (and its preface) are taken not from the MSS but from de Selincourt's text, *PW*, I.

show in *The Borderers* a man dominated by "pride and the love of distinction" who is "betrayed into a great crime" then "quits the world in disgust, with strong misanthropic feelings"; his moral skepticism, his "contempt for mankind," his inability to resist certain depraved temptations, drive him to plot the destruction of another man "by the most atrocious means." Wordsworth's intentions outran Coleridge's, for they centered not simply on the events in which the protagonist acts out his malignity, but on his studied effort to reenact his own seduction on another victim who has done him the unforgivable injury of saving his life. Wordsworth characteristically cited the "moral" which he hoped to impress: "to shew the dangerous use which may be made of reason when a man has committed a great crime."

Wordsworth's play, being a study of motivation as well as behavior, thus reaches for a psychological depth that lay beyond Coleridge, as the latter seemed to acknowledge when he confessed that "the growth of Osorio's character is nowhere explained" (*STCPW*, II, 1114). In turn, of course, *The Borderers*, as an anatomy of character, lacks some important qualities of a good stage piece, as Wordsworth recognized. It should have had a more complex plot, showing a greater variety of behavior, of what Wordsworth liked to call "manners." As it was, he later said, "my care was almost exclusively given to the passions and the characters, and the position in which the persons in the Drama stood relatively to each other, that the reader (for I had then no thought of the Stage) might be moved, and to a degree instructed, by lights penetrating somewhat into the depths of our nature."[55]

The nature of Wordsworth's central character, Rivers (Oswald in the revised version), is lit up for us in Act IV by Rivers himself when he recounts his story. It is the story of the ancient mariner, of a voyage and a crime and a penance.

> The wind fell;
> We lay becalmed week after week, until
> The water of the vessel was exhausted;
> I felt a double fever in my veins,

55. These remarks were made to Miss Fenwick in 1843; see *PW*, I, 342.

> Yet rage suppressed itself;—to a deep stillness
> Did my pride tame my pride;—for many days,
> On a dead sea under a burning sky,
> I brooded o'er my injuries, deserted
> By man and nature;—if a breeze had blown,
> It might have found its way into my heart.
>
> (*PW*, I, 195)

But no breeze came, and Rivers was betrayed by the crew into helping to murder their Captain. Upon their return to society "the tale was spread abroad," and from the despair that overwhelmed him Rivers recovered by defying the world's soft morality. He throws off remorse and forges a career of action into which he tries to draw Mortimer (later Marmaduke), through the purgatory of suffering. Once he succeeds, as he thinks, he exults over his victim, now become his partner:

> . . . for ever you must yield to me.
> But what is done will save you from the curse
> Of living without knowledge that you live:
> You will be taught to think, and step by step
> Led on from truth to truth, you soon will link
> Pleasure with greatness, and may thus become
> The most magnificent of characters.
>
> (*PW*, I, 203)

Rivers' tactics of argument have fascinated readers who search the play for evidence of Wordsworth's break from Godwinism. But to the reader who looks for signs of Wordsworth's maturing technique the tactics of character revelation become the most important thing in it. For here *The Borderers* stands apart from Coleridge's companion play. Not only is Osorio a flatter character than Rivers; he is set before us in a less subtle, essentially less dramatic way. We hear about him from other characters in Act I, and we listen to him describe his villainous intentions in Act II. We watch him experience what Coleridge later called "the Anguish & Disquietude arising from the Self-contradiction introduced into the Soul by Guilt"[56]—that is, a

---

56. Coleridge was writing to Southey about his *Remorse*, 9 February 1813; *STCL*, III, 433.

series of fairly conventional crises of spirit. However before we learn anything of Wordsworth's Rivers, save a dark suspicion or two, we watch him in action and from his behavior we infer his character. Slowly, skillfully, he plays his victim, nerving him up to the murder of an innocent old man, teasing him sardonically, feeding his apprehensions, pretending skepticism of ideas he seeks to plant in Mortimer's mind, arguing perversely and brilliantly from "mercy" and with more and more insistent urgency from "justice."

Toward the close of Act II Rivers steps forward in a soliloquy to detail his malignity, and some of the motives of it. It rises in part, we learn, from the resentment he feels at being indebted to his victim.

> ... this Stripling
> Must needs step in, and save my life. The look
> With which he gave the boon—I see it now!
> What if he did the deed in love—so be it
> I hate him not—now I begin to love him.

And what if the deed he now urges his victim to were to be called, like the deed of his own past, "murder"?

> Of whom? of what? we kill a toad, a newt,
> A rat—I do not believe if they who first,
> Baptised the deed had called it murder, we
> Had quailed to think of it. How many fools
> Would laugh if I should say this youth may live
> To thank me for this service! I have learned
> That things will work to ends the slaves o' the world
> Do never dream of. I *have* been what he—
> This boy—when he comes forth with bloody hands—
> Might envy, and am now,—but he shall know
> What I am now—

> (*PW*, I, 165–166)

Coleridge echoed this soliloquy just at the turning point in his own play, which was significantly both the point (in Act III) where Osorio's character hardens abruptly and the point Coleridge had reached when he heard *The Borderers* read. Convinced of a plot against him, Osorio throws off his indecision:

Love—love—and then we hate—and what? and wherefore?
Hatred and love. Strange things! both strange alike!
What if one reptile sting another reptile,
Where is the crime? The goodly face of Nature
Hath one trail less of slimy filth upon it.
Are we not all predestined rottenness
And cold dishonour? Grant it that this hand
Had given a morsel to the hungry worms
Somewhat too early. Where's the guilt of this?
That this must bring on the idiotcy
Of moist-eyed penitence—'tis like a dream!

                                   (*STCPW*, II, 558–559)

There is something of Iago in both these speakers—a good deal more in Wordsworth's, if only because of Rivers' particular designs—but there are important differences. The complex moral nature of Wordsworth's speaker is only beginning to come into full view, and we continue to follow its dramatic revelation through Rivers' actions and his discourse. Osorio's rather uncomplicated rejection of conscience and his dedication to revenge seem by contrast essentially melodramatic, as do the psychological crises he experiences.

Yet it is Wordsworth who is commonly charged with having no dramatic genius or instinct. The charge has been made most strongly by some of Wordsworth's most perceptive critics, early and late. Reviewing *The Excursion*, Hazlitt found that "an intense intellectual egotism swallows up everything" and concluded that "Mr. Wordsworth's mind is the reverse of dramatic" (see Moorman, II, 261–263). More recently John Jones suggests that Wordsworth understood quite early his "desperate poverty in dramatic talent" and, moreover, that after writing *The Borderers* he realized "that his talent was not only undramatic in its kind, but in a positive sense the denial of drama."[57]

---

57. *The Egotistical Sublime* (London: Chatto and Windus, 1954), pp. 55, 61. On the other hand, one of the best modern appraisals of Wordsworth's dramatic power was, I think, made by Marjorie Latta Barstow in *Wordsworth's Theory of Poetic Diction* (New Haven: Yale University Press, 1917). Of recent studies, the wisest is Jonathan Wordsworth's chapter on "The Dramatic Framework" of the "Ruined Cottage," *The Music of Humanity*, pp. 87–101.

Whatever Wordsworth may have known or felt, a reading of *The Borderers* alongside *Osorio* does not teach us this lesson. Coleridge's play is a more vivid and theatrical stage piece, partly because it picks up some of Schiller's magical power, making good use of theatrical apparatus like dreams and fortune-telling and disguise. Wordsworth's play is less glamorous, more thoughtful, more penetrating, rather slower and heavier. But the elements of drama are there in some abundance. Besides the techniques of character revelation, it is richer in dramatic irony than Coleridge's play, and has sharper, more abundant suspense. Wordsworth makes particularly skillful use of dialogues in which one speaker is eager to find something out, while the other, either unaware of his listener's desire or incapable of reacting to it, rambles slowly to the point. Mortimer keeps Rivers (and us) on edge when he returns from his first attempt to murder the old Baron Herbert; Robert, the simple countryman, is maddeningly slow to reveal that he has found the old Baron alive, then abandoned him.

There is one other way in which Wordsworth's dramatic instinct reveals itself, and again it involves a point of difference with Coleridge. Shortly after finishing his play Coleridge complained to Bowles that he found it highly imperfect, but singled out the "style" as one thing that satisfied him. "I have endeavoured to have few sentences which *might not* be spoken in conversation, avoiding those that are *commonly* used in conversation" (*STCL*, I, 355–356). This distinction was an important one to Coleridge, and we find it restated in various ways, in various contexts, throughout his critical writings, particularly where he speaks of Wordsworth's experimental poems. Wordsworth took a different view of this matter, even as early as *The Borderers*, and we find him often insisting in his critical writings that the language of his characters was exactly as he had actually heard it uttered. The language of his play is generally less vivid, less passionate, than Coleridge's, but it is also more natural, closer to the language of common life (and not only because Wordsworth used passages of prose).

Moreover, it varies more subtly according to the speaker.

The language that Mortimer characteristically employs—

> Should he, by tales which would draw tears from iron,
> Work on her nature, and so turn compassion
> And gratitude to ministers of vice,
> And make the spotless spirit of filial love
> Prime mover in a plot to damn his Victim—
>
> (*PW*, I, 171)

can be distinguished from the language of old Baron Herbert—

>   A little boy,
> A shepherd-lad, ere yet my trance was gone,
> Hailed us as if he had been sent from heaven,
> And said, with tears, that he would be our guide—
> I had a better guide—that innocent Babe—
> Who to this hour has saved me from all evil
> From cold, from death, from penury and hunger—
>
> (*PW*, I, 181)

and from the language of Robert, the simple-minded, garrulous peasant—

> I was abroad, the search of a stray heifer
> While yet the moon was up had led me far
> Into the wildest part of this wild heath
> When hearing as I thought a sudden voice
> I stopped and listened not without much fear
> Upon me as the time and place might breed
> I looked, but neither could I hear or see
> Aught living—
>
> (*PW*, I, 208)

or the language of the "female Beggar"—

> Sweet heavens! I told him
> Such tales of your dead Father!—God is my judge,
> I thought there was no harm: but that bad Man,
> He bribed me with his gold, and looked so fierce.
> Mercy! I said I know not what—oh pity me—
> I said, sweet Lady, you were not his Daughter.
>
> (*PW*, I, 219)

There is variety of discourse in *Osorio*, but most of it is founded on a wholly different principle, following a different propriety. After he revised *Osorio* for the stage, Coleridge told Southey he thought one of its best qualities was "the variety of metres, according as the Speeches are merely transitive; or narrative; or passionate; or (as in the Incantation) deliberate & formal Poetry. It is true, they are all or most Iambic Blank Verse; but under that form there are 5 or 6 perfectly distinct metres" (*STCL*, III, 434). In short, where Wordsworth adapted the language of his speakers to their characters and situations—an essentially dramatic maneuver—Coleridge adapted the metrical pattern of his speakers' utterance to the genre of the utterance—a maneuver that is essentially poetic. In the experiments at collaboration that followed, this difference became of fundamental importance.

CHAPTER 3

The Ballad as Drama: I

The publication in 1954 of Robert Mayo's admirable paper "The Contemporaneity of the *Lyrical Ballads*"[1] has made it seem incautious if not foolhardy to claim novelty of theme or technique for the volume of 1798. As Mayo appears to have shown, the *Lyrical Ballads* conformed in nearly all respects to the patterns prevailing in magazine poetry of the 1790's; the volume's "originality" lay less in any innovations it attempted than in the freshness and intensity with which it developed already familiar conventions. As for the "experiments" alluded to in the 1798 Advertisement and the 1800 Preface, they were, as the comments of Coleridge and others seem to confirm, largely experiments in language alone, and wholly within the boundaries of popular taste.

Yet, despite Mayo's abundant and persuasive evidence, something remains to be said about these experiments. For one thing, whether or not they were innovative, they appear to have been regarded as such by Wordsworth, who repeatedly cited their divergence from popular styles. If the carefully worded Advertisement "seems to claim more than it actually does" (Mayo, 491), it betrays concern about the response of readers of two important kinds: not only those "accustomed to the gaudiness and inane phraseology of many modern writers," but also those "of superior judgment," who may feel that the author, in avoiding "the prevalent fault of the day," adopted too low a style (Owen, 3). Fearing these readers' disapproval, Wordsworth had not looked for the volume to find early acceptance, and Dorothy was able to report in Sep-

1. *PMLA*, 69 (June), 486–522.

tember 1800 (*EY*, 297–298) that it had "sold much better than we expected, and was liked by a much greater number of people."

At about the same time Wordsworth, explaining why he felt it necessary to write the Preface, described his poems as "materially different from those, upon which general approbation is at present bestowed," and went on (in the Preface) to enumerate more than one "circumstance which distinguishes these Poems from the popular Poetry of the day" (Owen, 155–159). After sending off the last sheet of manuscript for the 1800 edition, Wordsworth explained to his publisher that "the Lyrical Ballads are written upon a theory professedly new, and on principles which many persons will be unwilling to admit" (*EY*, 310). In 1801 Wordsworth announced to his brother that the reputation of the book was spreading constantly, though slowly, "as might be expected from a work so original" (*EY*, 337). By 1815 Wordsworth was able to look back seventeen years to "the taste that prevailed when some of these poems were first published," and invite his readers to observe "to what degree the poetry of this Island has since that period been coloured by them."[2] Statements of this kind— indeed, the whole line of argument of the "Essay, Supplementary to the Preface"—make it clear that when Wordsworth declared "that every author, as far as he is great and at the same time *original*, has had the task of *creating* the taste by which he is to be enjoyed," he was thinking of his own career, specifically of the history of the experiments contained in *Lyrical Ballads*.

A second point to be made about these experiments concerns their nature. Whether or not Wordsworth believed them to be original, it may be argued that such originality as they had was limited, that they were largely or exclusively experiments in language alone. Coleridge has helped to give this argument authority. When he recognized in 1802 the "*radical* Difference" between his views of poetry and Wordsworth's, he proposed to "go to the Bottom" of the difference in a forthcoming

2. "Essay, Supplementary to the Preface," *PW*, II, 426.

volume of critical essays.[3] And when the proposal finally matured, in scattered chapters of *Biographia Literaria*—almost fifteen years later—Coleridge announced it at the outset to be one of his main objects "to effect, as far as possible, a settlement of the long continued controversy concerning the true nature of poetic diction."

Yet it seems improbable that diction, however real an issue, could have lain at the bottom of this difference, or that Coleridge could have thought it did. We have already looked at some of the problems that lay deeper than diction—problems like the relation of Nature to Art, or the structure of philosophical poetry. As he worked into his analysis, Coleridge seemed, further, to acknowledge that any experiments in the language of poetry inevitably involved larger matters than language—matters like the choice of a speaker, characterization, dramatic propriety, and the like. "We do not adopt the language of a class," he asserted in the *Biographia* (II, 43–44), "by the mere adoption of such words exclusively, as that class would use, or at least understand; but likewise by following the *order*, in which the words of such men are wont to succeed each other." And order, along with other properties of language, he had explained, is determined by the speaker's power of mind, his education, his station in life *(BL,* II, 41–42).

A few pages earlier Coleridge had summed up sharply his dissent from the theories of poetry laid down in the preface to *Lyrical Ballads.* He grounded it (II, 29) on Wordsworth's notion that the language of poetry should be taken "from the mouths of men in real life," but since he singled out to illustrate his views poems that were "more or less dramatic" in form, what began as a discussion of language soon turned into a discussion of dramatic technique. The central issue proved not to be a matter of language at all:

Here seems to be the point, to which all the lines of difference converge as to their source and centre. (I mean, as far as, and in whatever respect, my poetic creed *does* differ from the doctrines promulged

3. See his letters to William Sotheby (13 July) and Southey (29 July) 1802), *STCL,* II, 812, 830.

in this preface.) I adopt with full faith the principle of Aristotle, that poetry as poetry is essentially *ideal*, that it avoids and excludes all *accident*; that its apparent individualities of rank, character, or occupation must be *representative* of a class; and that the *persons* of poetry must be clothed with generic attributes, with the common attributes of the class . . .

Later, in the final chapter of the *Biographia* (II, 103), Coleridge singled out as "the great point of controversy between Mr. Wordsworth and his objectors" simply "THE CHOICE OF HIS CHARACTERS."

It is, I suggest, in remarks like these that Coleridge came closest to revealing the distinctive nature of Wordsworth's experiments in *Lyrical Ballads*. At one level, of course, the experiments did involve poetic diction. But at a deeper level they were, I think, experiments in dramatic form, in characterization, and in narrative technique. No one knows precisely what a "lyrical ballad" was supposed to be; consequently, the "few other poems" of the title page have been difficult to identify. But if we exclude (from Wordsworth's contributions) the three blank-verse pieces as having no ballad characteristics, we are left with sixteen poems. Of the sixteen, twelve are dramatic or semidramatic in form: five are spoken wholly or largely by a dramatic character; three are spoken in a colloquial voice adopted by the poet; four are in large part dialogues between the poet and another person. Only four of the sixteen are spoken solely by the poet in his own character. These facts should not, after all, be surprising. In poems whose purpose was to follow fluxes and refluxes of the mind and at the same time to imitate the real language of men, the adoption of dramatic form was virtually inevitable.

Wordsworth's choice of the ballad for his experiments took place near the beginning of the *annus mirabilis*, but it is unclear what role in the choice was played by his newly formed intimacy with Coleridge. Coleridge's own metrical experiments had been varied, and he had worked in a number of eighteenth-century genres, one or two of them involving a ballad stanza, though his bent seemed to lie toward the philosophical blank-verse discourse of "Destiny of Nations" and "Religious Musings." In poems like the "Aeolian Harp" and the "Nightingale" —low-keyed blank-verse meditations which he first called "Effusions," then came to call his "conversation poems"—he had, by relaxing the restraints of decorum, begun to develop a genre that was distinctive and (as he was later proud to acknowledge) widely influential.

Wordsworth's own experiments in form had carried him by the middle of 1797 through such types as the topographical (or "loco-descriptive") poem in couplets, the sentimental narrative in Spenserian stanzas or blank verse, the Gothic tale, and poetic drama. One ballad survives among his early manuscripts. Written, apparently about the age of seventeen, it recounts in lugubrious quatrains the broken-hearted death of Mary of Esthwaite.

> And soon these eyes shall cease to weep
> And cease to sob my breath
> Feel—what can warm this clay-cold hand?"
> —Her hand was cold as Death.
>
> To warm her hand a glove they brought
> The glove her Murtherer gave;
> She sigh'd (her mother shriek'd) the sigh
> That sent her to her grave.—[4]

One other juvenile poem, a quasi-Gothic "Dirge," imitated from Chatterton or Collins, shows traces of the style that later flowered in the Matthew elegies:

> Dumb is the ploughman's whistle shrill,
> The milkmaid at her pail is dumb,
> The schoolboys laughing game is still,
> And mute all evening's mingled hum.
>
> They laid him while each heart did bleed
> To cavern dark for wizard worms,
> Fair as some green ash left to feed
> The mountain flocks in winter storms.

What may seem remarkable is not that these two pieces have shown up among Wordsworth's juvenilia—neither was printed

4. This and the following poem are found in DC MS. 2; they are printed in *PW*, I, 265–267 and 268.

until 1940—but rather that so little else can be found there to foreshadow the sudden taste for the ballad that appears to have seized Wordsworth about the middle of 1797. It has been observed that Wordsworth confessedly lacked any natural feeling for the ballad ("The moving accident is not my trade"), and in fact developed a theory of poetry which wholly disavowed the purpose of any traditional ballad, the telling of a story for its own sake.[5] But this observation is misleading. In his Alfoxden notebook (DC MS. 14) Wordsworth wrote of the "Scotch Songs . . . Scotch poetry, old Ballads & old tales" he had loved as a boy (see *PW*, V, 406), and he later confessed that he was "indebted to the North" for more than he could ever acknowledge.[6] Even cheap street ballads, printed on half-penny sheets, moved Wordsworth to write some of his own "songs, poems, and little histories" with the thought of circulating them in the same form.[7] It ought to be clear that a number of features of the eighteenth-century English and Scottish ballad would have attracted him powerfully, notably the ballad's directness and simplicity, and its closeness to common life. In the 1800 Preface Wordsworth probably referred to ballads when he gave implicit approval to poems "written upon more humble subjects, and in a still more naked and simple style" than his own (Owen, 171) .

The fact that the ballad commonly told a tragic tale, a story of suffering, would also have been important to Wordsworth. The notion that a story of suffering could produce beneficial effects in the listener or reader was one principle of sentimental morality that Wordsworth clearly accepted. The effects were, in fact, curiously like the "vivifying Virtue" of the "spots of time" (*Prelude*, XI, 258, 260). Mortimer, in *The Borderers* (*PW*, I, 186), put the matter succinctly in a terse aside:

> In terror,
> Remembered terror, there is peace and rest.

Wordsworth himself tried to put it more elaborately in bringing the story of Margaret to a close. His first attempt is flat,

5. See Charles Stork, "The Influence of the Popular Ballad on Wordsworth and Coleridge," *PMLA*, 29 (1914), 300.

6. To Allan Cunningham, 23 November 1823; *LY*, I, 218.

7. As he told Wrangham, 5 June 1808; *MY*, I, 248.

but revealing *(PW, V, 400)*. Musing over the tragic events and
looking at the ruins of the cottage, the poet finds his response
to be oddly comforting:

> I know not how
> But to some eye within me all appeared
> Colours and forms of a strange discipline.
> The trouble which they sent into my thought
> Was sweet, I looked and looked again, and to myself
> I seemed a better and a wiser man.

There was an even broader principle involved here, esthetic
as well as moral, as Wordsworth reminded us emphatically in
1800: "Poetry is passion: it is the history or science of feelings"; "passion," he later observed, "is derived from a word
which signifies *suffering*."[8]

Above all, the ballad, however objective, was in one particular sense, as Wordsworth revealed by his classification of it in
1815, a "lyrical" form, one which required music or, at the very
least, "an animated or impassioned recitation" *(PW, II, 433,
435)*. What made the ballad "lyrical" was chiefly its meter, and
we have noticed that an important purpose of the 1800 Preface
was to assert the power of meter as a stimulant of esthetic
pleasure. "The metre of the old Ballads is very artless," declared Wordsworth in a comment added in 1802 (Owen, 172),
"yet they contain many passages which would illustrate this
opinion, and I hope, if the following Poems be attentively
perused, similar instances will be found in them."

Whatever the logic of Wordsworth's interest in the ballad,
and whatever his childhood experience of English and Scottish
ballads, he drew his immediate inspiration in 1797 from German sources, not Schiller this time—though Schiller wrote
some ballads—but Gottfried Bürger. The simple event that pre-
cipitated his interest and led to the brief intense concentration
on ballads was probably the appearance of a new journal, the
Monthly Magazine, containing some ballads of Bürger in
William Taylor's translations. When Wordsworth had talked
of founding a "monthly Miscellany" in 1794, he had hoped

8. Note to "The Thorn," *PW*, II, 513; "Essay, Supplementary to the
Preface" [of 1815], *PW*, II, 427.

to include a selection of poetry to counteract "the trash which infests the magazines" (*EY*, 125–126). The *Monthly Magazine* announced in its first number (February 1796) a similar program of poetic reform. "The term *Magazine-poetry*, has usually been considered as synonymous with the most trivial and imperfect attempts at writing verse. It has been their [the editors'] earnest wish, to establish a very different character of the pages devoted to this pleasing object in the Monthly Magazine." It was evidently as contributions to this program that the Taylor translations were published—"Lenora" in March, "The Lass of Fair Wone" in April, two others in May. The editor, or Taylor himself, published a brief paragraph of appraisal to introduce "Lenora," part of which must have struck Wordsworth's eye. Bürger's "extraordinary powers of language," it was explained, "are founded on a rejection of the conventional phraseology of regular poetry, in favour of popular forms of expression, caught by the listening artist from the voice of agitated nature."

The Bürger-Taylor ballads were received with rare enthusiasm. Scott said later that "Lenora" inspired him to be a poet.[9] Southey found "Lenora" derivative, but was deeply taken with the ballad that followed it ("I know no commendation equal to its merit").[10] Lamb was no less smitten and wrote to Coleridge about Bürger in July.[11] It was probably about this time that Coleridge laid plans for a study of "English Ballads illustrated by the Translations of the Volkslieder of all countries."[12] Before the end of 1796 Lamb, Southey, and Coleridge all published poems of their own in the new journal. Wordsworth's acquaintance with it may have been slower. We know

9. J. W. Robberds, in his *Memoir of. . . William Taylor*, 2 vols. (London, 1843), I, 92–93, quotes a letter from Mrs. Barbauld to Taylor.

10. To Grosvenor Bedford, 31 July 1796; C. C. Southey, ed., *The Life and Correspondence of Robert Southey*, 6 vols. (London, 1849–1850), I, 287.

11. E. V. Lucas, *The Letters of Charles Lamb*, 3 vols. (London: J. M. Dent and Methuen, 1935), I, 37.

12. His plan for a "History of English Poetry" in eight or more essays, found in MS. Egerton 2800 in the British Museum, was quoted by Kathleen Coburn, *Inquiring Spirit* (London: Routledge and Kegan Paul, 1951), p. 152.

only that he was sent a bundle of back copies in March 1797 (see *EY*, 186n), and that, in the year that followed, Bürger's influence showed itself in several ways.

Bürger's extraordinary powers of language (as rendered by Taylor) left their mark on several of the *Lyrical Ballads*. "The Idiot Boy," for instance, echoes what the editors of the *Monthly Magazine* had called the "hurrying vigour" of Bürger's "impetuous diction" (Wordsworth composed "The Idiot Boy" "almost extempore," and he described the narration of the poem as "so rapid and impassioned" that a suitable place to insert a description of the boy could not be found"[13]). The following stanzas illustrate a few of the many verbal patterns in "Lenora" imitated by Wordsworth:

> Halloo! halloo! away they goe,
> Unheeding wet or drye;
> And horse and rider snort and blowe,
> And sparkling pebbles flye.

> How swift the hill, how swift the dale,
> Aright, aleft, are gone!
> By hedge and tree, by thorpe and towne,
> They gallop, gallop on.

Compare a stanza of Wordsworth's:

> In high and low, above, below,
> In great and small, in round and square,
> In tree and tower was Johnny seen,
> In bush and brake, in black and green,
> 'Twas Johnny, Johnny, every where.[14]

If "The Idiot Boy" is to some degree a mock-heroic poem ("I never wrote anything with so much glee," Wordsworth said later[15]), "Lenora" clearly served as one of the heroic originals, the macabre, terrifying, midnight ride of Bürger's ghostly lovers being burlesqued in the half-comic, blundering ride of Wordsworth's idiot, clinging happily to his pony, pursued by his anxious mother.

13. Fenwick note, *PW*, II, 478; to John Wilson, June 1802, *EY*, 357.
14. Lines 217–221 of the 1798 version; Owen, 92.
15. To Isabella Fenwick, *PW*, II, 478.

Coleridge took "Lenora" more seriously than his partner. He picked up in "The Ancient Mariner" the supernatural qualities of the ballad—the "ghostlie crew" that whirled and danced over the lovers' heads, and the like. He also echoed some of Bürger's language:

> To and fro they are hurried about;
> And to and fro, and in and out
>   The stars dance on between.

At the same time he must have appreciated his partner's parody, for he evidently honored it with one of his own. "Recantation, Illustrated in the Story of the Mad Ox," published in the *Morning Post* on 30 July 1798 (see *STCPW*, I, 299–303) echoes again the hurrying vigor of Bürger's narrative:

> The victor ox drove down the street,
>   The mob fled hurry-scurry.
>
> Through gardens, lanes and fields new-plough'd,
>   Through *his* hedge, and through *her* hedge,
> He plung'd and toss'd and bellow'd loud—
> Till in his madness he grew proud
> To see this helter-skelter crowd
>   That had more wrath than courage.

The "Mad Ox" also has the colloquial language of "The Idiot Boy" and some of its casual tone; it is broken by asides to the "gentle reader" and a jocular reference to the Muse. These shared features only serve to point up the distinctive qualities of Wordsworth's poem. Not only did he filter out the supernatural, confining himself to details of common life, but he sharply modified Bürger's method of narration. He focused his poem not on the events themselves but on the fears they inspired in the mind of the distraught mother. "The Idiot Boy," he explained in 1800 (Owen, 158), was one of the poems designed "to follow the fluxes and refluxes of the mind" specifically by "tracing the maternal passion through many of its more subtle windings." The mother's passion is revealed in her dramatic soliloquies and her dialogues with Susan Gale, just as Lenora's passion was in part revealed in the taut dia-

logues with her mother. But Wordsworth, significantly, over-
laid her passion with the exuberant emotions of the teller of
the story. Adopting himself the role of narrator and speaking
in a casual, colloquial manner, Wordsworth assumed a personality and intruded it into the ballad, addressing intermittent,
half-jocular remarks to his muse, to the reader, and to the
characters in the tale. The result is a curious amalgam of ballad
qualities with qualities distinctive of the lyric: the poem's passion arises almost as much from the speaker's play of mind and
turns of emotion as from the characters' speech or behavior.

The second of Bürger's ballads to appear in the *Monthly
Magazine* evidently impressed Wordsworth and Coleridge as
deeply as the first: "The Lass of Fair Wone" set patterns they
were to follow in several poems. It may, moreover, have inspired them to the active formal collaboration they undertook
in the summer or fall of 1797. Whether any very formal program was shaped this early,[16] the experiments—and the poetic
"revolution"—represented by *Lyrical Ballads* must be thought
of as dating from this collaboration.

The three works on which Wordsworth and Coleridge
labored jointly in 1797—"The Three Graves," "Cain," and
"The Ancient Mariner"—are of unequal value as revelations of
a difference between their authors. All were abortive as joint
undertakings, and only the first, "The Three Graves," contains
extensive pieces of writing by both partners. The history of this
work, however, is not entirely clear. Parts I and II were printed
for the first time as Coleridge's in 1893, by J. Dykes Campbell
(reprinted in *STCPW*, I, 267–275). When de Selincourt dis-
covered that Wordsworth, not Coleridge, was the author, he
argued that in Parts III and IV Coleridge, out of uncritical
admiration, had taken up a subject which Wordsworth had
"thrown aside."[17] Wordsworth did, it would appear, begin the
ballad, probably in 1797, but once his beginning was made,
"The Three Graves" may well have been planned on the same
pattern as "Cain," the first canto of which was to have been

16. See Mark Reed's admirable account, "Wordsworth, Coleridge, and
the 'Plan' of the *Lyrical Ballads*," *UTQ*, 34 (April 1965), 238–253.
17. *The Early Wordsworth*, (n.p.: The English Association, 1936), p. 24.

written by Wordsworth, the second by Coleridge, the third by "which ever had *done first*."[18] "The Three Graves" was to have had six parts. Wordsworth, we now know, wrote the first two, and Coleridge, in publishing the second two in the *Friend*, 21 September 1809, announced that the last two "may be given hereafter, if the present should appear to have afforded pleasure."[19]

Thomas Hutchinson seems to have been the first to observe that the three collaborative poems of 1797 developed the same theme.[20] Grouping them with two of Wordsworth's poems of 1798—*Peter Bell* and "Goody Blake and Harry Gill"—Hutchinson argued that the five poems "have a common psychological basis, and may be described as studies in mental pathology. Each in its own fashion illustrates the tremendous effect upon the imagination (and through it upon the physical organism) of a painful *idea* vividly and suddenly impressed upon the mind. The *idea* is the same in all five cases—that of a *curse*."[21] Hutchinson's grouping is meaningful, but Wordsworth's "Thorn," which shows close affinities to "The Three Graves" (and to Bürger's "Lass of Fair Wone") must be included, together with several poems added to the *Lyrical Ballads* in 1800. When all these "curse poems" are studied side by side, some significant features of Wordsworth's poetic technique come into view.

Bürger's (that is, Taylor's) "Lass of Fair Wone," which was to cast a long shadow, has its setting at a place that is blighted by a withering curse. As the ballad opens, a voice is asking questions about the place:

> Beside the parson's bower of yew
> Why strays a troubled spright,
> That peaks and pines, and dimly shines
> Thro' curtains of the night?

18. According to Coleridge's "Prefatory Note" of 1828, reprinted *STCPW*, I, 286.

19. See Barbara Rooke's edition of *The Friend*, 2 vols. (Princeton: Princeton University Press, 1969), II, 88–89.

20. Thomas Hutchinson's edition of *Lyrical Ballads: 1798* (London, 1898).

21. I quote Hutchinson's "Notes to the Appendix," p. 255.

> Why steals along the pond of toads
> A gliding fire so blue,
> That lights a spot where grows no grass,
> Where falls no rain nor dew?—

In answer to the questions another voice (presumably) recites the tragic story of a maid cast off by her lover. Fleeing "thro' the hissing sleet, / Thro' thorn and brier, thro' flood and mire," she reaches the shelter of the bower, where she gives birth to her baby, kills it, and buries it. At the close of the ballad, the blighted spot is once more described, this time with the reader fully aware of its terrible history:

> Hard by the bower her gibbet stands:
> Her skull is still to show;
> It seems to eye the barren grave,
> Three spans in length below—

> That is the spot where grows no grass;
> Where falls no rain nor dew:
> Whence steals along the pond of toads
> A hovering fire so blue.

> And nightly, when the ravens come,
> Her ghost is seen to glide;
> Pursues and tries to quench the flame,
> And pines the pool beside.

"The Three Graves," so far as we can piece it together, shows roughly the same pattern. This ballad, too, opens at the scene of a parson's bower, a spot cursed not with the absence but with a curious abundance of the marks of nature. After summarizing Parts I and II in the *Friend*, Coleridge observed that the ballad "is supposed to be narrated by an old Sexton, in a country Church-yard to a Traveller, whose curiosity had been awakened by the appearance of three Graves, close by each other."[22] But Coleridge omitted a significant feature. Wordsworth's poem began not with the three graves but with a blossoming tree, which the old Sexton points out to his listener as he begins to reminisce:

> Beneath this thorn when I was young
>   This thorn that blooms so sweet

22. Rooke, ed., *The Friend*, II, 89.

> We loved to stretch our lazy limbs
> In summer's noon-tide heat.

He is interrupted by insistent questions:

> "Then tell me, Sexton, tell me why
> The toad has harbour here.

> "The Thorn is neither dry nor dead
> But still it blossoms sweet;
> Then tell me why all round its roots
> The dock and nettle meet.

> . . .

> "Why these three graves all side by side
> Beneath the flow'ry thorn
> Stretch out so green and dark a length
> By any foot unworn?"

In answer the Sexton embarks on the tragic tale. As it unfolds he remains relatively objective, intruding his own feelings only in an occasional sally. But a Bürgeresque fragment probably intended to close Part II shows that Wordsworth meant to bring the focus back on the thorn and the narrator and his listener:

> Now ask you why the barren wife,
> And why the maid forlorn,
> And why the ruthless mother lies
> Beneath the flowery thorn?

> Three times, three times this spade of mine
> In spite of bolt or bar,
> Did from beneath the belfry come,
> When wandering spirits are.

> And when the mother's soul to Hell
> By howling fiends was borne
> This spade was seen to mark her grave
> Beneath the flowery thorn.

> . . .

> And 'tis a fearful, fearful tree;
> The ghosts that round it meet
> 'Tis they that cut the rind at night,
> Yet still it blossoms sweet.[23]

23. Wordsworth's share of the poem is quoted from the version printed in *STCPW*, I, 269–275.

In a notebook Wordsworth used at Racedown, and perhaps later (DC MS. 11), there are a number of ballad stanzas concerning Edward and Mary and "the barren wife," intended for "The Three Graves." They are scrawled on unused portions of pages used for the translation of Juvenal, hence are later, and some of them are mingled with various lines of the Yew-tree poem, which we assume dates from the spring or early summer of 1797. Probably they were rejected or modified when Wordsworth developed the parts of the ballad he turned over to Coleridge (six leaves have been cut out of the notebook where the ballad fragments fall, and enough letters remain on one of the stubs to show that it contained stanzas from Part I of "The Three Graves"[24]). Their main interest here is that some of them reveal the same mode of narration as Wordsworth's share of the published poem. The old Sexton appears to be telling something of his own role in the events of long ago. Mary has been excited by the apparition of her dead lover's "gallant greyhound" dashing past her:

> Peace gentle [*deleted to* sweetest] Lady peace I said
> And took her by the hand
> There is no shape that cometh quick
> Across the meadow land
>
> I saw [*deleted to* marked] the greyhound scour along
> And lost him in yon wood
> And I will go with your good will
> And see what is his food
>
> What dost thou say thou aged man
> Art thou again a child
> And then she checked herself and wept
> She was of nature mild.

Instead of turning at once to Coleridge's portion of this poem, we need to connect Wordsworth's portion with the

24. For example:
> Wh [y these three graves all side by side,]
> Be [neath the flow'ry thorn]
> St [retch out so green and dark a length]
> By a [ny foot unworn]

See *STCPW*, I, 270.

related poems he wrote during the following year. For by doing so we get a clear sense of the boldly innovative character of his experiments. In "The Thorn," written in March and April 1798, Wordsworth developed themes and techniques he had employed in "The Three Graves," some of them drawn from Bürger, some formed in reaction to Bürger. But before then he had faced and begun to solve in his own way two major problems raised by "The Three Graves" and the other two collaborative pieces.

The first problem, as most critics have recognized, concerned the use of the supernatural. On the approaches to it the partners diverged, and we recognize in the Prologue to *Peter Bell* a summary of their disagreement. With a show of regret Wordsworth there refuses an invitation to rise free from the world of real events and explore "a deep romantic land," a "land of fairy," replete with "streams & bowers & ladies fair / The shades of palaces and kings."[25] In later versions of the Prologue Wordsworth spelled out his refusal:

> There was a time, a time indeed
> A time when Poets liv'd in clover;
> What boots it now to keep the key
> Of Fairyland? for, woe is me!
> Those blessed days are over.
>   . . .
> Why wander then to faery walks
> To forests and enchantments drear
> If I at home may see the sight
> Of conscience, and the dread delight
> Of phantasy and inward fear.[26]

Peter Bell itself, together with two other "curse" poems of 1798—"Goody Blake and Harry Gill" and "The Thorn"—represent Wordsworth's side of this disagreement. Though each poem treats of matters that appear to lie outside the realm of probability, there is in fact nothing supernatural in any of them: every event has a physical explanation. As Words-

25. Quoted from the earliest version of *Peter Bell*, DC MS. 18.
26. Quoted from DC MS. 60 (MS. 5 of *Peter Bell*). Wordsworth never published either stanza in this form. De Selincourt shows the first one, *PW*, II, 336n, but omits the second.

worth's own comments make clear, the poems are studies of the ability of the imagination to respond to natural events as though they were supernatural. *Peter Bell*, as Wordsworth explained in his prefatory letter to Southey, dated 7 April 1819, "was composed under a belief that the Imagination not only does not require for its exercise the intervention of supernatural agency, but that, though such agency be excluded, the faculty may be called forth as imperiously, and for kindred results of pleasure, by incidents within the compass of poetic probability, in the humblest departments of daily life" (*PW*, II, 331). In "Goody Blake and Harry Gill" Wordsworth "wished to draw attention to the truth that the power of the human imagination is sufficient to produce such changes even in our physical nature as might almost appear miraculous"— that is, supernatural (1800 Preface; Owen, 174). "The Thorn," written "to exhibit some of the general laws by which superstition acts upon the mind," is narrated by a man who, though "utterly destitute of fancy," possesses "a reasonable share of imagination, by which word I mean the faculty which produces impressive effects out of simple elements" (1800 note; *PW*, II, 512–513).

The second problem raised by the efforts at collaboration was a problem of technique. Besides sharing a common theme, these works share a common narrative pattern: each is related in the voice of a narrator, not in the poet's own voice. The problem which each of them raised, therefore, was a problem of narrative method, involving such matters as the narrator's language, his character, his role in the events he recounted.

Wordsworth again presented his own answers to the problem in his "curse poems" of 1798. More clearly than any of his other poems, *Peter Bell*, "Goody Blake and Harry Gill," and "The Thorn" appear to have been "experiments . . . written chiefly with a view to ascertain how far the language of conversation in the middle and lower classes of society is adapted to the purposes of poetic pleasure" (1798 Advertisement; Owen, 3). But at another level they are all experiments in narrative technique. In *Peter Bell* the poet adopts a colloquial voice much like that of "The Idiot Boy" and addresses his listeners as though the poem were an oral narration, telling of "Spirits of the Mind" that had teased and deceived him, infusing the story with his own feelings and memories. (The earlier versions of the ballad are more colloquial, and more dramatic, than the later.) Even more boldly in "Goody Blake and Harry Gill" (Owen, 50–55) the poet adopts the point of view and the idiom of a rustic commentator. The poem begins with a series of questions, marked by repetitions like those of Bürger:

> Oh! what's the matter? what's the matter?
> What is't that ails young Harry Gill?
> That evermore his teeth they chatter,
> Chatter, chatter, chatter still.

In his answer the speaker exhibits a certain loquaciousness, an interest in homely and not particularly significant detail, and a colloquial turn of phrase.

> By the same fire to boil their pottage,
> Two poor old dames, as I have known,
> Will often live in one small cottage,
> But she, poor woman, dwelt alone.
> 'Twas well enough when summer came,
> The long, warm, lightsome summer-day,
> Then at her door the *canty* dame
> Would sit, as any linnet gay.
>
> But when the ice our streams did fetter,
> Oh! then how her old bones would shake!
> You would have said, if you had met her,
> 'Twas a hard time for Goody Blake.

Moreover, the narrator, unaware that his story only illustrates "the power of the human imagination," clearly believes in the reality of Harry Gill's affliction. He thus reveals something of the way his own imagination works, and the poem verges on the dramatic monologue form.

The most daring experiment among Wordsworth's "curse" poems, though it represents in some ways only an extension of earlier techniques, is "The Thorn," for which he returned to the pattern of "The Lass of Fair Wone" and "The Three Graves." "The Thorn" is a poem that illustrates, among other things, Wordsworth's sense of place. In Dorothy's Alfoxden journal the entry for 19 March 1798 opens: "Wm. and Basil [Montagu] and I walked to the hill-tops, a very cold bleak day. We were met on our return by a severe hailstorm." The scenes of this walk were familiar, but during the storm Wordsworth's eye was caught and his imagination fired by a solitary, aged tree. Dorothy marked the event by noting laconically as she closed the day's entry: "William wrote some lines describing a stunted thorn." Forty-five years later William corroborated her account of the genesis of this lyrical ballad. "The Thorn," he told Miss Fenwick, "arose out of my observing, on the ridge of Quantock Hill, on a stormy day, a thorn which I had often passed in calm and bright weather without noticing it. I said to myself, 'Cannot I by some invention do as much to make this Thorn permanently an impressive object as the storm has made it to my eyes at this moment?' " (*PW*, II, 511–512).

The lines in which Wordsworth tried to make impressive his vision of a tree in a hailstorm have excited a good deal of critical attention. De Selincourt summed up majority opinion when he called them "the extreme example of W.'s experiment 'to ascertain how far the language of conversation in the middle and lower classes of society is adapted to the purposes of poetic pleasure' " (*PW*, II, 513). The poem was experimental, but the nature of the experiment has, I believe, been misunderstood, and the poem almost universally misread. Of the dozens of critics who have commented on "The Thorn," hardly one appears to have discerned who the central character is, and what the poem is about. The readings fall, roughly, into two traditions. One holds that the narrator mars the poem: "The Thorn" would have been more satisfying had Wordsworth spoken it in his own voice. The other overlooks the narrator, focusing on the story he tells, the tragedy of Martha Ray: "The Thorn" is a haunting and powerful study in social morality. In the one view, "The Thorn" is a bad poem because of the narrator; in the other, a good poem in spite of the narrator.

It would be hard to decide which view is the more misleading, for what neither recognizes is that the narrator is not only
the central figure, but in a sense the subject of the poem. As its
author conceived it, "The Thorn" is not a poem about an abandoned mother and her murdered infant, as nearly all critics
have supposed, nor a poem about the maternal passion. It
would be more accurate to call it a poem, first, about a tree, and
second, about a man. It was intended to be a psychological
study, a poem about the way the mind works. The mind whose
workings are revealed is that of the narrator, and the poem is,
in effect, a dramatic monologue—that is, loosely, a poem in
which the events related are meaningful not in themselves
but as they reveal the character of the person who relates
them. (Actually, "The Thorn" is a dialogue, but the second
voice enters only to ask questions in language that echoes the
narrator's, giving the effect—probably intentional—of a ballad
refrain.)[27]

That Wordsworth's design should have been lost sight of
seems astonishing, for he took unusual pains to make it clear.
In the Advertisement to the first edition of *Lyrical Ballads* he
had singled out five poems for comment. Besides touching on

27. Prior to the publication of my reading of the poem in 1957 (*ELH*,
24, 153–163), George McLean Harper, almost alone among Wordsworthians, gave evidence of reading "The Thorn" in this way. "This
poem is generally misunderstood," he wrote in his notes to the Oxford
Standard *Wordsworth* (Oxford: Oxford University Press, Clarendon
Press, 1933) "through failure to observe that it is a dramatic monologue,
supposed to be uttered by a retired sea-captain who has heard a tale of
superstition in a village." Harper carried his reading no further, and
his notes, tucked in behind Hutchinson's, have not attracted the attention they deserve; they were dropped from de Selincourt's "New Edition"
of 1950. Of more recent readings, perhaps the fullest and most sensitive
are John Danby's in *The Simple Wordsworth* (London: Routledge and
Kegan Paul, 1960), pp. 57–62—singled out by Owen, p. xxxiin, as particularly "subtle"—and Albert S. Gérard's "global analysis," "Of Trees
and Men," *E in C*, 14 (July 1964), 237–255. Danby, however, like most
other readers, seems unwilling to give Wordsworth any credit for knowing what he was about: "nothing could be more misleading," he says,
p. 58, than the poet's "defensive rationalization of the intention behind
the poem." Gérard is more understanding, finding the device of the narrator "both necessary and successful," though like other readers he per-
sists in finding the "actual theme" of the poem to be not the narrator's
imagination but "the truth of human misery."

the sources of three and on the style of another, he had remarked meaningfully: "The poem of the Thorn, as the reader
will soon discover, is not supposed to be spoken in the author's
own person: the character of the loquacious narrator will
sufficiently shew itself in the course of the story" (Owen, 4).
In 1800, after the narrator's character had totally failed to
show itself, Wordsworth attached a lengthy note telling precisely what he had intended to do in "The Thorn" (*PW*, II,
512–513). He began by confessing that "this Poem ought to
have been preceded by an introductory Poem," implying that
he would have sketched there the history of "The Thorn's"
narrator, then went on to supply the information that poem
might have contained. He asked the reader to visualize "a man,
a Captain of a small trading vessel, for example, who being
past the middle age of life, had retired . . . to some village or
country town of which he was not a native." Why a man of
this sort? Because, the poet explained, reaching his point de-
liberately and then summing it up, "such men, having little to
do, become credulous and talkative from indolence; and from
the same cause, and other predisposing causes . . . they are
prone to superstition. On which account it appeared to me
proper to select a character like this to exhibit the general laws
by which superstition acts upon the mind."

Could any statement of poetic intent be plainer? As Wordsworth conceived it, "The Thorn" is a portrayal of the superstitious imagination. More literally than any other poem it
carries out the principal object of *Lyrical Ballads:* to trace in
situations of common life "the primary laws of our nature,"
chiefly "as regards the manner in which we associate ideas in
a state of excitement." For the manner in which the narrator
associates ideas is precisely what "The Thorn" is about. The
ideas themselves—that is, the "events" of the poem—are unimportant except as they reflect the working of the narrator's
imagination. In fact, the point of the poem may very well be
that its central "event" has no existence outside of the narrator's imagination—that there is no Martha Ray sitting in a
scarlet cloak behind a crag on the mountain top, that the
narrator has neither seen nor heard her, that what he has

seen is a gnarled old tree hung with moss, and what he has heard (besides the creaking of the branches or the whistling of the wind) is village superstition about a woman wronged years ago.

This reading of "The Thorn," differing sharply from any traditional reading, alters the poem radically. It becomes not a poem about a woman but a poem about a man (and a tree); not a tale of horror but a psychological study; not a ballad but a dramatic monologue. Based as the reading is on Wordsworth's statements of intent, the question it may seem to raise is whether the poem Wordsworth meant to write resembles the poem he did write. To take the question seriously is to show a singular skepticism about Wordsworth's understanding of his own craft (his careful statements of intent were written after the poem, not before). Yet once raised it must be answered. If we look carefully at the poem Wordsworth did write in 1798 we find, I think, that it does correspond to the poem he later told us he had meant to write.

The design of "The Thorn" is revealed in the order in which the narrator associates ideas—the order, that is, in which the poem's "events" pass through his mind. The poem begins, as it began in Wordsworth's mind, with the tree.

> There is a thorn; it looks so old,
> In truth you'd find it hard to say,
> How it could ever have been young,
> It looks so old and grey.

As the narrator's imagination begins to work (stanza 2), he sees the old tree, "hung with heavy tufts of moss," engaged in a drama of nature:

> Up from the earth these mosses creep,
> And this poor thorn they clasp it round
> So close, you'd say that they were bent
> With plain and manifest intent,
> To drag it to the ground . . .

After this brief flight, the narrator drops to prosaic detail, describing the thorn's location, the "little muddy pond," and the hill of moss "like an infant's grave in size." Not until stanza 6 does he mention "a woman in a scarlet cloak," and when his listener asks why the unhappy creature sits by the thorn crying her doleful cry, the flat answer is (stanza 9):

> I cannot tell; I wish I could;
> For the true reason no one knows . . .

But two stanzas later it turns out that the narrator can tell what everyone does know—and the story of Martha Ray begins slowly to unfold. His imagination warming, the old mariner relates what he has learned about the incidents that took place "some two and twenty" years ago (long before he came to the village): Martha's abandonment, her pregnancy, and her madness. But again he breaks off abruptly (stanza 15):

> No more I know, I wish I did,
> And I would tell it all to you;
> For what became of this poor child
> There's none that ever knew:
> And if a child was born or no,
> There's no one that could ever tell;
> And if 'twas born alive or dead,
> There's no one knows, as I have said . . .

Again, the professions of ignorance prove not to be serious, for we learn at once that Martha was seen that summer on the mountain, and that cries were later heard there, some "plainly living voices," others, it was believed, "voices of the dead" (stanza 16). Here the narrator exhibits a nice skepticism:

> I cannot think whate'er they say,
> They had to do with Martha Ray.

To this point, the pattern of the poem has been consistent: as the narrator's loquacity ebbs and flows he retails, piece by piece, village recollection and superstition about Martha Ray. With stanza 17, however (some two thirds of the way through the poem), he suddenly offers first-hand testimony. He claims actually to have seen the woman by the tree. His testimony is highly important because he has already suggested that no one else has seen her there. Inviting his listener (stanza 9) to view the spot, he had cautioned him to make sure first that Martha was in her hut ("Pass by her door—tis seldom shut"), adding meaningfully:

> I never heard of such as dare
> Approach the spot when she is there.

He would not, we gather, now venture to approach it himself; he had stumbled on it unknowingly (stanza 17),

> When to this country first I came
> Ere I had heard of Martha's name . . .

On that occasion, the narrator and the poet now take impressive pains to point out (stanzas 17 and 18), the visibility was wretched—virtually zero:

> A storm came on, and I could see
> No object higher than my knee.
>
> 'Twas mist and rain, and storm and rain,
> No screen, no fence could I discover,
> And then the wind! in faith, it was
> A wind full ten times over.
> I looked around, I thought I saw
> A jutting crag, and off I ran,
> Head-foremost, through the driving rain . . .

But instead of a crag he thinks he saw "A woman seated on the ground." After a glimpse of her face through the rain he "turned about," then, above the wind, heard her cry, "O misery! O misery!"

Encouraged, perhaps, by the sound of his own testimony, and with his imagination now glowing hot, the narrator lets fall (stanzas 20 to 22) the terrible superstitions he has been holding back: some say that Martha hanged her child, some that she drowned it, but all agree that it lies buried in the little mound; some say that the moss is red with blood, some that the infant's face can be seen on the pond, and some that the ground shook when the little tomb was threatened. After these revelations the narrator subsides abruptly, returning in the final stanza to the tree with which he had begun and the testimony he has offered.

I cannot tell how this may be,
But plain it is, the thorn is bound
With heavy tufts of moss, that strive
To drag it to the ground.
And this I know, full many a time,
When she was on the mountain high,
By day, and in the silent night,
When all the stars shone clear and bright,
That I have heard her cry,
'O misery! O misery!
'O woe is me! oh misery!'

From this review of its "events" the design of the poem should be clear. Stimulated by his memory of a tree, the narrator begins to relate village gossip about a woman. Some of it is factual, some not. Martha Ray and her lover did evidently exist twenty years ago, and the tree, the pond, the mound, and a "hut" nearby with a woman in it evidently exist now. On the other hand (Wordsworth was not, it is generally agreed, a poet of the supernatural), the ghostly voices from the mountain head, the shaking grass and the stirring moss, the "shadow of a babe" on the pond are superstitions, products of the villagers' imaginations. But as the narrator retails these superstitions, his own imagination is roused to activity, and he proceeds to show how superstition acts upon his mind. By the end of the poem he clings to two ideas: that the moss on the tree is struggling to drag it down, and that near the spot he has heard the woman's cry. Both ideas are colored with imagination—"the faculty which produces impressive effects out of simple elements." They may, moreover, be closely related: the first showing how the narrator first saw the tree, the second suggesting how he saw it later, under the influence of village superstition —and that is perhaps why they fall together in the last lines of a poem designed to make a tree "impressive."

For consider the second idea in its context. After indicating that no one else could have seen the woman under the thorn, the narrator claims (but only after working deep into his story) to have glimpsed her once himself, at the height of a blinding storm! Wordsworth left ambiguities in the poem, but to leave one here—to suggest that Martha Ray was really on view by the tree in storms some twenty years after—would have been to throw away his best opportunity both of making the tree "impressive" and of exhibiting the "laws by which superstition acts upon the mind." Martha's presence in the poem surely illustrates one law: that when a credulous old seaman catches sight in a storm of a suggestively-shaped tree hung with moss and later crams his head with village gossip, then his imagination can turn the tree into a woman, the brightly-colored moss into her scarlet cloak, and the creaking of the branches into her plaintive cry, "O misery! O misery!"

In Taylor's translation of Bürger's "Lenore" Wordsworth would have read the line, "The blasts athwarte the hawthorn hiss." But in his own juvenile lines on the "Vale of Esthwaite" he had described an evening "when the wintry blast / Through the sharp Hawthorn whistling pass'd" (*PW*, I, 279), and in his "Haunted Tree," composed in 1819 (*PW*, II, 290–291), he wrote:

>   . . . some there are
> Whose footsteps superstitiously avoid
> This venerable Tree; for, when the wind
> Blows keenly, it sends forth a creaking sound
> (Above the general roar of woods and crags)
> Distinctly heard from far—a doleful note!
>   . . .
>   . . . nor is it unbelieved,
> By ruder fancy, that a troubled ghost
> Haunts the old trunk; lamenting deeds of which
> The flowery ground is conscious.

The same effect was evidently created on 19 March 1798 by the imagination of a poet who had already crammed his head with German and Scottish ballads and tragedies of real life. One feature of the poem that has been called inexplicable might, on this assumption, be quite simply explained: this is the naming of Martha Ray after the grandmother of little Basil Montagu, who was being looked after at Alfoxden by the Wordsworths. When we remember that the boy went along on the walk past Quantock Hill, we may conceivably have a revelation of the way the tree looked to Wordsworth during the hailstorm. By giving the creature in the poem the name of the creature who flashed before his eyes, Wordsworth may have been obeying a law of association, even one of the "laws by which superstition acts upon the mind."

For the growth of the poem in the mind of its author almost certainly parallels the growth of the story in the mind of its narrator. In this connection, the sources of "The Thorn" have been as widely misunderstood as its subject. Most critics have attached heavy importance to parallel recitals of the poem's "events." In his commonplace book (DC MS. 26) Wordsworth copied out some stanzas of a ballad from David Herd's *Ancient and Modern Scottish Songs* that celebrates an abandoned mother and a murdered infant:

> And there she's lean'd her back to a thorn
> Oh! and alas-a-day, oh, &c
> And there she has her baby born . . .

Rivers, in *The Borderers*, had told the same story, dressing it out with small details and pretending belief in it as a device for deceiving Mortimer:

> She eats her food which every day the peasants
> Bring to her hut; and so the Wretch has lived
> Ten years; and no one ever heard her voice;
> But every night at the first stroke of twelve
> She quits her house, and, in the neighbouring Churchyard
> Upon the self-same spot, in rain or storm,
> She paces out the hour 'twixt twelve and one—
> She paces round and round, still round and round
> And in the Churchyard sod her feet have worn
> A hollow ring; they say it is knee-deep—
>
> (PW, I, 143)

To find other parallels in Wordsworth one might even range back to the "Vale of Esthwaite" or forward to the *Excursion*, Book VI, where the Vicar (entirely without passion) tells the story of an abandoned mother who haunts a little mound of turf encircled by a trodden path.

But these are superficial analogies and throw little light on the genesis of "The Thorn." If one must find a literary source for this poem about a tree, as good as any would be Charlotte Smith's "Apostrophe to an Old Tree":[28]

> Where thy broad branches brave the bitter North,
> Like rugged, indigent, unheeded, worth.
> Lo! Vegetation's guardian hands emboss
> Each giant limb with fronds of studded moss,
> That clothes the bark in many a fringed fold
> Begemm'd with scarlet shields and cups of gold,
> Which, to the wildest winds their webbs oppose,
> And mock the arrowy sleet, or weltering snows.

But far more important than any literary source are the objects in nature that haunted Wordsworth's imagination, often seeming to come alive and take on human shape or significance: the rock in the shape of an old woman seated on Helm Crag, the "Stone-Man" on the top of a hill at Grasmere, the lonely whistling hawthorns and ghostly yews in Somerset and the Lakes, the "Hart's-Horn tree" and the "Round Thorn" (a sycamore) near Penrith,[29] "The single sheep, and the one blasted tree" of the *Prelude* (XI, 378), the single "Tree, of many, one" of the "Intimations" ode.

Late in his life Wordsworth cited as one of the important events in his poetical history the moment when (at the age of fourteen) he caught sight of an oak tree between Hawkhead and Ambleside: "I date from it my consciousness of the infinite variety of natural appearances which had been unnoticed by the poets of any age or country . . . and I made a resolution to supply, in some degree, the deficiency."[30] The way in which such materials could work on a youthful poet's fancy, or imagination, is told in the *Prelude*, not only in the "spots of time" passages but more explicitly where Wordsworth speaks of certain habits of his early "wilfulness of fancy and conceit" (VIII, 511–541):

28. Found in Charlotte Smith's *Elegaic Sonnets and Other Poems*, 2 vols. (London, 1797), II, 50–53.
29. See the Fenwick note to "Suggested by a View . . . ," *PW*, III, 534.
30. Fenwick note to *An Evening Walk*; *PW*, I, 319.

> From touch of this new power
> Nothing was safe: the Elder-tree that grew
> Beside the well-known Charnel-house had then
> A dismal look; the Yew-tree had its Ghost,
> That took its station there for ornament.

No common sight, no common event, could escape exaggeration. If a widow were seen to visit her husband's grave once or twice,

> The fact was caught at greedily, and there
> She was a Visitant the whole year through,
> Wetting the turf with never-ending tears,
> And all the storms of Heaven must beat on her—

just as they beat on Martha Ray, in the old Captain's superstitious imagination. Again, in *Peter Bell* the poet testifies to the power of "Spirits of the Mind" who seize control of men's faculties, "Disordering colour form and stature."

> Your presence I have often felt
> In darkness & the stormy night
> And well I know, if need there be
> Ye can put forth your agency
> Beneath the sweet moonlight.[31]

A few stanzas later, the vision that Peter sees under the Spirits' influence, when "Distraction reigns in soul and sense,"[32] strikingly resembles the vision that haunted "The Thorn's" narrator. Peter's vision begins with a shrub—not a thorn, but a "flowering furze"—and features an abandoned female wailing a rhythmic lament:

> And stretched beneath the furze he sees
> The Highland girl—it is no other
> And hears her crying, as she cried
> The very moment that she died,
> My mother! oh! my mother!

Wordsworth left fewer ambiguities in *Peter Bell* than in "The Thorn" (perhaps because while still working on it he had the

---

31. *PW*, II, 368 and 375, but quoted from DC MS. 33.
32. The reading is from 1819; see *PW*, II, 375.

instructive experience of seeing "The Thorn" misread), but he must have felt that even in "The Thorn" he was planting ample evidence that the narrator's vision was the handiwork of "Spirits of the Mind," called up not by guilt but by superstition.

That evidence is complemented by one fact of the poem's later history: Wordsworth did not, it became clear, consider "The Thorn" to be essentially a poem about the maternal passion. The title alone might suggest this fact, but plainer suggestions lie in the way the piece was classified. In the letter to Coleridge of 5 May 1809 in which Wordsworth first spoke of arranging his poems (*MY*, I, 331–336), he designated as a separate class "those relating to Maternal feeling, connubial or parental," and named as examples "The Sailor's Mother," "The Emigrant Mother," "The Affliction of Margaret," "The Mad Mother," and "The Idiot Boy." In the collected edition of 1815 all these pieces, together with "The Complaint of a Forsaken Indian Woman" and others, turned up as "Poems founded on the Affections."

But not "The Thorn." It was not linked with any of these titles. In 1809 Wordsworth placed it in a class of poems "relating to human life." His account of the class is somewhat diffuse, but a meaningful distinction does emerge: "This class of poems I suppose to consist chiefly of objects most interesting to the mind not by its personal feelings or a strong appeal to the instincts or natural affections, but to be interesting to a meditative and imaginative mind either from the moral importance of the pictures or from the employment they give to the understanding affected through the imagination and to the higher faculties." The distinction is between the "affections" and the "imagination," and as might be expected "The Thorn" turned up in 1815 among "Poems of the Imagination," where it remained in later editions.

The way in which Wordsworth transformed the literary analogues of "The Thorn" throws a flood of light not only on his experiments of 1798 but on his growing disagreements with Coleridge. The difference between Bürger's "Lass of Fair Wone" and "The Thorn" is plainly the difference between a ballad and a lyrical ballad. "The Three Graves" is rather less

simple, for the difference between the parts Wordsworth himself wrote and "The Thorn" may seem less striking than the
similarity. A major aim of each work appears to have been to
invest an object of nature—a tree—with significance. Each
work is a verse dialogue. In each an aged narrator recounts to
a stranger some local beliefs concerning a thorn with a grave, or
row of graves, beneath, revealing as he does so his own superstitious character. In each an incongruity is set up between the
brightly colored tree (hung with scarlet moss in "The Thorn,"
with blossoms in "The Three Graves") and the tragic horror
connected with the spot. And in each the narrator's language
is governed by the needs of dramatic propriety. All these, and
other, similarities suggest that Wordsworth's "Thorn" may
be regarded as a development of the major themes and techniques of his unfinished "Three Graves."

When Coleridge presented his own "Three Graves" in 1809,
he seemed to suggest even further similarities between this
poem as a whole and Wordsworth's "Thorn." He announced
that his poem (just like "The Thorn") was a psychological
study, a study of the working of the imagination. He had been
attracted to the story, he said, "from finding in it a striking
proof of the possible effect on the imagination, from an idea
violently and suddenly impressed on it." He had been reading
about the effects of witchcraft, and "conceived the design . . .
of illustrating the mode in which the mind is affected in these
cases, and the progress and symptoms of the morbid action on
the fancy from the beginning" (*STCPW*, I, 269).

But it is time to recognize the all-important difference. The
imagination whose working Wordsworth studied in "The
Thorn" belongs to the narrator; the imagination whose working Coleridge studied in "The Three Graves" belongs to a
person in the narrator's story. In "The Thorn," therefore, the
narrator is actually the central figure, the subject of the poem;
the poem's "events" take place mainly in his imagination. In
"The Three Graves," as developed by Coleridge, the narrator
is relatively unimportant; the old Sexton—though he does,
like Wordsworth's old seaman, draw some attention to himself—describes events that are meaningful in themselves, not

for what they reveal about their describer. In "The Thorn" dramatic propriety is highly important, for the poem is, in effect, a dramatic monologue. In "The Three Graves" dramatic propriety, in spite of Coleridge's announced attempt to achieve it, is virtually meaningless, and what Coleridge later called the "homeliness of the diction"[33] is, ironically, just what he considered it to be in Wordsworth's ballads, a pointless blemish.

In later years these two poems have occasionally been compared, to Wordsworth's disadvantage. Swinburne was among the first to indicate a preference, finding more "tragic exactitude," less crude realism, and less horror in "The Three Graves."[34] Later critics have followed Swinburne. But Wordsworth's own opinion was quite different. Coleridge, he told Barron Field, was unable to project himself dramatically into his characters; having "always too much personal and domestic discontent," he could not "afford to suffer / With those whom he saw suffer." "I gave him the subject of his Three Graves," Wordsworth continued, "but he made it too shocking and painful, and not sufficiently sweetened by any healing views. Not being able to dwell on or sanctify natural woes, he took to the supernatural, and hence his Antient Mariner and Christabel."[35]

Wordsworth's remark clearly implies that "The Ancient Mariner"—the partners' third attempt at collaboration—embodied Coleridge's solution to the problems presented by their first attempt, "The Three Graves." It should by now be equally clear that "The Thorn," in turn, embodied Wordsworth's solution to the same problems. One problem concerned the supernatural. Here we need only observe that the way in which Wordsworth "sweetened" and made endurable the theme of a curse was to make the terrible "events" of "The Thorn" not supernatural, or even real, but only products of the superstitious imagination.

33. When he reprinted Parts III and IV in *Sibylline Leaves* (1817); see *STCPW*, I, 267.
34. Algernon Charles Swinburne, *Miscellanies* (London, 1886), p. 140.
35. Field's MS "Memoirs" are quoted by de Selincourt, *The Early Wordsworth*, p. 28n.

Another problem concerned narrative technique in the ballad. Here Wordsworth's disapproval of "The Ancient Mariner" takes on, I think, a new significance. In October 1800, in preparation for the second edition of *Lyrical Ballads*, Wordsworth gave "The Ancient Mariner" and "The Thorn" a close critical review. To the letter in which he mailed to the printer the draft of his Preface he appended two long notes (for insertion at the end of Volume I), one listing "defects" in his partner's poem, the other giving a detailed interpretation of his own (*EY*, 303): "(N.B. The following notes are to be printed at the end of the first volume with References to the last page of the poems to which the notes belong. I do not recollect whether the 'Thorn' or the 'Antient Mariner' is printed first. If the Thorn be printed first the note to the Thorn must likewise be printed first & vice versâ.)" In singling out defects in "The Ancient Mariner" Wordsworth seems to have had in mind the sharply different narrative technique of his own poem. It has been held that he objected mainly to the supernatural quality of the events in "The Ancient Mariner" and to their lack of relation to one another. For the edition of 1800 Coleridge did attempt, presumably at his partner's urging, to reduce what has been called the "dreamlike inconsequence" of the events[36] and did add a subtitle—"A Poet's Reverie"—apparently designed to justify the inconsequence that remained. But this objection came third in Wordsworth's list of "defects" in "the Poem of my Friend." First on the list was "that the principal person has no distinct character"; second, "that he does not act, but is continually acted upon." What Wordsworth appears to suggest is that his friend's poem lacked an entire dimension, that which might have been provided by the narrator's personality—the very dimension in which, he was simultaneously at pains to point out, the real subject of his own poem (as of any dramatic monologue) lay.

Wordsworth's poem is of central importance in the experiments of 1798 for another reason. By turning a ballad into a psychological study, Wordsworth showed how the "feeling"

36. Hutchinson, ed., *Lyrical Ballads: 1798*, p. 218.

developed in his *Lyrical Ballads* could give "importance to the action and situation and not the action and situation to the feeling," as in "the popular Poetry of the day" (Owen, 159). Moreover, while explaining the way in which this particular poem was supposed to work, Wordsworth came as close as he ever did to explaining what a "lyrical Ballad" was. Once he had chosen as the subject of his study a narrator from humble life (the situation in which the "essential passions of the heart," the feelings, and the manners are all more simple and more vivid), Wordsworth faced a problem common to all the "lyrical ballads" that were made up wholly or in part of dramatic utterance. The problem was to make sure that the narrator's language, in his mind "impregnated with passion," should "convey passion to Readers who are not accustomed to sympathize with men feeling in that manner or using such language"—readers, that is, inhibited by theories of character and expression centered on decorum. The solution that occurred to Wordsworth was a simple one. "It seemed to me that this might be done," he explained in his 1800 note, "by calling in the assistance of Lyrical and rapid Metre," by which means a poem that had to move slowly in order to be "natural" might yet "appear to move quickly" (*PW*, II, 512–513).

The appearance of rapidity was achieved in part by adding lines to the ballad quatrain, and thereby prolonging the rhyme pattern, as Coleridge had occasionally done in "The Ancient Mariner." With regard to the term "lyrical," Robert Langbaum has conjectured that Wordsworth could only have meant "lyrical in the sense of subjective," and has gone on to read some of the poems of 1798 as incipient or partial dramatic monologues.[37] Wordsworth may have meant lyrical partly in this sense, but he talked about it in the primary sense of musical (or metrical); the two senses of the word seem to have been closely related in his mind, perhaps through their common connection with passion. He touched on the "metrical" meaning when he justified using verse instead of prose for the other "curse poem" in the 1798 volume. "Goody Blake and

37. Robert Langbaum, *The Poetry of Experience* (London, Chatto and Windus, 1957), Chap. I: "The Dramatic Lyric and The Lyrical Drama."

Harry Gill," he felt, was better able to communicate passion
for its having been "narrated as a Ballad, and in a more impressive metre than is usual in Ballads" (Owen, 175).

A "lyrical ballad," then, we may venture, was distinctively
lyrical in two respects: its passion ("Poetry is passion") arose,
as in any lyric, from the mind of the speaker; and this passion
was communicated in heightened, hence more lyrical, ballad
meter.

CHAPTER 4

The Ballad as Drama: II

The concept of originality in literary art is notoriously elusive, not to say illusory. Nothing, we know, is ever wholly new: no theme, no form, no tactic seems ever to appear without a precedent in earlier literature and suggestive parallels in the literature of its time. These commonplaces may help to keep alive our skepticism about Wordsworth's claims to originality. However clear it may seem that the *Lyrical Ballads* of 1798 were experiments in dramatic and narrative technique, it may still be asked whether they were truly innovative, or whether they simply represented experimental genres that had already become popular. Literary ballads—modern imitations of old German and Scottish ballads—did enjoy a vogue, as Robert Mayo has shown,[1] in the later 1790's, not only on broadsides and in the magazines but in collections of verse. It would not be surprising to find, upon a fresh search of the magazines and miscellanies, that some of these ballads were semidramatic in form.

But there is another way of judging just how innovative Wordsworth's experiments were, a way that acknowledges some important parallels. For Robert Southey was experimenting widely in these years with dramatic and semidramatic narratives. The *Monthly Magazine* printed one of his "monodramas"—dramatic soliloquies in blank verse, spoken by a historical or legendary character. The first of what he later called his "Ballads and Metrical Tales" appeared in *Poems*, 1797. A typical specimen, "Mary, the Maid of the Inn," con-

1. In his *PMLA* article already cited: "The Contemporaneity of the *Lyrical Ballads*," 69 (June 1954), 486–522.

tained dialogue which drew Coleridge's praise: "You have properly enough made the diction colloquial."[2] And by 1797 Southey had begun writing his "English Eclogues," most of them, like the earlier "Botany Bay Eclogues," dialogues in blank verse. Not only the themes and the manner but the titles of several—especially those he wrote after he had seen the *Lyrical Ballads*—were strikingly Wordsworthian: "The Sailor's Mother," "The Ruined Cottage," "The Last of the Family." Mayo has discerned (pp. 496–497) a close resemblance between one of the Eclogues, "Hannah," and Wordsworth's "Thorn." "Hannah" was published in the *Monthly Magazine*, October 1797, and much admired by Coleridge (see *STCL*, I, 345–346). It tells the pathetic history of a girl who, with her child, is abandoned by her sailor-husband; after a long struggle against poverty and sickness she lies now in a fresh grave in the churchyard,

> and none,
> Who trod upon the senseless turf would think
> Of what a world of woes lay buried there!

All in all, Southey's poems of 1794 to 1799 so closely resembled the *Lyrical Ballads* that one of the easiest ways to measure the originality of Wordsworth's experiments might be to examine Southey's response to them. That response was forthright and uncomplicated. When Southey reviewed the volume in October 1798,[3] he had little good to say about any of the ballads in it. "The Idiot Boy" he considered to be the "most important" of the "experimental" poems, but he found

2. 17 July 1797; *STCL*, I, 333–334. Coleridge never approved of dramatic poetry, however. Three years earlier he had told Southey flatly, "I *detest* Monodramas" (*STCL*, I, 116), and in 1801 he counseled John Thelwall against publishing "A *dramatic Legend*," for he found that term not to be "a happy combination": "The Etyma of the words 'dramatic' & [']legend' directly contradict each other—tho' not so absurd as the phrase 'speaking Pantomime' it is too much of the same class" (*STCL*, II, 723).

3. For the *Critical Review*; the review is reprinted in Elsie Smith, *Estimate of William Wordsworth* (Oxford: Oxford University Press, 1932), pp. 30–33.

it, one gathers, disturbingly naturalistic: the poem resembled a Flemish painting "in the worthlessness of its design and the excellence of its execution." The other ballads, Southey felt, were equally "bald in story" and "not so highly embellished in narration." What he apparently meant by this Southey disclosed in his criticism of "The Thorn." Pointing out that the poem was not told by the author but by "some loquacious narrator," Southey complained sharply: "The author should have recollected that he who personates tiresome loquacity, becomes tiresome himself." (This opinion, reinforced by Coleridge's paraphrase of it in *Biographia Literaria*, was to echo for a century and a half of "Thorn" criticism.) "Goody Blake and Harry Gill" Southey considered "perhaps a good story for a ballad," but he feared that Wordsworth's presentation of it as "well authenticated" might "promote the popular superstition of witchcraft." Of all the dramatic pieces in the volume, Southey found it possible to praise only the "Foster-Mother's Tale," by Coleridge, which he pronounced to be "in the best style of dramatic narration," and "The Female Vagrant," from which he quoted ten stanzas.

These opinions reveal amost total insensitivity to Wordsworth's experiments. The excerpt from Coleridge's *Osorio* is a straightforward piece of dialogue in the course of which one character tells a story to another. The story is told for its own sake; the teller of it betrays only moderate feeling as she recites a tragic history. There is no dramatic self-revelation, nor any dramatic propriety, and the reader's interest is fixed wholly on the events. At the same time, the truly dramatic element of such a poem as "The Thorn"—the narrator's unconscious self-revelation—seems to have been lost upon Southey: the narrator, he apparently felt, got in the way of the "events," interfering with the reader's perception of them. For Southey, similarly, to express fear that the events of "Goody Blake and Harry Gill" might promote superstition was to have read the poem literally, for the events alone, and to have missed its dramatic dimension—the emotions of the ballad narrator.

Southey's own version of similar events, "The Witch," is

prudently presented as a dialogue, with the speeches clearly labeled, and his ballad "The Idiot"[4] differs from Wordsworth's "Idiot Boy" in the speaker's detachment from the events and characters he describes. As if to confirm his insensitivity to Wordsworth's dramatic experiments, Southey wrote a number of other loosely, though often imperceptively, imitative pieces in the months that followed his reading of *Lyrical Ballads*. "The Cross Roads," which he dated 1798 and published in 1799,[5] is a fair specimen. Like "The Thorn" it is a story told by an old man to a listener at the side of a grave, a spot cursed by the tragedy of the girl who lies therein. A prefatory note explains that the events in the ballad really "happened about forty years ago in a village adjacent to Bristol. A person who was present at the funeral, told me the story . . ." The flatness and simplicity of the language make the ballad read like parody, but it is characteristic of Southey's pieces that these qualities are not attached to any particular voice, hence have no dramatic justification. We hear painfully literal details not from a garrulous old man speaking in character, but from the poet himself, introducing the narrative:

> There was an old man breaking stones
>   To mend the turnpike way,
> He sat him down beside a brook
> And out his bread and cheese he took,
>   For now it was mid-day.
>
> He lent his back against a post,
>   His feet the brook ran by . . .

In 1799 Southey described his own English Eclogues, in which he might have found affinities to *Lyrical Ballads*, many of them being manifestly imitative, as bearing "no resemblance to any poems in our language"; their models were German, he explained. Having found "The Ancient Mariner" "a Dutch

4. Published in the *Morning Post*, 30 June 1798; see B. R. McElderry, Jr., "Southey, and Wordworth's 'The Idiot Boy,' " *N & Q*, n.s. 2 (November 1955), 490–491.

5. In Vol. II, added to his *Poems*, published by Longman (London, 1799); Vol. I was the 3rd ed.

attempt at German sublimity," as he described it in his review, Southey had resolved, evidently, to make an honest English attempt. What Wordsworth thought of the English Eclogues we do not know, but his comment on Southey's 1797 *Poems*, which contained the Botany Bay Eclogues, is revealing. He complained to Coleridge, as the latter at once reported to Joseph Cottle, April 1797, that "Southey writes *too much at his ease*—that he seldom 'feels his burthened breast / Heaving beneath th' incumbent Deity' " *(STCL, I, 320)*. Southey's narrative poems Wordsworth later found empty of any characters that "interest you much" (Dorothy thought the characters insufficiently distinct), but the fault, he believed, lay even deeper. *Madoc*, despite its beauties, "fails in the highest gifts of the poet's mind Imagination in the true sense of the word, and knowledge of human Nature and the human heart."[6]

Southey's insensitivity to *Lyrical Ballads* cannot in itself prove that the ballads were innovative, or original, or out of tune with popular styles. Yet taken with all the other evidence it carries, I think, great significance. For Southey of all contemporary readers might have been expected to understand experiments in dramatic and narrative technique had the experiments been, like his own "mono-dramas," for instance, conventional. He conspicuously failed to recognize what we might in one sense consider the "lyrical," in another the "dramatic" qualities of the ballads—the feeling revealed by the speaker or narrator of a ballad-like tale. Whether the feeling belonged to a wholly invented character, to a colloquial voice assumed by the poet, or even, as in "Simon Lee" and some of the shorter pieces in ballad stanzas, to the poet himself, it was, I suggest, a distinctive, even original feature of these experiments in ballad form.

What now seems, in fact, mistaken is not to grant the innovative quality of these experiments, but to trace them mainly as I have provisionally done to German origins. For once one defines a lyrical ballad as an experiment in dramatic form, and

6. Wordsworth to Beaumont, 3 June 1805 *(EY,* 595) and Dorothy to Lady Beaumont, 11 June 1805 *(EY,* 600).

follows Wordworth's variations on the theme of a curse, one has to recognize that Wordsworth reacted against Bürger more than he imitated him.

His fundamental dissent from Bürger's poetic tactics—and his heavy obligation to English sources—began to come out after the first edition of *Lyrical Ballads* was published. During the year that Wordsworth and Coleridge spent in Germany they got acquainted with Bürger in the original. Coleridge took to him from the start—"Bürger of all the German Poets," he wrote to his wife on 8 November 1798 (*STCL*, I, 438), "pleases me the most"—and he found "Lenore" "greatly superior to any of the Translations." Wordsworth found it in several passages inferior, complaining, late in 1798, that Bürger, however much delight he gave, left little permanent impression (*EY*, 234). "I remember a hurry of pleasure, but I have few distinct forms that people my mind, nor any recollection of delicate or minute feelings which he has either communicated to me, or taught me to recognize." The reason for this probably lay in the significant failing which Wordsworth then cited: "I do not perceive the presence of character in his personages. I see everywhere the character of Bürger himself; and even this, I agree with you, is no mean merit. But yet I wish him sometimes at least to make me forget himself in his creations. It seems to me, that in poems descriptive of human nature, however short they may be, character is absolutely necessary, &c.: incidents are among the lowest allurements of poetry." It was, of course, this failing that Wordsworth had corrected in his own modifications of Bürger's themes, throwing the focus not on his own character, nor on the incidents of his poems, but on the characters he created, whether these were simply voices adopted for narrative purposes (as in "The Idiot Boy") or fully sketched personalities (like the narrator of "The Thorn"). Wordsworth did admire Bürger's "manner of relating," finding it "almost always spirited and lively, and stamped and peculiarized with genius." But he artfully summed up Bürger as "the poet of the animal spirits." "I love his '*Tra ra la*' dearly," he concluded, "but less of the horn and more of the lute—and far, far more of the pencil."

Bürger is mentioned in one other letter from Germany, probably written later. Coleridge had evidently challenged his partner's notion of character, provoking this qualification (*EY*,
255): "I do not so ardently desire character in poems like
Burger's, as manners, not transitory manners reflecting the
wearisome unintelligible obliquities of city-life, but manners
connected with the permanent objects of nature and partaking
of the simplicity of those objects." In Burns, he suggested,
manners abound; in Bürger they are absent. Coleridge seems
again to have defended Bürger ("not that I thought Bürger a
great poet, but that he really possessed some of the excellences
which W. denied to him"), and the argument came to an end,
as he reported to Taylor on 25 January 1800, "in metaphysical
disquisitions on the nature of character" (*STCL*, I, 566).

By 1815, when he wrote the "Essay, Supplementary to the
Preface," Wordsworth found Bürger inferior to the English
master whose *Reliques*, "so unassuming, so modest in their
pretentions," had inspired the ballad revival in Germany and
"absolutely redeemed" the poetry of England. Bürger lacked
the "fine sensibility" of Percy, Wordsworth said, as he offered
a specimen in which Bürger had "deserted his original only to
go astray" (*PW*, II, 424, 422). And by 1824 Wordsworth was
ready to acknowledge his debt to Percy, Burns, and Cowper
for having "powerfully counteracted the mischievous influence" of Darwin and Schiller and "that of other German
writers upon my taste and natural tendencies."[7]

Percy, Burns, and Cowper here stand identified as the three
major English influences on *Lyrical Ballads*. Wordsworth's
tributes to their power are scattered, often casual, but unre-
strained. If it was Percy who had "absolutely redeemed" the
poetry of his country, Burns ranked second only to Chaucer as
a "natural and sensual" poet, a poet of flesh and blood (*HCR*,
II, 562), and of all the poets of his own day Wordsworth, as he
once testified, read and remembered hardly one, "with the
exception of Burns and Cowper."[8]

---

7. See the long note he appended to one of his poems on Burns, *PW*,
III, 440–442.
8. To R. P. Gillies, 22 December 1814; *MY*, II, 179.

How well Wordsworth knew Percy's volumes before buy-
ing copies in Germany, along with Bürger's poems, is uncertain. Coleridge, it is clear, knew several pieces in them, notably
"Sir Cauline," which left marks on "The Ancient Mariner"
and "Christabel," and which he mentioned to Wordsworth in
a letter of 23 January 1798 (*STCL*, I, 379). "Sir Cauline" has a
minor affinity with one of Wordsworth's "curse poems" in
the marking of the spot where Christabelle's champion chal-
lenges the "paynim" knight: "Upon Eldridge hill there groweth
a thorne, / Upon the mores broding." More meaningful, however, is the affinity between another ballad in Percy's collection, "Lady Anne Bothwell's Lament,"[9] and Wordsworth's
"Mad Mother." The way in which he altered the pattern he
found again reveals the tendency of Wordsworth's experiments in 1798.

Percy's ballad belonged to a conventional genre, the complaint. Spoken by a mother who has been abandoned, it followed to a limited degree the movement of the speaker's mind.
Talking to her infant, the mother let fall a casual stream of
reminiscence, admonition, and affection. Her last stanza pointed
a conventional moral:

> I wish all maides be warned by mee
> Nevir to trust mans curtesy.

Wordsworth's mad mother (after an introductory stanza in
which the poet assures us that she was speaking "the English
tongue") runs through many of the same utterances. But her
speech (which may owe something to one of Percy's "Mad
Songs"[10]) is far more passionate and distracted. Swinging from
her visions of "fiendish faces" to the baby at her breast, to the
breeze in the tree, to the waves, the "high crag" and "leaping
torrents," thence back to the cruel father, her mind travels
erratically over her experience and her plans for the future.
The poem ends with her disordered resolve to "find thy father
in the wood."

9. Found in H. B. Wheatley's edition of the *Reliques*, 3 vols. (London,
1885), II, 209–213.
10. See de Selincourt's note, *PW*, II, 486.

The speech of Percy's lady was of interest partly for what it revealed of her attitude toward her betrayer, which was consistent and intelligible: though he had been false and cruel, she loved him still. But the speech of Wordsworth's mad mother is of interest largely for what it reveals of her state of mind, "that deranged state," as Coleridge put it admiringly, "in which from the increased sensibility the sufferer's attention is abruptly drawn off by every trifle, and in the same instant plucked back again by the one despotic thought . . ." (*BL*, II, 123). Toward the close of the poem, with the baby still peacefully at her breast, she bursts out:

> —Where art thou gone my own dear child?
> What wicked looks are those I see?
> Alas! alas! that look so wild,
> It never, never came from me:
> If thou art mad, my pretty lad,
> Then I must be for ever sad.

As we follow the fluxes and refluxes of the speaker's imagination, we are aware, in Wordsworth's poem, of a heightened contrast between what she says and what we know about her. Wordsworth's speaker thus stands before us in dramatic perspective, as Percy's speaker had not. Once again Wordsworth had turned a conventional ballad into something that verged upon the dramatic monologue.

Yet it should be easy to see from these examples alone how much more Wordsworth owed to Percy than to Bürger—how much less he had to modify the pattern he found to achieve the effect he seemed to desire. Bürger's ballad did contain dramatic conversation, but they were mainly recitals of events, wholly lacking in revelation of feeling on the part of the narrator or observer of the events; their lyrical qualities lay only in their meter. Percy's "complaint," on the other hand (and this is often true of other pieces in the *Reliques*), resembled a lyric to begin with, in the sense that the speaker's feelings made up a significant part of it. Though Wordsworth drove deeper into the speaker's psychology, heightened her passion (and the reader's), and above all made her utterance more dramatic, he worked out a pattern already set by Percy.

The *Lyrical Ballads* of 1798 included (besides "The Female Vagrant") two other complaints. Both, though relatively conventional, showed the marks of Wordsworth's interest in dramatic technique. The first, "The Complaint of a Forsaken Indian Woman," avowedly written to "follow the fluxes and refluxes of the mind . . . by accompanying the last struggles of a human being at the approach of death, cleaving in solitude to life and society" (Owen, 158), closely resembles "The Mad Mother" and again verges on the dramatic monologue form. Since Wordsworth gave us in a prefatory note an outline of the woman's situation, her utterance is of interest to us for what it reveals of her mental state. We find her as the poem opens calling for death:

> Before I see another day,
> Oh let my body die away!

At the end of stanza 2 ("here contented will I lie; / Alone I cannot fear to die") the mood of resignation is broken by rising passion as her thoughts fix upon the child that has been taken from her,[11] and she presently voices an agonized resolve to follow her companions through the snow:

> In spite of all my weary pain,
> I'll look upon your tents again.

Another break, and the poem ends in despair, with an echo (in the 1798 version) of the opening lines:

> I feel my body die away,
> I shall not see another day.

The dying woman's shifts of mood and conflicts of passion allow Wordsworth to present what the conventional complaint rarely presented, a semidramatic portrait of the speaker.

The other complaint, "The Last of the Flock"—far more

11. A detail not in Wordsworth's source, Samuel Hearne's *Journey* (1795). It is worth noting that the overflow stanzas from this poem (*PW*, II, 475–476) accord perfectly with the poem's expressed design, four of them showing the forsaken woman "cleaving" to the society of her friends, the fifth showing her grasping poignantly after symbols of life. But none mentions the child; had they been retained they would have blurred the focus Wordsworth evidently resolved to fix—on the woman's bereaved motherhood.

homely and prosaic, though Wordsworth would not have felt it less pathetic—also centers on the passion arising from bereavement. Wordsworth may have wished to point an anti-Godwinian moral,[12] but the important thing about the poem is the character of the rustic speaker, as revealed in his dramatic address to the poet. The subdued yet deeply emotional language represents, as in many of the "lyrical ballads," Wordsworth's attempt to achieve dramatic propriety—to "imitate," as he put it in the 1800 Preface, "and, as far as possible, to adopt the very language of men."

> A woeful time it was for me,
> To see the end of all my gains,
> The pretty flock which I had reared
> With all my care and pains,
> To see it melt like snow away!
> For me it was a woeful day.

Again, in order to engage the reader's sympathy, the meter was made "more lyrical and rapid" than that customary in ballads.

Wordsworth's obligations to Percy are not always easy to separate from his obligations to other writers of semidramatic ballads or songs, for a number of the forms that Percy used were widely imitated. About the obligations to Burns, however, there can be little uncertainty. We may recall how the Pedlar—commonly agreed to represent Wordsworth as he might have been—used to "repeat / The songs of Burns" as he strolled the hills, "his eye / Flashing poetic fire."[13] Wordsworth had read Burns's Scottish poems as soon as they appeared, and in 1803 stood at Burns's graveside to praise the poet

> Whose light I hailed when first it shone,
> When, breaking forth like Nature's own,
>   It showed my youth
> How verse may build a princely throne
>   On humble truth.[14]

12. As Emile Legouis first suggested; see de Selincourt's note, *PW*, II, 476.

13. Lines 318–320 of Jonathan Wordsworth's text of "The Pedlar," *The Music of Humanity* (London: Thomas Nelson and Sons, 1969), p. 182.

14. While the sentiment arose in 1803, the words are from 1842; see *PW*, III, 66.

It is not hard to find Wordsworthian parallels to poems like "Despondency: An Ode," or "A Bard's Epitaph." The epistles to J. Lapraik ("Gie me ae spark o' Nature's fire, / That's a' the learning I desire") may well be the models for William's dialogues with Matthew about Nature's teachings. We might even see in Lucy a shadow of Burns's Highland Mary. These obligations and others like them are numerous and important.

But more important here are the obligations that Wordsworth implied when he summed up Burns's poetic virtues in 1816. "A Letter to a Friend of Robert Burns" bluntly denies Burns a place among those poets of "transcendent genius" whose personal feelings remain wholly invisible—poets like Homer, Virgil, or Shakespeare. Burns himself always shows through his "effusions": in the relatively few narratives he wrote "he himself bears no inconsiderable part, and he has produced no drama." Yet Burns's genius was essentially dramatic, and in a way that interested Wordsworth profoundly. "On the basis of his human character," Wordsworth explained, Burns "has reared a poetic one" which shows itself throughout his earlier, and better, poems. This poetic character, or "poetic self," as Wordsworth also called it, Burns "introduced as a dramatic personage" into his poems, "for the purpose of inspiriting his incidents" and giving force and meaning to his opinions (Grosart, II, 12, 14).

This is, as we have seen, substantially what Wordsworth had done in some of his most interesting experimental ballads. How much the speaking voice of *Peter Bell*—to take perhaps the best example—inspirits the incidents of that poem may be argued, but clearly it plays a dramatic role not in but above and around the poem's events, commenting, reacting, setting the events in perspective, filtering them to the reader. Constructed out of Wordsworth's own self—"I am as much Peter Bell as ever," he once remarked[15]—the voice becomes a poetic self through whose sensibilities the poem's power is felt.

Wordsworth's obligations to Cowper are of smaller interest to us here because their marks were left largely on the *Prelude* and the *Excursion*. Humphrey House has reminded us that

15. To Basil Montagu, 21 October 1831; *LY*, II, 578.

Coleridge's "Brook" was to have imitated "The Task," and shown how Coleridge developed his "conversation poems" from the "divine chit-chat" of Cowper, whom he spoke of in 1798 as "the best modern poet."[16] Abbie Potts has explained how Cowper taught Wordsworth "to deal with homely and humorous matters in blank verse and to sharpen and refine the diction of his ironic and critical passages,"[17] and we may recall how Wordsworth echoes "The Task" in a sonnet: "There is a pleasure in poetic pains / Which only Poets know" (*PW*, III, 29). Jonathan Wordsworth has recently shown how Wordsworth and Southey both were influenced "in their treatment of emotion by the Cowper of 'Crazy Kate.' "[18] Cowper had other lessons to teach as well, and other qualities that Wordsworth would have admired: echoes of the jocular vigor, the wit, and the plainness of "John Gilpin," for instance, have been heard by readers of "The Idiot Boy." In 1802, writing to John Wilson (*EY*, 356), Wordsworth implicitly praised Cowper who was "passionately fond of natural objects," for challenging however hesitantly the decorum of eighteenth-century nature poetry. By that time, and probably earlier, he could have read some of Cowper's complaints and dramatic pieces. A few of these, like "Pity for Poor Africans"[19] in the ballads on slavery, were fully-formed dramatic monologues, colloquial in flavor, rich in crude but unconscious self-revelation. One can perhaps measure the depth of Cowper's influence from Crabb Robinson's bizarre account of Dorothy's imbecility: in her later years, Robinson observed, she used to say over and over to herself "without intermission" little poems that she and her brother had written or liked, and Robinson remembered hearing scraps of Isaac Watts and Cowper (*HCR*, II, 477).

Wordsworth's obligations to his three eighteenth-century masters may, once again, be thought to limit his own claims

16. Humphrey House, *Coleridge* (London: R. Hart-Davis, 1953), pp. 71–73.

17. *Wordsworth's Prelude* (Ithaca: Cornell University Press, 1953), pp. 350–357.

18. *Music of Humanity*, pp. 61–62.

19. Published in an Appendix to the 11th ed. of Cowper's *Poems*, Vol. I, 1800.

to originality. He himself noted Burns's great obligations to Fergusson but pronounced them unimportant, since, he said, he "considered it a much higher effort of genius to excel in degree, than to strike out what may be called an original poem."[20] The way in which Wordsworth could excel in degree is summed up admirably by Coleridge in a passage of the *Biographia* (I, 59) quoted by Robert Mayo to support his view that the *Lyrical Ballads* only developed prevailing conventions: "It was the union of deep feeling with profound thought; the fine balance of truth in observing, with the imaginative faculty in modifying the objects observed; and above all the original gift of spreading the tone, the *atmosphere*, and with it the depth and height of the ideal world around forms, incidents, and situations, of which, for the common view, custom had bedimmed all the lustre, had dried up the sparkle and the dew drops." As a matter of fact, Coleridge's remarks are ambivalent. They could easily be read as a testimony to the only kind of originality ever achieved in literary art. But however the remarks are read, it must be observed that Coleridge was speaking here of "Salisbury Plain," not the *Lyrical Ballads*. It is important, moreover, that his enthusiasm for that poem was aroused less by the narrative of the Female Vagrant, which was dramatic in form, than by the murderer's narrative, which was not.[21] In his shocked dissent elsewhere in the *Biographia* from his partner's bolder experiments Coleridge testified with acid eloquence to their originality, to their differences from anything he recognized as poetry.

Though the force of Coleridge's influence is difficult to measure, one supposes that it was mainly his dissent expressed in conversation together with reviewers' coolness to the volume of 1798 that led Wordsworth to modify his dramatic and narrative techniques. Whatever the reason, the poems he published in 1800 are quite different from the poems of 1798, and the

20. As reported by Lady Richardson, November 1846; Grosart, III, 453.
21. As Legouis first noticed, *The Early Life of William Wordsworth*, trans. J. W. Matthews (London and Toronto: J. M. Dent; New York: E. P. Dutton, 1921), p. 334n.

principal differences, which mark a fresh stage in Wordsworth's poetic development, are illustrated best in the poems that were meant to be ballads.

"Ellen Irwin," for instance, was based on a Scottish original "in the simple ballad strain," as Wordsworth explained. But "desirous of throwing the reader at once out of the old ballad, so as, if possible, to preclude a comparison between that mode of dealing with the subject and the mode I meant to adopt," Wordsworth compared Ellen with a Grecian maid, "Adorned with wreaths of myrtle," and adopted the stanza of Bürger's "Lenora" with a minor change in the rhyme scheme.[22] The difference is that "Ellen Irwin" omits most of Bürger's verbal tricks—alliteration, repetition, "hurrying vigour" of pace. There are occasional flashes of the old style, as when an insistent voice questions the narrator:

> But what is Gordon's beauteous face?
> And what are Gordon's crosses
> To them who sit by Kirtle's Braes
> Upon the verdant mosses?
> Alas that ever he was born!
> The Gordon, couched behind a thorn,
> Sees them and their caressing,
> Beholds them blest and blessing.

But the flashes are not sustained. The ballad seems placid, its terror muted, its speaker (who could be the poet himself) relatively passionless, even in his parting invitation to view "the grave of lovely Ellen" in Kirkonnel churchyard.

For another example, two poems in the 1800 collection revive the theme of a curse—a curse implanted not upon the mind but upon a spot in nature. The first, a fragment later called "The Danish Boy," appears to carry on the pattern of "The Lass of Fair Wone," "The Three Graves," and "The Thorn." Written in the "Thorn" stanza (save that lines 1 and 3 rhyme), the poem was "intended as a prelude to a ballad poem never written" (*PW*, II, 493). ("The Thorn," we may remember, had been a poem for which a prelude, though needed, was never

22 See his Fenwick notes to "Ellen Irwin" (*PW*, III, 443) and to "Ode to Lycoris" (*PW*, IV, 422)

written.) The ballad was to have told the story of a Danish
Prince whose murder brought down a curse: "the Spirit of the
Youth it was believed, haunted the Valley where the crime
had been committed."[23] One stanza of the poem, published in
1800 but later dropped, might almost have come from "The
Three Graves" or "The Thorn":

> When near this blasted tree you pass,
> Two sods are plainly to be seen
> Close at its root, and each with grass
> Is cover'd fresh and green.
> Like turf upon a new-made grave
> These two green sods together lie,
> Nor heat, nor cold, nor rain, nor wind
> Can these two sods together bind,
> Nor sun, nor earth, nor sky,
> But side by side the two are laid,
> As if just sever'd by the spade.

(PW, II, 158n)

Like the creature who is believed to haunt the scene of her
crime, the Danish Boy is insubstantial: "A spirit of noon day
is he; / He seems a Form of flesh and blood." Whether he is
visible only to the imagination, or whether the poem is, as
some critics have called it, a venture into the supernatural,[24]
cannot be guessed from the fragment. But the poem as we

23. Wordsworth's note of 1827; *PW*, II, 493.
24. E.g., F. W. Bateson, *Wordsworth*, 2nd ed. (London: Longmans,
Green, 1956), p. 151. It might be added that "The Danish Boy" shows
striking affinities of tone with still another curse poem, probably supernatural, the single surviving stanza of "Cain" which Coleridge said he
wrote in 1798 when he published it in *Aids to Reflection* (1825); see
STCPW, I, 285–287:

> Encintured with a twine of leaves,
> That leafy twine his only dress!
> A lovely Boy was plucking fruits,
> In a moonlight wilderness.
> The moon was bright, the air was free,
> And fruits and flowers together grew
> On many a shrub and many a tree:
> And all put on a gentle hue,
> Hanging in the shadowy air
> Like a picture rich and rare.
> It was a climate where, they say,
> The night is more belov'd than day . . .

have it gives little promise of becoming a psychological study and lacks the dimension that made "The Thorn" unique, that of the narrator's imagination. The recital is straightforward, untinged by passion, and again, for all one can tell, the poet himself speaks.

Another curse poem, written about a year later, is "Hart-leap Well," which appears to be loosely based on a ballad of Bürger's, "Der Wilde Jaeger," translated as "The Chase":

> Earl Walter winds his bugle horn;
>   To horse, to horse, halloo, halloo!
>
>   . . .
> Upsprings, from yonder tangled Thorn
>   A Stag more white than mountain snow;
> And louder rung Earl Walter's horn,
>   "Hark forward, forward, holla, ho"[25]

Like "The Thorn," which it followed in "Poems of the Imagination," "Hart-leap Well" began in the poet's mind with his observation of a scene which he desired to commemorate. The history of the scene he learns from an old shepherd who, like "The Thorn's" narrator, retails superstitions in language that is to a degree dramatically appropriate, revealing, perhaps, something of his own character:

> There's neither dog nor heifer, horse nor sheep,
> Will wet his lips within that Cup of Stone;
> And oftentimes, when all are fast asleep,
> This water doth send forth a dolorous groan.

This curious testimony resembles that offered by "The Thorn's" superstitious narrator, who vows that Martha Ray is known to haunt the mountain top, but adds: "I never heard of such as dare / Approach the spot when she is there." And here, much as in "The Thorn," a contrast is set up between the beauty of the scene, now vanished, and the pathos of the event connected with it. The hart, the old shepherd conjectures, had loved the spot:

> In April here beneath the scented thorn
> He heard the birds their morning carols sing.

25. From excerpts printed in the *Critical Review*, 20 (August 1797), 422–426.

This natural beauty had been supplanted by the gorgeous "House of Pleasure" with which the knight paid tribute to the hart's endurance. But all is now wasted and lifeless. The oddly buoyant effect which the tragic story left on the poet's mind is described in a fragment of the *Recluse* (*PW*, II, 515). A suggestion of it can be felt in the poem's conclusion, where Wordsworth assures the shepherd that Nature will bloom again at the scene. The shepherd's own feeling is communicated vividly, and in fact comes close to being the subject of Part II.

But the major difference between this poem and some of its forerunners is that the story of the chase (Part I) is not put into the shepherd's mouth but is related directly by the poet— the shepherd is allowed to speak only afterward. As the story is being related, therefore, our interest focuses on its incidents, not on the speaker's psychology. Hence the poem is only in a limited sense dramatic. While it represents a maturing of certain techniques of the earlier "lyrical ballads," it represents an abandonment of others, more daring and more original.

The same thing is true of another poem, composed at about the same time as "Hart-leap Well." "The Brothers," a "pastoral poem," follows certain patterns of the curse poems. It begins with an animated address uttered by an old priest; he complains petulantly to his wife about the manners of tourists:

> some glance along,
> Rapid and gay, as if the earth were air,
> And they were butterflies to wheel about
> Long as their summer lasted: some, as wise,
> Upon the forehead of a jutting crag
> Sit perched, with book and pencil on their knee,
> And look and scribble, and scribble on and look,
> Until a man might travel twelve stout miles,
> Or reap an acre of his neighbour's corn.[26]

The stranger who had provoked this complaint, the poet now informs us, had been standing in the churchyard gazing at a row of graves. The priest having presently joined him there, they commence the dialogue which makes up the bulk of the

26. *PW*, II, 1. The readings are from 1800.

poem. The stranger (Leonard), long absent from the village and haunted by the fear that his brother may lie in one of the graves, circles cautiously in to the point, asking first about a grave in which he evidently knows his grandfather is buried: "who is he that lies / Beneath yon ridge, the last of those three graves?" Upon hearing the priest discourse on the old man's kindness to his grandsons, Leonard breaks down into tears. We learn of his behavior through the priest's comments, highly charged with dramatic irony:

> If you weep, Sir,
> To hear a Stranger talking about Strangers,
> Heaven bless you when you are among your kindred!
> Aye. You may turn that way—it is a grave
> Which will bear looking at.

As the poem proceeds, dramatic tension arises from the conflict between Leonard's intense, fearful desire to know the fate of his brother, and the priest's casual, garrulous, unwitting evasion of the crucial questions. The poem centers, in fact, on this conflict. As the priest interrupts his story, rambles through reminiscences that are painfully and pathetically familiar to his listener, moving slowly toward his fatal disclosure, the reader shares Leonard's apprehension and senses the passion that fills his mind. Like the early curse poems, "The Brothers," "written with a view to shew that men who do not wear fine cloaths can feel deeply" (*EY*, 315), focuses on the psychology of passion, and the feeling developed in it clearly gives importance to the action and situation, not the other way around.

But there are important differences. Here, the place of the narrator is taken by the old priest, whose function is less to communicate his own passion than to evoke passion in the mind of his listener. The rich dramatic irony involved in the performance of this function makes the poem more sophisticated than the earlier complaints and dramatic monologues. Moreover, the passion felt by Leonard, as he learns gradually of his brother's death, is made known to the reader less through direct speech than through dramatic implication. But the most important difference is that "The Brothers" is not a ballad, let alone a "lyrical ballad." Its passion is communicated neither in "Lyrical and rapid metre" nor in hurried, repetitious, impulsive utterance, but in muted understatement. Gone is the lyrical excitement of "The Thorn," in its place a subdued rendering of deep emotion. Gone, too, is the rude, colloquial language of common life, in its place a somewhat heightened, yet natural and easy talk, representing Wordsworth's compromise between two kinds of propriety.

Nowhere is Wordsworth's dramatic achievement better illustrated than in "The Brothers." Within its limits the poem is an impressive compound of dramatic irony, pathos, and psychological realism, a fine example of Wordsworth's mature technique. It is ironic, however, that Wordsworth should have gained his greatest dramatic success by abandoning the ballad form in which his dramatic experiments had been cast. It is no less ironic that having gained the success he should have begun to move away not only from the experimental techniques but from the dramatic method in general. Yet that he did so is a fact which hardly needs to be documented. In the elegant poems he wrote in Germany he had already begun to use the ballad stanza for lyrical utterance in his own voice, charged with his own feeling. Similarly, in "Michael," which he might have cast in dramatic form, he himself assumed the role of narrator, viewing a tragic scene—the "straggling heap of unhewn stones" that formed the sheepfold—and relating its history directly to the reader. The poem contains some conversation, but the pathos which pervades it arises from the utterance of the poet himself, speaking in his own character.

Another poem of 1800, "The Reverie of Poor Susan," is based on Bürger's "Des Armen Suschens Traum,"[27] but where Bürger's piece is spoken by the girl, Wordsworth's is spoken by the poet. In "The Affliction of Margaret" of 1801 or 1802,[28]

27. Which Wordsworth said he read in 1798 (*EY*, 234) and which he found "the most perfect and Shakespearean" of Bürger's poems (as reported by Coleridge to William Taylor; *STCL*, I, 566).

28. Published in *Poems in Two Volumes*, 1807. The original title, from DC MS. 41, was "The Affliction of Mary——— of ———."

a complaint of the usual sort, Wordsworth abandoned any effort to keep the speaker's discourse realistic:

> He was among the prime in worth,
> An object beauteous to behold;
> Well born, well bred; I sent him forth
> Ingenuous, innocent, and bold:

The afflicted woman sums up her lament with a kind of late-Wordsworthian elegance:

> Beyond participation lie
> My troubles, and beyond relief.

A number of other examples might be cited. One might compare "The Seven Sisters" (written in 1800) with earlier ballads from German sources, or "The Emigrant Mother" (1802) with "The Mad Mother" of 1798, or the Matthew poems in the 1800 volume with those of 1798. All would confirm, I think, what we have already seen happening to the ballad techniques developed in 1798.

Even as he followed a decisive turn away from the dramatic and narrative tactics that had made his experiments distinctive—and this is another of the curious ironies that make up the history of *Lyrical Ballads*—Wordsworth composed his reasoned, critical defense of the experiments. It has been noticed that the Preface of 1800 applies mainly to the poems of 1798 (Wordsworth's first intention, relinquished only toward the end, had been to write a separate preface for the new volume of 1800). No less do the substantial additions of 1802, which preceded a fresh outburst of boldly experimental writing in the spring of that year. The lag between practice and theory is not hard to account for. By 1800 Wordsworth had seen his poems misread by reviewers; by 1801 and 1802 he had felt Coleridge's dissent hardening.

Only after the revised Preface appeared do Coleridge's views on the central issues of disagreement come into sharp focus, in his two letters of July 1802 to Sotheby and Southey *STCL*, II, 808–813 and 828–834). The second letter is the more detailed of the two:

I am far from going all lengths with Wordsworth. He has written lately a number of poems (32 in all) some of them of considerable Length / (the longest 160 Lines) the greater number of these to my feelings very excellent Compositions / but here & there a daring Humbleness of Language & Versification, and a strict adherence to matter of fact, even to prolixity, that startled me / his alterations likewise in Ruth perplexed me / and I have thought & thought again / & have not had my doubts solved by Wordsworth.

The poems that startled Coleridge are not hard to identify. When he turned, in Chapter XVIII of *Biographia Literaria*, to the problems of meter and language, he cited five poems of Wordsworth's which he found so plain that they would have been "more delightful" to him in prose (II, 53). Three of these —"Alice Fell," "The Beggars," and "The Sailor's Mother"— are among the poems of early 1802 (as Dorothy's Journal for 13 and 14 March shows). As if to suggest what it was in these pieces that he disliked, Coleridge took care to praise "the beauties which are to be found in each of them where the poet interposes the music of his own thoughts."

It was, then, the dramatic passages, where the poet presented the thoughts of his characters or spoke with their voices, not his own, in which Coleridge found "Humbleness of Language & Versification" and "adherence to matter of fact." "The Beggars," to be sure, appears to be spoken mainly by the poet, but in its original form the speaking voice took on a (rather pale) identity, betrayed in some of its utterances *(PW*, II, 222n):

> What other dress she had I could not know;
> Only she wore a Cap that was as white as snow.

"Alice Fell" is spoken by a more distinctive voice, as the earliest version again reveals best. Sara Hutchinson's transcript of the poem (DC MS. 41), taken before Wordsworth altered it in response to her criticisms (see *PW*, II, 542), opens:

> "The sky grows wild—a storm is near
> Clouds gather and the moon is drown'd—
> What is that strange sound I hear?
> What is the meaning of that sound?

> As if the wind blew many ways
> I hear the noises more and more.

It might be noted, too, that Sara's transcript of "The Sailor's Mother" *(PW,* II, 538) contains dialogue which is plainer and more matter-of-fact than any that survived in the version Wordsworth published:

> "The room in which he lodg'd was small,
> "And few effects were in it, when
> "I reach'd the place; I sold them all,
> "And now am travelling home again.
> "I live at Mary-port, a weary way!
> "And scarcely what I have will for my journey pay.

Coleridge's perplexity about revisions in "Ruth," which two years earlier (17 September 1800) he had pronounced "the finest poem in the collection" *(STCL,* I, 623), rose from a similar source. Talking to Crabb Robinson on 13 August 1812, Coleridge explained how Wordsworth's alterations had damaged the poem. Censuring Schiller "for a sort of ventriloquism in poetry"—which Robinson found "a happy term to express that common fault of throwing the feelings of the writer into the body, as it were, of other personages—the characters of the poem"—Coleridge went on to apply the term to Wordsworth. "In *Ruth* as it stands at present, there is the same fault; Wordsworth had not originally put into the mouth of the lover many of the sentiments he now entertains and which would better have become the poet himself" *(HCR,* I, 107).

Some years later, in *Biographia Literaria,* Coleridge was to follow up this charge against Wordsworth, making use again of the term "ventriloquism." But a large part of that later discussion seems to have been provoked by another composition of Wordsworth's published in 1802, referred to briefly in a letter to Southey. When Coleridge talked of the Preface as "half a child of my own Brain," he took care to say that he meant only the 1800 version, and went on to report that his partner had since made numerous additions *(STCL,* II, 830). Most of them evidently displeased Coleridge, for he pronounced the latter half of the new Preface (where the additions were) "obscure beyond any necessity." To Sotheby two weeks earlier he had been more specific:

In my opinion every phrase, every metaphor, every personification, should have its justifying cause in some *passion* either of the Poet's mind, or of the Characters described by the poet—But *metre itself* implies a *passion*, i.e. a state of excitement, both in the Poet's mind, & is expected in that of the Reader—and tho' I stated this to Wordsworth, & he has in some sort stated it in his preface, yet he has [not] done justice to it, nor has he in my opinion sufficiently answered it. In my opinion, Poetry justifies, as *Poetry* independent of any other Passion, some new combinations of Language, & *commands* the omission of many others allowable in other compositions / Now Wordsworth, me saltem judice, has in his system not sufficiently admitted the former, & in his practice has too frequently sinned against the latter.—Indeed, we have had lately some little controversy on this subject—& we begin to suspect, that there is, somewhere or other, a *radical* Difference [in our] opinions.   (*STCL*, II, 812)

I have already identified some of the practice in which Wordsworth sinned by including inappropriate combinations of language. The system, Coleridge suggests, in which he failed to admit that poetry justified certain "new combinations of language" was that set down in the revised Preface of 1802. The controversy, then, that Coleridge mentions evidently accompanied Wordsworth's additions to the Preface, which made the new version half again as long as that of 1800.

One addition, in particular, touches the heart of the disagreement between the partners—what Coleridge called the problem of "ventriloquism." To the passage in which in 1800 he had compared the languages of prose and verse—finding no "essential difference" between them—and explored the powers of meter, Wordsworth added in 1802 some ten paragraphs (Owen, 164–170). In them he made a fundamental distinction between two kinds of poetry, one in which "the Poet speaks through the mouths of his characters," the other in which "the Poet speaks to us in his own person and character." In the first kind Wordsworth insisted on dramatic propriety. In imitating the natural language of passion the poet will want to suppress "any foreign splendour" of diction peculiar to him as a poet or to poets in general. He will, moreover, want to project himself dramatically into his characters, "to bring his feelings near to those of the persons whose feelings he describes, nay, for short spaces of time perhaps, to let himself slip into an entire delusion, and even confound and identify his own feelings with theirs"; consequently, as everyone of good sense must agree, "the dramatic parts of composition are defective, in proportion as they deviate from the real language of nature, and are coloured by a diction of the Poet's own." After presenting his lofty characterization of the poet and his "sublime notion of Poetry," Wordsworth returned in his summary to dramatic technique: "What has been thus far said applies to Poetry in general; but especially to those parts of composition where the Poet speaks through the mouths of his characters."

It was, in short, by adopting the dramatic form—even the very tactic of ventriloquism, though not quite the way in which Robinson had understood it—that Wordsworth endeavored to carry out the aims of *Lyrical Ballads:* to trace "the primary laws of our nature; chiefly, as far as regards the manner in which we associate ideas in a state of excitement," and to create in poetry "the image of man and nature," "the breath and finer spirit of all knowledge."

Coleridge immediately showed his skepticism about these designs, particularly the part about the poet's confounding and identifying his own feelings with those of his characters. "It is easy to cloathe Imaginary Beings with our own Thoughts & Feelings," he avowed to Sotheby (*STCL,* II, 810), "but to send ourselves out of ourselves, to *think* ourselves in to the Thoughts and Feelings of Beings in circumstances wholly & strangely different from our own / hoc labor, hoc opus / and who has atchieved it? Perhaps only Shakespere." But the issue to which Coleridge mainly addressed himself was not whether Wordsworth was capable of projecting himself into his characters, but whether he ought to try. As early as 1797, in his little preface to the second edition of his poems, Coleridge had implied some doubts about dramatic verse: "the most interesting passages in our most interesting poems are those in which the author develops his own feelings. The sweet voice of [Ossian's] Cona never sounds so sweetly as when it speaks of itself" (*STCPW*, II, 1144), and in *Paradise Lost* he found the opening of Book III especially moving. Where the tactics of dramatic writing were adopted, as Wordsworth persisted in doing, then Coleridge thought the simple matter of dramatic propriety was all very well—"every phrase . . . should have its justifying cause in some *passion*"—but overriding its demands were the demands of the verse itself: "Poetry justifies, as *Poetry* . . . some new combinations of Language, & *commands* the omision of many others."

Wordsworth had used similar terms in his 1800 note to "The Thorn," which Coleridge may have been echoing in 1802: "the Reader cannot be too often reminded that Poetry is passion: it is the history or science of feelings" (*PW*, II, 513). But the crucial difference lay in Wordsworth's adoption of the dramatic method in his ballads, and Coleridge's rejection of it. To put it in the simplest way, the passion that Wordsworth expressed in poetry was likely to be that of his characters; the passion that Coleridge looked for was mainly that of the poet. For Wordsworth, the passion could appear only if the poet maintained strict dramatic propriety; for Coleridge, the passion was obscured unless the poet spoke in his own voice. As against Wordsworth's dramatic propriety, Coleridge cited what he might have called poetic propriety.[29]

Beyond the simple issue of dramatic propriety, out in the wider reaches of this controversy, the major issues are all closely connected. Wordsworth's concern with truth as the object of poetry is, for instance, related to his espousal of dramatic method. For the truth revealed in poetry was psychological truth, and it was revealed most plainly in dramatic utterance, in the language really spoken by men in a state of passion. The poet's business was to subdue his own feelings

29. In a marginal note on Beaumont and Fletcher, Coleridge once defined "poetic" as opposed to "tragic" as "capable of being narrated by the Poet in his own person in the same words, with strict adherence to the character of the Poet"; see Roberta F. Brinkley, *Coleridge on the Seventeenth Century* (Durham, N.C.: Duke University Press, 1955), p. 660.

and to project himself into the feelings of his characters, in much the same way as, while recollecting emotion in tranquillity, he allowed himself to be transported out of his present feelings into feelings that had possessed him at some earlier time. Only by this sort of dramatic projection could he grasp the truth of man's nature. "It was well for Shakespeare," Wordsworth remarked to Aubrey de Vere (Grosart, III, 488), "that he gave himself to the drama. It was that which forced him to be sufficiently human." For Coleridge, on the other hand, the poet's business was not to subdue his feelings but to arouse them to creative activity. Where Wordsworth—to put the matter in another way—sought to imitate nature (half believing it the equal of art) by simulating dramatically the passions of real men, Coleridge sought to reconcile nature and art in the working of the poet's synthetic imagination.

Wordsworth's revised Preface and some of his poems of 1802 served to fix and widen the differences that had been opened between the partners in *Lyrical Ballads* by their early experiments and exchanges of view. The following year Coleridge, aware that the differences involved only a few poems, reported to Thomas Poole (14 October 1803) that he had been urging Wordsworth to abandon the ballad altogether and turn to the philosophical mode: "I have seen enough, positively to give me feelings of hostility towards the plan of several of the Poems in the L. Ballads" (*STCL*, II, 1013). Most of Coleridge's hostility remained hidden for years, illuminated only by a few letters or notes, a few remarks recorded in Crabb Robinson's diary, and some glancing comments in Coleridge's lectures on poetry. But in 1815, when Coleridge at last began to set down a relatively ordered statement of his critical opinions, he brought once more into clear focus the issue of dramatic method .

In Chapter XVII of *Biographia Literaria* Coleridge proceded to outline his dissent from the theories of poetry laid down in the Prefaces to *Lyrical Ballads*. As he moved in to the point "to which all the lines of difference converge as to their source and centre," he declared, as we have noticed, his wholehearted allegiance to Aristotle, insisting that "poetry as poetry is essentially *ideal*, that it avoids and excludes all *accident*"; that the persons it represents must be typical and generic, not individual (II, 32–34). Coleridge followed this declaration of poetic faith by applying these (essentially Aristotelian) doctrines to five of Wordsworth's poems, all of them from the *Lyrical Ballads*. "In "The Brothers" and "Michael" he found the "verisimilitude and representative quality" of character he required; in "Goody Blake and Harry Gill" and in "The Idiot Boy" he found at least "the *feelings*" to be "those of human nature in general." But in the fifth poem, "The Thorn," to which Coleridge devoted more attention in the *Biographia* than any other poem of Wordsworth's, Coleridge found fundamental errors of conception, and in his analysis of it he returned once more to the heart of the old disagreements.

Coleridge began by quoting Wordsworth's "Thorn" note of 1800, in which Wordsworth had introduced his "credulous and talkative" speaker and explained the rambling, repetitive nature of his discourse. "But in a poem," Coleridge replied abruptly (II, 36), "still more in a lyric poem (and the NURSE in Shakespeare's Romeo and Juliet alone prevents me from extending the remark even to dramatic *poetry* . . . it is not possible to imitate truly a dull anr garrulous discourser, without repeating the effects of dullness and garrulity." As a consequence, "The Thorn" is made up of good parts and bad parts. The good parts are the passages "which might as well or still better have proceeded from the poet's own imagination, and have been spoken in his own character"; the bad parts are the passages "exclusively appropriate to the supposed narrator."

The trouble lay deeper than language; it lay in Wordsworth's choice of characters. For once the choice is made, Coleridge took pains to show, language becomes a secondary issue (II, 38–39). The language of an uneducated rustic, he says, if "purified" to a degree, would be exactly like the language "of any other man of common-sense." What is significant is that the ideas of the rustic—the content, not the manner, of his discourse—will be different. With his limited faculties, his "scanty experience," and his superstition, he will tend to talk in particulars and give a fragmentary view of his subject, while the educated man will talk in generalities, and, seeing the *"connections* of things," will give a whole and organized view. Nor is it helpful to suggest as Wordsworth does that the rustic might rise to poetic discourse when *"in a state of excitement,"* for excitement cannot create, but only set in motion what is already stored in the mind (II, 42). Turning back to "The Thorn" at the close of the chapter (it ends with a quotation from Wordsworth's "Thorn" note of 1800), Coleridge delivered a final thrust at the way in which Wordsworth had followed the fluxes and refluxes of the narrator's imagination: "It is indeed very possible to adopt in a poem the unmeaning repetitions, habitual phrases, and other blank counters, which an unfurnished or confused understanding interposes at short intervals, in order to keep hold of his subject, which is still slipping from him, and to give him time for recollection; or in mere aid of vacancy . . . But what assistance to the poet, or ornament to the poem, these can supply, I am at a loss to conjecture."

This astonishing confession shows how wide a gulf had opened between the partners in *Lyrical Ballads*. By 1816, at any rate, Coleridge seems to have had no sympathy with Wordsworth's immediate aim in "The Thorn"—to show how superstition acts upon the mind—and little understanding (or recollection) of Wordsworth's ultimate aim—to make a tree "impressive." He seems, moreover, to have rejected absolutely the tactics by which Wordsworth had set out to achieve his aims. For in "The Thorn," as we have seen, Wordsworth had created something very close to a dramatic monologue. As the narrator rambled through his tale of horror, halting at crucial places, repeating himself, darting abruptly ahead into fresh terrors, he was engaged not just in telling a story but in revealing his own character. It is one thing for Coleridge to say that Wordsworth lacked dramatic skill, or that he chose his narrator unwisely. It is quite another to suggest that Wordsworth should have dispensed with the narrator and related the "events" of the poem himself—that it was a mistake for

Wordsworth to have made the narrator dull and garrulous but a greater mistake to have employed him at all. Coleridge appears not to have accepted the idea that the events of the poem might be a product of the narrator's imagination, that "The Thorn" was not a ballad but a lyrical ballad, something resembling a dramatic monologue. If Coleridge was troubled by the narrator's homely diction, he was even more troubled, it seems clear, by the whole theory of poetry embodied in his partner's experimental poem.

Even "The Three Graves" now suffered Coleridge's condemnation. In 1816 he jotted into the margin of the poem, "I regret that I wrote this in verse."[30] Reprinting Parts III and IV in *Sibylline Leaves* (1817), he set down some terse remarks in explanation of their style. He seemed concerned to make it clear that dramatic propriety had governed his choice of diction, but so acute was his discomfort, evidently, with these verses, composed some twenty years earlier, that he pointedly declined to call them poetry. "The language," he explained, "was intended to be dramatic; that is, suited to the narrator; and the metre corresponds to the homeliness of the diction. It is therefore presented as the fragment, not of a Poem, but of a common Ballad-tale" (*STCPW*, I, 267–268). Uncertain "whether this is sufficient to justify the adoption of such a style, in any metrical composition not professedly ludicrous," Coleridge for a second time excluded the work from the realm of poetry: "It is not presented as poetry, and it is in no way connected with the Author's judgment concerning poetic diction." The implication of these blunt remarks is inescapable: no work cast in a dramatic form, in which diction is governed by dramatic propriety, qualified as a poem—it could only be a "common Ballad-tale."

This arbitrary separation of genres will be seen to restrict severely the possibilities of poetic drama, or dramatic poetry. Yet, in making it Coleridge was being consistent with the opinions about Shakespeare he had voiced in his London and Bristol lectures. Shakespeare's characters, he repeatedly de-

30. See Jonathan Wordsworth, "Some Unpublished Coleridge Marginalia," *TLS*, 14 June 1957, p. 369.

clared, were typical as well as particular: they represent "a class, and not an individual," "a class individualized," "*genera* intensely individualized," "ideal realities."[31] Coleridge commonly cited the Nurse in *Romeo and Juliet* as a possible exception; yet, though "the nearest of anything in Shakespeare to borrowing [?from] observation," she too remains typical for the reason that in very old age, as in childhood, "the individual in nature is a representative. Like larch trees, in describing one you generalize a grove."[32] Consequently, the language talked by Shakespeare's characters was a general language, appropriate not so much to the particular individual who uttered it as to the class of individuals he represented.

Even this propriety was sharply limited by two other kinds of control, so that it can hardly be called dramatic propriety at all. The language of Shakespeare's speakers was appropriate, that is, not to their personalities but to the passions they experienced, and in this connection Coleridge on several occasions cited the "Sublime tautology" of the Song of Deborah[33] ("nature is the poet here"), which Wordsworth had cited in his "Thorn" note of 1800. Second, into this language throughout, owing to Shakespeare's unique gift for dramatic self-projection, was subtly infused the voice of the poet himself, and the infusion represented the harmony of poetry and drama. One observation jotted down for a lecture on *Macbeth* suggests what Coleridge meant: "The poet lost in his portraits contrasted with the poet as a mere ventriloquist; wonderful union of both in Shakespeare."[34] In an occasional early work like *Romeo and Juliet*, to be sure, the poet and the dramatist were not yet "entirely blended," with the result that some of the characters speak a language that is really the poet's—"Shakespeare, for a moment forgetting the character, utters his own

31. These phrases appear in Thomas Raysor's edition of Coleridge's lecture notes together with reports on the lectures by those who heard them: *Samuel Taylor Coleridge: Shakespearean Criticism*, 2nd ed., 2 vols. (London: J. M. Dent; New York: E. P. Dutton, 1960), II, 29; I, 64; I, 122; and II, 125.

32. *Ibid.*, I, 39.

33. *Ibid.*, I, 86, 193; II, 102.

34. *Ibid.*, I, 73.

words in his own person."[35] But apart from these early lapses, Shakespeare's language is both universal and distinctive.

In the *Biographia* (II, 77–78) Coleridge compared Shakespeare and Wordsworth in these connections. Anyone, he said, who has studied three or four of Shakespeare's plays will be able to recognize as Shakespeare's a quotation, however brief, from any other play. "A similar peculiarity, though in a less degree, attends Mr. Wordsworth's style, whenever he speaks in his own person; or, whenever, though under a feigned name, it is clear that he himself is still speaking, as in the different dramatis personae of the 'RECLUSE.' Even in the other poems, in which he purposes to be most dramatic, there are few in which it does not occasionally burst forth." In brief, Shakespeare's virtue appeared to be that he made no use of strict dramatic propriety; one of Wordsworth's minor faults was that he could not sustain it—but the major fault was that he attempted it at all.

No less revealing than Coleridge's 1816 strictures on "The Thorn" and "The Three Graves" are his other strictures of about the same date, the chapters he wrote to fill out the second volume of the *Biographia*. Stubbornly reiterating his opposition to all the techniques that distinguish the dramatic monologue, most of which his partner had experimented with in *Lyrical Ballads*, Coleridge brought the heart of the disagreement once more into sharp focus. He found five major "defects" in his partner's poetry (Chapter XXII). The first, "INCONSTANCY" or "*disharmony*" of style, had already been cited in "The Thorn," where it amounted simply to dramatic impropriety—the poet's own style showing through that of the narrator. The second, "*matter-of-factness*," Coleridge found not only in the poet's utterances but in his characterizations, in which too often Wordsworth showed "a *biographical* attention to probability."[36] In discussing these faults Coleridge summed up again his position on "the great point of contro-

---

35. *Ibid.*, II, 102–103.

36. Coleridge had recently spoken forcefully to Wordsworth on this subject in giving his appraisal of the *Excursion* (30 May 1815; *STCL*, IV, 572): "It is for the Biographer, not the Poet, to give the *accidents* of *individual* life. Whatever is not representative, generic, may be indeed most poetically exprest, but it is not Poetry."

versy between Mr. Wordsworth and his objectors; namely on THE CHOICE OF HIS CHARACTERS" (II, 103). Coleridge would rather, he explained, listen to the poet "speaking in his own person" than listen to an artificial person for whom the poet had invented a history and a character, but if a poem was to have characters they must, he insisted, be representative, not individual. The third defect appears almost to summarize the first two: "an undue predilection [on Wordsworth's part] for the *dramatic* form in certain poems, from which one or other of two evils result. Either the thoughts and diction are different from that of the poet, and then there arises an incongruity of style; or they are the same and indistinguishable, and then it presents a species of ventriloquism, where two are represented as talking, while in truth one man only speaks" (II, 109). The fourth defect particularizes the charges against Wordsworth's dramatic technique: "prolixity, repetition, and an eddying, instead of progression, of thought." Only the final defect in the list—"thoughts and images too great for the subject"—appears to be found exclusively in the passages where Wordsworth speaks in his own voice, and to have nothing to do, therefore, with the issue of dramatic method.

Long before these strictures appeared in print, Wordsworth had abandoned his experiments with dramatic method. We can only guess how large a part Coleridge may have played, in the early years, in turning his partner away from the dramatic monologue and toward the philosophic mode. But there is no need to guess at the impression left by *Biographia Literaria*. For the 1820 edition of his collected poems Wordsworth carefully revised the passages that Coleridge had singled out for criticism. There is a double irony in this event. Back in 1800 Wordsworth, fearing that the "strangeness" of "The Ancient Mariner" had hurt the reception of *Lyrical Ballads*, persuaded Coleridge to revise his poem for the second edition. Coleridge normalized the language by removing thirty or forty of the archaic words and some baldly colloquial expressions.[37] Twenty years later Wordsworth, persuaded by Coleridge's attack, normalized the language of "The Thorn" by

37. His revisions are listed in a letter to Biggs and Cottle, *STCL*, I, 598–602.

removing the plainest and most colloquial expressions, together with some of the biographical particulars. Coleridge's
revisions are generally thought to have improved "The
Ancient Mariner." But Wordsworth, by yielding to Coleridge's
charge against the language of his characters—that is, by ele-
vating it to make it conform more closely to Coleridge's notion
of poetic diction—laid himself more open to another, more
telling, charge, that in those poems dramatic propriety was
not sustained. He also obscured the *"radical* Difference" that
had begun to separate him from his partner more than twenty
years earlier. For by improving the language of his dramatic
pieces at the expense of their form, he made the central disagreement about dramatic method look like a disagreement
about poetic diction.

CHAPTER 5

The Ballad as Pastoral

One nearly forgotten episode in the history of *Lyrical Ballads* points up with wonderful irony the tensions of that unequal balance between poetry of the supernatural and poetry of common life: if Coleridge had been able to finish "Christabel" Wordsworth would never have written "Michael." The episode sprawled over the spring, summer, and autumn of 1800, coming to a climax in the first week of October. By this date Wordsworth had mailed off in a series of letters to his printer all his copy for the second volume of 1800, together with the celebrated Preface to be printed with Volume I.[1] While waiting for Coleridge to furnish the rest of "Christabel," Wordsworth commenced work on the critical essay he intended to print with Volume II. Meanwhile, Coleridge had come to the end of his inspiration, "stricken," as he shortly put it, "with barrenness" by the disgust which he had suffered in completing his translation of *Wallenstein*. His own account of his failure is probably half candid, half fanciful. "I tried & tried," he wrote to Josiah Wedgwood on 1 November (*STCL*, I, 643),

& nothing would come of it. I desisted with a deeper dejection than I am willing to remember. The wind from Skiddaw & Borrowdale was often as loud as wind need be—& many a walk in the clouds on the mountains did I take; but all would not do—till one day I dined out at the house of a neighbouring clergyman, & some how or other drank so much wine, that I found some effort & dexterity requisite to balance myself on the hither Edge of Sobriety. The next day, my verse making faculties returned to me, and I proceeded suc-

1. The letters that survive are printed in *EY*, 285–312.

cessfully—till my poem grew so long & in Wordworth's opinion so impressive, that he rejected it from his volume as disproportionate both in size & merit, & as discordant in its character.

A little earlier Coleridge had reported to Poole that "Christabel" had "swelled into a Poem of 1400 lines" (*STCL*, I, 634), but since all that survives in any form is 677 lines, we are left to wonder how far the rest ever reached material substance in the forge of Coleridge's mind.

All we know is that on the evening of 4 October Coleridge abruptly left his house at Keswick and walked down to Grasmere, where he read to William and Dorothy the beginning of Part II of "Christabel." After hearing the poem a second time the next morning with "increasing pleasure" (as Dorothy recorded in her journal), William composed a paragraph discussing "Christabel," to be inserted toward the end of his Preface; that night Dorothy mailed it to the printer. But the very next day (6 October) the partners "Determined not to print Christabel with the L.B.," as Dorothy bleakly noted— perhaps because Wordsworth found the style "discordant" from his own (as he did tell Longman on 18 December; *EY*, 309), but more probably because he recognized at last that the shaping spirit of his partner's imagination had expired under the weight of its afflictions.

To make up the loss of his long poem Coleridge evidently agreed to furnish some of the "Poems on the Naming of Places" (as Wordsworth revealed in another hasty letter to his printers, canceling the paragraph about "Christabel"; *EY*, 304–305) —an agreement, of course, that Coleridge never kept. But a good deal more verse was required to fill the projected volume, the printing of which had already begun. To meet this requirement Wordsworth (having now abandoned his critical essay) set to work on a long and important poem which may have been taking shape in his mind for some time. The poem is not given a title in Dorothy's journal, but it clearly had a connection with the half-ruined sheepfold, "built nearly in the form of a heart unequally divided," which William and Dorothy went in search of and found during a walk up Greenhead Gill, 11 October. For the next two months William worked intermittently "at the sheep-fold" (both the location and the poem, we gather, for on one occasion they were "salving sheep" there), and finished the poem on 9 December.[2] By Christmas the 490-odd lines of "Michael" had been copied out (some by Coleridge) and mailed to Bristol (see *EY*, 308). Within five weeks of that date the second edition of *Lyrical Ballads* was on sale in the bookshops. "Michael: A Pastoral Poem" was the last piece in the collection, in the place originally reserved for "Christabel," and was given the additional honor of a separate title page.

When he turned in earnest to the composing of "Michael," Wordsworth probably had available scraps of two earlier treatments of this important subject. On the one hand there was the blank verse he had written for the *Recluse* or the poem on his own life, describing the heroic figure of an old shepherd in the Cumberland hills. Scrawled over the pages of Coleridge's 1796 *Poems* and over blank leaves in one of Dorothy's journals, these scraps tell mainly of one incident in the life of old Michael and his son—the search for a lost sheep. Some of them later found their way into "the Matron's Tale" in Book VIII of the 1805 *Prelude;* a few Wordsworth used for "Michael." The other treatment of Michael and Luke, which lay unnoticed for a century and a half in one of the Dove Cottage notebooks (MS. 15), consisted of six roughly-drafted stanzas of a ballad, touching on Michael's misfortunes in a semi-jocular way. From these Wordsworth evidently drew the central image of the sheepfold (scarcely mentioned in the blank-verse lines), together with the central incident of the old man's tragic disappointment.

The intended order of the stanzas is difficult to fix, but this might have been the first one:

> Two shepeherds we have the two wits of the dale
> Renow'd for song satire epistle & tale
> Rhymes pleasant to sing or to say
> To this sheepfold they went & a doggrel strain
> They carved on a stone in the wall to explain
> The cause of old Michael's decay.

Next, apparently, a snatch of this doggerel strain, in the words

2. Dorothy recorded these events in her *Journals*, ed. Mary Moorman (Oxford: Oxford University Press, 1971), pp. 42–54.

of the shepherd-wits, written higher on the same leaf of the notebook:

Deep read in experience perhaps he is nice
On himself is so fond of bestowing advice

These lines are deleted, and a fresh start made:

Perhaps the old man is a provident elf
So fond of bestow[ing] advice on himself
And of puzzling at what may befall
So intent upon baking his bread without leaven
And of giving to earth the perfection of heaven
That he thinks and does nothing at all.

Then, evidently, the poet's voice is heard, commenting wryly (and here the draft is partly illegible):

The verses were trim & stood [small?] on their [feet?]
But all their suggestions & taunts to repeat
Twas absolute scandal no less.

Or alternatively,

And all that sly malice so bitter & Sweet
My pen it would sadly distress;
When I say that our maidens are larks in their glee
And fair as the moon hanging over the sea
The drift of those rhymes you will guess

Now from this day forward to tie up your [tongues?]
To teach you to make better use of your lungs
An hour will I spend to relate
What old Michael once told me while on a loose [stone]
One sweet summers morning depressd [and] alone
By the edge of his sheepfold he sate.

Here another version of this last stanza:

That pastoral ballad is sung far & near
So thoughtless a falsehood it greives me to hear
And therefore I now will relate
What old Michael once told [me] while on a loose stone
One sweet summers morning depressd & alone
By the side of his sheepfold he sat[e].

Then a snatch of Michael's own voice, counseling his son at the sheepfold:

> Thy foreelders dwelt in the fear of their Go[d?]

The entire line is deleted in favor of:

> Weve loved and weve cherished the fear of our [God?]
> Should [thou] stir from the path which thy fath[ers trod?]

Finally a fresh start:

> Then think of this sheepfold my Son let it be
> Thy Anchor and watch tower a bond between thee
> And all that is good in thy heart
> You have heard of the end to which Archiba[ld came?]
> Should thou stumble or faint from the path [*illegible*]
> Should thou ever one tittle depart
>
> He stopped & beginning to weep
> He wept like an infant & [?]

And here the attempt breaks off.[3]

Readers who have learned to like "Michael"—readers who

3. These stanzas, which are exceptionally difficult to decipher, are given in their revised form, with miswritings and some illegible parts omitted. Full transcripts showing all variants together with facing photographs are provided in *BWS*, pp. 72–75. In 1963 I read the stanzas aloud as part of a paper presented to the Modern Language Association of America, but no lines from them were published until 1967, when Mark Reed printed five in *Chronology*, p. 323, conjecturing that they spoke of Coleridge. It is possible that an early version of the first stanza to be written on the page was bound into the "ballad Michael" by a change in the opening couplet, "Deep read in experience perhaps he is nice / On himself is so fond of bestowing advice," to include specific references to an old man: "Perhaps the old man is a provident elf / So fond of bestow[ing] advice on himself." In April 1970 Robert Woof published most of the stanzas in "John Stoddart, 'Michael' and Lyrical Ballads," *Ariel*, 1, 7–22, conjecturing that they represented the surviving scraps of a substantial ballad version of "Michael" entitled the "Sheepfold" which was "burnt" by Wordsworth on 9 November 1800 (see Dorothy's *Journals*, p. 50). The ensuing debate over these matters, joined by Mr. Woof, Mark Reed, and myself, was initiated by Jonathan Wordsworth, who discerned that at the stage when the poem referred to Coleridge "the two wits of the dale" must have been the two partners in *Lyrical Ballads*; see *Ariel*, 2 (April 1971), 66–79, and *Ariel*, 3 (April 1972), 70–83.

have, as Lionel Trilling once put it, passed the ultimate test of their tolerance for Wordsworth's poetry of understatement—may be dismayed by this crudely comic treatment of a tragic theme. Miss Helen Darbishire expressed shock and disbelief when she was shown these stanzas in 1959, scrawled into the notebook which contains the earliest version of "Christabel," though she courteously helped to decipher them. Yet the mode they represent is common enough in Wordsworth's poetry from the years of *Lyrical Ballads*. One poem in the volume of 1800, "Rural Architecture," though it treats a lighter subject, has the same meter and stanza form as the "ballad Michael." Its central image is a heap of stones, stacked into the crude shape of a man by three playful schoolboys.

> They built him of stones gather'd up as they lay,
> They built him and christen'd him all in one day,
> An Urchin both vigorous and hale;
> And so without scruple they call'd him Ralph Jones.
> Now Ralph is renown'd for the length of his bones;
> The Magog of Legberthwaite dale.

The tone and diction of the poet's voice, when it enters, are identical with those of the "ballad Michael":

> —Some little I've seen of blind boisterous works
> In Paris and London, 'mong Christians or Turks,
> Spirits busy to do and undo:
> At remembrance whereof my blood sometimes will flag . . .

Another similar poem, the only poem Wordsworth ever titled a "pastoral ballad," treats one of the major themes of "Michael"—that is, what Wordsworth later called "the love of property, *landed* property."[4] (It was a theme he had touched in some earlier poems, among them the "Female Vagrant," where the misfortunes started when the "old hereditary nook" was lost.) "Repentance: A Pastoral Ballad" (later dated 1804 by Wordsworth—*PW*, II, 476—but more likely written in 1802) tells the story of an old couple who gave up their land. Spoken entirely in the voice of the countryman's wife, the

4. In a letter to Thomas Poole, 9 April 1801; *EY*, 322.

poem is a lament for the cruel loss. The subject should be moving, but its pathos is tempered by the same sort of bouncing meter and homely manner, particularly marked in the earlier versions of the poem,[5] as that which distinguishes the "ballad Michael."

> O fools that we were—we had land that we sold
> Snug fields that together contentedly lay,
> They'd have done us more good than another man's gold
> Could we but have been as contented as they.
>
> When the fine Man came to us from London, said I
> Let him come with his bags proudly grasp'd in his hand
> But Thomas, be true to me, Thomas, we'll die
> Before he shall go with an inch of the Land.

But this resolution dissolved; the land was sold, the son deprived of his birthright and condemned to the life of a wanderer; and the poem ends in despondency:

> But we traiterously gave the best Friend that we had
> For spiritless pelf—as we feel to our cost.
>
> When my sick crazy Body had lain without sleep
> What a comfort did sunrise bestow when I stood
> And looked down on the fields & the kine & the sheep
> From the top of the hill—'twas like youth in my blood.
>
> Now I sit in the house and am dull as a snail
> And oftentime hear the Church bell with a sigh
> When I think to myself we've no land in the Vale
> Save six feet of earth where our Fore-fathers lie.

This poem has sometimes been compared with "The Last of the Flock" (de Selincourt drew attention to the resemblances; *PW*, II, 476). The differences show something of what happened to the strain of sentimental pathos in 1800 and 1802. The old shepherd's distress in the poem of 1798 is revealed in the terrible eloquence of his own simple speech:

5. Found in DC MS. 80, from which the readings are taken. W. J. B. Owen has traced language in these early versions to conversation recorded in Dorothy's *Journals* for 24 November 1801 (pp. 61–62 in the Moorman edition); see his *Wordsworth as Critic* (Toronto and London: University of Toronto Press, 1969), pp. 80–82.

> To wicked deeds I was inclined,
> And wicked fancies cross'd my mind;
> And every man I chanc'd to see,
> I thought he knew some ill of me.
> No peace, no comfort could I find,
> No ease, within doors or without,
> And crazily, and wearily,
> I went my work about.

By contrast, the couple's distress in the poem of 1802 is muted, for all its homely realism, by a curious artifice of language and meter which gives the incident a fanciful flavor.

The same kind of loss is treated in another poem published in 1800, "The Farmer of Tilsbury Vale: A Character,"[6] and again one can hear in some of its lines, spoken this time by an observer in a jaunty, colloquial voice, the distinctive tone and diction of the later ballads:

> There's an old man in London, the prime of old men,
> You may hunt for his match through ten thousand and ten,
> Of prop or of staff, does he walk, does he run,
> No more need has he than a flow'r of the sun.

Old Adam has lost his farm, run through the "ill-gotten pelf" that begging and borrowing brought him, then fled to London. The speaker's moral comment is pointed dramatically at his listener:

> You lift up your eyes, "O the merciless Jew!"
> But in truth he was never more cruel than you;
> In him it was scarce e'en a business of art,
> For this he did all in the ease of his heart.

The poem closes with scenes of the old man in Covent Garden, the Haymarket, and Smithfield, sustained, like poor Susan, by visions of the pastoral life he has left behind:

> Where the apples are heap'd on the barrows in piles,
> You see him stop short, he looks long, and he smiles;
> He looks, and he smiles, and a Poet might spy
> The image of fifty green fields in his eye.

6. Published in the *Morning Post*, 21 July 1800, from which the readings are taken.

Other examples of what begins to look like a particular species of ballad come readily to mind. "The Two Thieves" in the 1800 volume opens with a characteristically exuberant address, though Wordsworth never ventured to print the original version (found in DC MS. 29):

> Oh! now that the box-wood and graver were mine
> Of the Poet who lives on the banks of the Tyne!
> Who has plied his rude tools with more fortunate toil
> Than Reynolds e'er brought to his canvas and oil.
>
> Then, Books and Book-learning! I'd ring out your knell:
> The Vicar should scarce know an A from an L;
> And for hunger & thirst and such troublesome calls,
> Every ale-house should then have a feast on its walls.

One thinks also of two other "pastorals" in the volume of 1800. "The Idle Shepherd-boys," like the early blank-verse scraps of "Michael," tells the story of a lost lamb, but in a joyous, half-serious tone. One stanza anticipates, or echoes, the "Intimations" ode:

> A thousand Lambs are on the rocks,
> All newly born! both earth and sky
> Keep jubilee; and more than all,
> Those Boys with their green Coronal.

The boys' gleeful games take up more of the poem than the unfortunate lamb, who has to be rescued by the poet himself, stepping providentially into the scene:

> And gently did the Bard
> Those idle Shepherd-boys upbraid,
> And bade them better mind their trade.

"The Pet-Lamb," also subtitled "A Pastoral," is spoken by a young girl but overheard by the poet with such feeling that as he "retrac'd the ballad line by line" it seemed to him "that but one half of it was hers, and one half of it was mine." If style alone were to be the criterion, one might add to this group poems like the galloping ballad "Written in Germany, On one of the coldest days of the Century," or even the "Character," probably of Coleridge, that Wordsworth wrote in the summer and autumn of 1800:

> I marvel how Nature could ever find space
> For the things and the nothings you see in his face
> There's thought and no thought, and there's paleness and
>   bloom,
> And bustle and sluggishness pleasure & gloom.[7]

In later years an occasional poem appears to echo this style, as though Wordsworth were slow in abandoning a design that interested him. One notable example is the "Power of Music," which Wordsworth said he wrote in 1806, and published in 1807. The scene of the street musician in London arousing in his listeners the same sort of transport as moved "old Adam" and "poor Susan" is presented in familiar anapests, and in a familiar tone:

> That errand-bound 'Prentice was passing in haste—
> What matter! he's caught—and his time runs to waste—
> The News-man is stopped, though he stops on the fret;
> And the half-breathless Lamp-lighter he's in the net!
>
> The Porter sits down on the weight which he bore;
> The lass with her barrow wheels hither her store;—
> If a Thief could be here he might pilfer at ease;
> She sees the Musician, 'tis all that she sees!
>
> He stands, back'd by the Wall;—he abates not his din;
> His hat gives him vigour, with boons dropping in,
> From the Old and the Young, from the Poorest; and there!
> The one-pennied Boy has his penny to spare.

The difficulties of defining a genre like the "pastoral ballad" while at the same time using the definition to identify members of the genre are sufficiently sobering. Precisely what the phrase meant to Wordsworth we cannot know. We are unsure,

7. The version is an early one, from DC MS. 16. It may be worth observing that just ahead of the "ballad Michael" in DC MS. 15 a number of leaves have been torn out; writing that survives on the stubs shows that "Rural Architecture," "The Farmer of Tilsbury Vale," and "A Character" were among the poems once entered there (see *Chronology*, 322–324).

for instance, whether he would have applied it to his "ballad Michael" as a whole, or only to the shepherds' "doggrel strain" therein. There is a further difficulty here. As we begin to enumerate Wordsworth's ballad pieces in which subjects from common life that inspire pathos are treated in a semi-jocular manner, this genre seems to widen out in the poetry of 1797 to 1802 in such a way that one scarely knows where to draw its limits. That is, a "pastoral ballad" comes to look very much like certain forms of a "lyrical ballad."

But here, I think, is the point. The importance of this some-what undistinguished species, the "pastoral ballad," is not that it shows us Wordsworth writing in a semi-comic vein, or manip-ulating his subjects or his speaking voices in unusual ways—however interesting these matters are. Its importance is that it combines and brings into focus two eighteenth-century con-ventions that Wordsworth modified distinctively in his vol-umes of 1798 and 1800—the convention of the ballad and the convention of the pastoral. The second of these has had less attention than the first, in the background of *Lyrical Ballads*, and it needs to be set into perspective.

It is on the whole surprising that anyone could overlook the importance to Wordsworth of the pastoral mode. Only five poems in the 1800 volume are formally subtitled "Pastorals," all of them containing shepherds, but Wordsworth's design was revealed by Coleridge in a letter to Southey in April 1800, at the beginning of work on the second edition: "Wordsworth publishes a second Volume of Lyrical Ballads, & Pastorals" (*STCL*, I, 585). By 1802 the title-page of the collection read *Lyrical Ballads, With Pastoral And Other Poems*. One of the important poems therein, "The Brothers," which Wordsworth referred to at its inception as "The Pastoral of Bowman" (*EY*, 277) was "intended to be the concluding poem of a series of pastorals, the scene of which was laid among the mountains of Cumberland and Westmoreland" (Wordsworth's note of 1800). Although Wordsworth may have thought of "Michael" as the only other finished poem in this series, "The Old Cumberland Beggar: A Description" would have needed no more than a shift of focus—perhaps from the old man himself to the so-called domestic affections he inspired—or the addition of a moving accident to fit it for the series.

Most revealing of all is the way in which Wordsworth later ranked and analyzed the poetic genres. This is not to say that his efforts to divide his own poems into classes have been helpful; shifting and tentative to begin with, they appear to have multiplied confusion for even the most perceptive of later critics. Thus in recent generations we can find H. W. Garrod declaring that the *Lyrical Ballads* contains only one ballad; George Harper inventing such classifications as "The Story" and "The Short Reflective Poem"; and John Jones lumping together as "landscape poems" "The Brothers," "Hart-leap Well," and "Tintern Abbey"—poems which Wordsworth himself seemed to consider, respectively, a pastoral, a ballad, and an ode.[8]

There is better sense to be made of these efforts. The group of unpretentious lyrics in the 1807 volumes which Wordsworth called "Moods of my own Mind" appears to have represented for him both something like a pastoral form and something central to his poetic designs. Trifling and brief as they may seem, Wordsworth once asked whether these poems did not, "taken collectively, fix the attention upon a subject eminently poetical, viz., the interest which objects in nature derive from the predominance of certain affections more or less permanent, more or less capable of salutary renewal in the mind of the being contemplating these objects? This is poetic, and essentially poetic, and why? because it is creative!"[9] When Wordsworth laid out for Coleridge in May 1809 a tentative arrangement of his poems (*MY*, I, 334–336), he came up with eight classes, grouping the poems by subject. Most subjects were associated with certain emotional or intellectual faculties. Thus the first class included poems "relating to childhood, and such feelings as rise in the mind in after life in direct

8. H. W. Garrod, *Wordsworth: Lectures and Essays*, 2nd ed. (Oxford: Oxford University Press, Clarendon Press, 1927), p. 148; George McLean Harper, *Literary Appreciations* (Indianapolis and New York: Bobbs-Merrill Co., 1937), p. 159; John Jones, *The Egotistical Sublime* (London: Chatto and Windus, 1954), pp. 135, 138.

9. In a letter to Lady Beaumont, 21 May 1807; *MY*, I, 147.

contemplation of that state." "The Brothers" was to be placed in the second class, among poems relating to "the fraternal affections, to friendship, and to love," and so on. "Michael" and "The Old Cumberland Beggar" were in the eighth class, poems relating to old age. Perhaps the most interesting class, one which Wordsworth confessed "would be numerous," was the class of poems "relating to natural objects and their influence on the mind." Some of the 1800 pastorals were to appear in this class, and it was to conclude with "Tintern Abbey."

In the collected edition of 1815 most of the classes of 1809 were formally defined by faculties or activities of the mind: thus, "Poems Proceeding from Sentiment and Reflection," "Poems of the Fancy," "Poems of the Imagination," and the like. "The Brothers" and "Michael" turned up among "Poems founded on the Affections," where they were later joined by "Repentance: A Pastoral Ballad"; "Tintern Abbey" was among "Poems of the Imagination." The class of poems "relating to natural objects" had disappeared and its contents were distributed.

At the same time, in the preface to his 1815 volumes (*PW*, II, 431–444), Wordsworth enumerated the "moulds" into which the materials of poetry could be shaped by the various faculties of the poet. There were six of these moulds, representing a telescoping and reduction of the usual eighteenth-century catalogue of genres. The first three were conventional enough: the "Narrative" (to include the Epic), the "Dramatic" ("in which the poet does not appear at all in his own person"), and the "Lyrical"—"containing the Hymn, the Ode, the Elegy, the Song, and the Ballad." The last three—the Idyllic, the Didactic, and the Satiric—were occasionally combined, Wordsworth said, into a composite form, and he offered as examples Young's "Night Thoughts" and Cowper's "Task." In the fourth of these forms, the Idyllium, was apparently preserved the provisional class of 1809 that Wordsworth had called "poems relating to natural objects and their influence on the mind." For Wordsworth defined the Idyllium as "descriptive chiefly either of the processes and appearances of external nature, as the Seasons of Thomson; or of characters, manners, and sentiments, as are

Shenstone's Schoolmistress, The Cotter's Saturday Night of
Burns, the Twa Dogs of the same Author; or of these in con-
jection with the appearances of Nature, as most of the pieces
of Theocritus, the Allegro and Penseroso of Milton, Beattie's
Minstrel, Goldsmith's Deserted Village" (*PW*, II, 433).

What is most striking about this definition is the way it
echoes some of the central passages of the 1800 Preface to
Lyrical Ballads, in particular the paragraph in which Wordsworth had defended his choice of "low and rustic life" (Owen,
156–157). In that situation, Wordsworth had explained, our
elementary feelings are best revealed "because the manners
of rural life germinate from those elementary feelings; and,
from the necessary character of rural occupations are more
easily comprehended; and are more durable; and lastly, because in that situation the passions of men are incorporated with
the beautiful and permanent forms of nature." In the long
addition to the Preface of 1802 Wordsworth had again seemed
to put the mode of the Idyllium close to the center of his poetic
concerns. The poet, in his exalted task of binding together the
"vast empire of human society," of creating an art that would
be "the first and last of all knowledge," principally works with
the common elements of man and the details of his ordinary
life in the setting of the natural world. "He considers man and
nature," Wordsworth summed it up (Owen, 167), "as essentially adapted to each other, and the mind of man as naturally
the mirror of the fairest and most interesting qualities of
nature."

In short, the program of *Lyrical Ballads*—if not the program
Wordsworth seemed to recommend for all great poetry—is a
program centered on the pastoral mode. It seems hardly too
much to say that the *Lyrical Ballads* with their critical prefaces
were simply Wordsworth's versions of pastoral, his contribution to the sustained eighteenth-century debate over the nature
and the value of pastoral poetry.

If we think of pastoral as a form which embodies nostalgic
memories of an imagined golden age, of the idealized purity
and nobility of a time and a race uncorrupted by civilization,

we can find equivalent memories in Wordsworth. His idealization of the common rural people of Cumberland and Westmorland—it caused some surprise among contemporaries who knew the peasantry better than he did—arose out of the deep impression made on his boyhood sensibilities by the solitary figures he met in his native hills. From the same origins, no doubt, arose the stately process of his conversion from Love of Nature to Love of Man. "Shepherds were the men who pleas'd me first," he revealed in Book VIII of the *Prelude* (182–212), not shepherds from Arcadian pastoral tradition, nor even "such as Spenser fabled," but men whose lives were "severe and unadorn'd," filled with "danger and distress, / And suffering." To enforce these distinctions, apparently, Wordsworth here inserted (in 1805) the "Matron's Tale" of an old shepherd and a strayed sheep and a lost boy. At the same time he made it clear that the shepherd he knew in his childhood could grow to more than human stature, could take on, if not archetypal, at least supernatural proportion and significance.

> A rambling Schoolboy, thus
> Have I beheld him, without knowing why
> Have felt his presence in his own domain,
> As of a Lord and Master; or a Power
> Or Genius, under Nature, under God,
> Presiding.
>
> (VIII, 390–395)

This figure could show itself under various aspects of terror and magnificence. Sometimes to the watching boy he would seem to be "a giant, stalking through the fog, / His Sheep like Greenland Bears" (VIII, 401–402); sometimes simply a "Form," "glorified / By the deep radiance of the setting sun"; sometimes an object, solitary,

> sublime,
> Above all height! like an aerial Cross,
> As it is stationed on some spiry Rock
> Of the Chartreuse, for worship.
>
> (VIII, 407–410)

In all these aspects the Shepherd represented man "ennobled," "exalted," "purified" by the imagination of the watching boy, and it was this image of man to which Wordsworth later turned when he wrote the studies of psychology and manners that make up the *Lyrical Ballads*.

We must, however, recognize that in shaping his version of pastoral Wordsworth decisively rejected the pastoral tradition that had prevailed through most Augustan writing. The shepherd, the man whose nature had aroused the youthful Wordsworth's "unconscious love and reverence," whose form became "an index of delight / Of grace and honour, power and worthiness" (as *Prelude* VIII continues),

> this Creature, spiritual almost
> As those of Books; but more exalted far,
> Far more of an imaginative form,
> Was not a Corin of the groves, who lives
> For his own fancies, or to dance by the hour
> In coronal, with Phillis in the midst,
> But, for the purposes of kind, a Man
> With the most common; Husband, Father; learn'd,
> Could teach, admonish, suffer'd with the rest
> From vice and folly, wretchedness and fear.
>
>   (416–427)

If Wordsworth failed, as he confessed, to realize this truth in his childhood, he understood it by the time he began to write pastoral poetry—in time, that is, to align himself against the strong current of eighteenth-century opinion that held the pastoral to be a low and vulgar form in so far as it departed from the groves of Corin and moved toward common life. This current of opinion derived, loosely, from Rapin, who had argued that pastoral ought to imitate the actions of a shepherd in the Golden Age, in a state of innocence.[10] In England the opinion drew authority from Pope, who had declared in a widely influential essay that the true business of pastoral con-

---

10. His remarks were translated and prefaced to an edition of the *Idylliums of Theocritus* (Oxford, 1684). J. E. Congleton, *Theories of Pastoral Poetry in England 1684–1798* (Gainesville, Fla.: University of Florida Press, 1952), gives an admirably full summary of these opinions. Leslie Broughton, *The Theocritan Element in the Works of William Wordsworth* (Halle: M. Niemeyer 1920), is also helpful.

sisted in "exposing the best side only of a shepherd's life, and in concealing its miseries."[11]

By 1750, Dr. Johnson had broadened the definition of pastoral by endorsing Virgil's: "a poem in which any action or passion is represented by its effects upon a country life."[12] At the same time he sharply limited the pastoral by declaring its subjects to be inevitably uninteresting, too confined and special to carry wide appeal. His declaration perfectly summarizes the view that Wordsworth tried to counter in 1800 when he set out "to make the incidents of common life interesting." Here is Johnson in *Rambler* no. 36:

Not only the images of rural life, but the occasions on which they can be properly produced, are few and general. The state of a man confined to the employments and pleasures of the country, is so little diversified, and exposed to so few of those accidents which produce perplexities, terrors and surprises, in more complicated transactions, that he can be shewn but seldom in such circumstances as attract curiosity.

Against this, set Wordsworth fifty years later (Owen, 156):

Low and rustic life was generally chosen because in that situation the essential passions of the heart find a better soil in which they can attain their maturity, are less under restraint, and speak a plainer and more emphatic language; because in that situation our elementary feelings exist in a state of greater simplicity and consequently may be more accurately contemplated and more forcibly communicated; because the manners of rural life germinate from those elementary feelings; and from the necessary character of rural occupations are more easily comprehended; and are more durable; and lastly, because in that situation the passions of men are incorporated with the beautiful and permanent forms of nature.

Elsewhere, in numerous scattered remarks, Johnson had

11. "A Discourse on Pastoral Poetry" (1717), reprinted by E. Audra and Aubrey Williams in the Twickenham Edition of Pope, Vol. I: *Pastoral Poetry and An Essay on Criticism* (London: Methuen; New Haven: Yale University Press, 1961), pp. 23–33. The essay appeared in Robert Anderson's *British Poets*, 13 vols. (London, 1795), VIII, 11–13.

12. *Rambler* 37; see Vol. III of *The Yale Edition of the Works of Samuel Johnson*, edited by W. J. Bate and A. B. Strauss, (London: Methuen; New Haven: Yale University Press, 1969), p. 201. Johnson used this definition in his Dictionary.

made clear his contempt for modern writers of pastoral, even Milton. Like Pope, Johnson further cherished a strong preference for one of the two classical masters of pastoral. Theocritus, he complained,[13] depicted "manners" that were "coarse and gross"; Virgil was "very evidently superior," having "much more description, more sentiment, more of Nature and more of art." Whether or not Wordsworth knew all these various opinions about pastoral, he probably knew those that Johnson articulated. It is worth remembering that he showed his awareness of Johnson by citing him in each of his major pieces of criticism (the 1800 Preface, the 1802 Appendix, the 1809 "Essays, upon Epitaphs," the 1815 Preface, and the 1815 "Essay, Supplementary to the Preface"). It is reasonable to suppose that when Wordsworth wrote to John Wilson in 1802 (*EY*, 352–358) about people who were "disgusted with the very mention of the words pastoral poetry, sheep or shepherds," he was thinking of Johnson, who in the life of Shenstone had ridiculed Shenstone's "Pastoral Ballad": "I cannot but regret that it is pastoral; an intelligent reader, acquainted with the scenes of real life, sickens at the mention of the *crook*, the *pipe*, the *sheep*, and the *kids*."[14]

Wordsworth must, moreover, have known the arguments for or against Virgil and Theocritus as models for writers of pastoral to imitate, for these arguments ran through nearly all eighteenth-century writings on the pastoral. It is significant that from his own earliest observations on the pastoral Wordsworth praised Theocritus for a range of virtues. Writing to Coleridge in Germany, 27 February 1799, on the subject of character and "manners," Wordsworth tried to explain why Bürger failed to satisfy him. His explanation touches several important matters.

When I had closed my last letter to you to which you have replied, I recollected that I had spoken inaccurately in citing Shenstone's

13. As Boswell reported, *Life of Johnson*, ed. George Birkbeck Hill, 6 vols. (Oxford: Oxford University Press, Clarendon Press, 1934–1950), IV, 2.

14. Samuel Johnson, *Lives of the English Poets*, ed. George Birkbeck Hill, 3 vols. (Oxford: Oxford University Press, Clarendon Press, 1905), III, 356.

schoolmistress as the character of an individual. I ought to have said of individuals representing classes. I do not so ardently desire character in poems like Burger's, as manners, not transitory manners reflecting the wearisome obliquities of city-life, but manners connected with the permanent objects of nature and partaking of the simplicity of those objects. Such pictures must interest when the original shall cease to exist. The reason will be immediately obvious if you consider yourself lying in a valley on the side of mount Ætna reading one of Theocritus's Idylliums or on the plains of Attica with a comedy of Aristophanes on your hand. Of Theocritus and his spirit perhaps three fourths remain of Aristophanes a mutilated skeleton; at least I suppose so, for I never read his works but in a most villainous translation. But I may go further read Theocritus in Ayrshire or Merionethshire and you will find perpetual occasions to recollect what you see daily in Ayrshire or Merionethshire read Congreve Vanbrugh and Farquhar in London and though not a century is elapsed since they were alive and merry, you will meet with whole pages that are uninteresting and incomprehensible. Now I find no manners in Burger; in Burns you have manners everywhere, Tam Shanter I do not deem a character, I question whether there is any individual character in all Burns' writing except his own. But every where you have the presence of human life. The communications that proceed from Burns come to the mind with the life and charm of recognitions. But Burns also is energetic solemn and sublime in sentiment, and profound in feeling. His Ode to Despondency I can never read without the deepest agitation. (*EY, 255–256*)

Shenstone, Theocritus, and Burns—three poets who were to be presented in 1815 as masters of the Idyllium—thus stand associated in 1799 as painters of humble manners. Wordsworth's earlier remarks about Shenstone are lost, but the tenor of them may be guessed from his later remark (in a letter of 15 January 1837) that Shenstone was one of the first poets who "fairly brought the muse into the Company of common life" (*LY*, II, 829). Of Wordsworth's veneration for Burns I have already spoken, and we will return to Burns in a moment. His veneration for Theocritus had deeper origins. "Child of the mountains, among Shepherds rear'd," he wrote in the *Prelude*,

> Even from my earliest school-day time, I lov'd
> To dream of Sicily.
>
> (X, 1007–1009)

And he went on to pay tribute to Theocritus by citing his seventh idyl, the story of "Divine Comates." What Wordsworth seemed to admire in all three poets was their ability to reach the deepest, most typical patterns of feeling and behavior through the simple surfaces of life in rural settings, to find the universal in the local. In depicting realistically the "manners" of Sicilian goatherds of the third century B.C. Theocritus had touched the permanent elements of human nature, just as Burns had done in his homely lyrics about Scottish peasants, and as Wordsworth hoped to do by giving "pictures" of eighteenth-century shepherds in Cumberland and Westmorland.

The word "manners," which figures in the 1799 letter to Coleridge, runs persistently through Wordsworth's critical vocabulary, from his talk of founding a monthly magazine in 1794, to be concerned principally with "Life and Manners" (*EY*, 125), to his notes on the *Borderers* in 1843 (*PW*, I, 342) distinguishing character from "manners," which he felt at that date should have been more prominent in the play. Wordsworth defined the term rather slackly in 1830 as "designating customs, rules, ceremonies, minor incidents and details, costume, etc. . . . almost everything except natural appearances, that is not passion or character, or leading incident" (*LY*, I, 506–507). What is important is that "manners" was a conventional term in eighteenth-century writings on the pastoral, used more often than not in a fairly derogatory sense (great poetry imitated universal passions, pastoral poetry could only imitate local manners). For Wordsworth to tell his readers in the "Advertisement" of 1798 that they would like his poems in proportion as they knew and liked writers who excelled in "painting manners and passions," as for him in the 1800 Preface to locate our "elementary feelings" in the "manners of rural life," was to propose a tradition of pastoral which broke with that defined by the critical authorities of his century.

It is hard to say how well Wordsworth may have known the dissenting tradition of pastoral with which he was aligning himself. In its seventeenth-century origins the contest between the two traditions can be taken as roughly analogous to the battle of the Ancients and the Moderns. Where Rapin had called for imitation both of Golden-Age shepherds and of classical models, Fontenelle had argued (in 1688) that the pastoral ought simply to reflect the psychological truth of rural life.[15] In England, the boldest follower of Fontenelle was Ambrose Philips, who wrote of English rustics in an English landscape. We can assume that Wordsworth knew the controversies that had swirled about the pastorals of Philips and the rival pastorals of Pope, for in 1815 he alluded to them in his "Essay, Supplementary to the Preface." Pope's extraordinary reputation, Wordsworth charged, was gained not by poetic merit but by the arts by which he "bewitched" and "dazzled" the nation. But he was "himself blinded by his own success." For "having wandered from humanity in his Eclogues with boyish inexperience, the praise, which these compositions obtained, tempted him into a belief that Nature was not to be trusted, at least in pastoral Poetry. To prove this by example, he put his friend Gay upon writing those Eclogues which their author intended to be burlesque." Wordsworth showed pleasure in reporting Johnson's summary of these events, in his life of Gay. Despite their ludicrous and disgusting passages, these burlesques were taken seriously, "became popular, and were read with delight, as just representations of rural manners and occupations" (*PW*, II, 418–419).

Later in the century a growing number of poets and critics called for a kind of pastoral that offered accurate portrayals of common life. A fair example was Hugh Blair, whose *Lectures on Rhetoric* became a standard text and ought to have been known to Wordsworth. Blair cautioned that a wholly realistic showing of peasant life, such as Theocritus had offered, would be too low for poetry; pastoral should not shock the reader with anything painful or disgusting, like a shepherd's "loss of a favorite lamb."[16] At the same time, he proposed that the topics of conventional pastoral be enlarged, that the pastoral be used as a means of probing the heart. "Human nature and human passions, are much the same in every rank of life; and wherever these passions, operate on subjects that are within the rural sphere, there may be a proper subject for Pastoral."

15. I am again indebted to Congleton, *Theories of Pastoral Poetry.*
16. Citations are from the 6th ed., 3 vols., of 1796; Lecture XXXIX, "Pastoral Poetry—Lyric Poetry," is in Vol. III, pp. 107–136.

Among the examples Blair found appropriate were some that
Wordsworth clearly fancied: "the attachment of friends and
of brothers," "the unexpected successes or misfortunes of fam-
ilies," and others. Blair reviewed the history of English pastoral and singled out Shenstone's "Pastoral Ballad" as a
particularly "elegant" achievement. Along the way he reported
that the program for pastoral poetry which he was outlining
had been fully realized in some recent German poems, the
Idyls of Salomon Gessner.

Gessner had been known in England for years, reviewed,
translated, widely praised. Wordsworth and Coleridge must
have talked about him at the start of their collaboration, for
"The Ancient Mariner" echoes "Der Erste Schiffer" (a poem
Coleridge later tried to put into blank verse, but gave up in "a
double disgust, moral & poetical"),[17] and "Cain" was patently
based on "The Death of Abel." Gessner's idyls were pastoral
narratives or dialogues of a conventional sort ("Climena and
Damon," "Corydon and Menalcas," and the like). Hardly one
could be taken as set in modern life, but they did make use of
sentiments and images drawn from nature and rural society.
While some of their humanitarian strains may have touched
Wordsworth, their larger importance is that they were modeled
frankly on Theocritus, whose simplicity and truth Gessner
praised without restraint.

How well Wordsworth knew Blair or Gessner has to remain conjectural. There is less doubt that he knew another
writer whose remarks on the pastoral are scattered through
some unimportant, little-read works. In a most interesting
article published in 1957,[18] A. A. Mendilow traced a number
of ideas and expressions in Wordsworth's Preface of 1800 to
Robert Heron, a champion of Burns who did a good deal of

17. As he told Godwin, 26 March 1811; *STCL*, III, 313. On 13 July
1802 (*STCL*, II 809–811) Coleridge had written to Sotheby about his
translation and spoken contemptuously of Gessner (it is the letter in
which he talks of the *"radical* Difference" that had begun to appear between his ideas of poetry and those of Wordsworth, who had left only
the day before).

18. A. A. Mendilow, "Robert Heron and Wordsworth's Critical Essays," *MLR*, 52 (July 1957), 329–338.

hack journalism, edited the "Seasons" of Thomson, and wrote a *Journey Through the Western Counties of Scotland* (1793), a book which Wordsworth's hunger for travel literature must have brought before his notice (Wordsworth alluded to the book in a footnote to *Excursion*, I, 341). Heron's memoir of Burns was published in two issues of the *Monthly Magazine* in 1797 (March and the June Supplement). In it he divided Burns's poems into two classes: "pastorals"—"in which rural imagery, and the manners and sentiments of rustics are chiefly described"—and "pieces upon common life and manners"—pieces, that is, "without any particular reference to the country."[19] Heron evidently found the pastorals more interesting. In *Journey Through the Western Counties* he had given special praise to "The Cotter's Saturday Night," which he found a strong corrective to Gay's burlesque, *The Shepherd's Week:* it proved "that Pastoral Poetry need not to employ itself upon fictitious manners and modes of life, but may, with higher poetical advantages, paint the humble virtues, the simple pleasures, the inartificial manners of our peasantry, such as they actually exist."[20]

There were other important statements on the pastoral available to Wordsworth, and a reasonable case can be made for the influence upon him of one or another of them. It would be surprising if he did not know something of the essays by Joseph and Thomas Warton, or by Francis Fawkes, whose translations of Theocritus Wordsworth would have read in Robert Anderson's *British Poets*. But the only major influence we need to recognize is again the influence of Burns, who shows up here, as in other central traditions behind the *Lyrical Ballads*, as Wordsworth's principal British model.

Burns had presented his Kilmarnock edition of 1786—the volume from which Wordsworth had learned his first enthusiasm for Burns—as a volume of pastoral poetry, but not pastoral of the classical kind, as the opening of his little preface made clear:

19. Quotations are from the separate publication, *A Memoir of the Life of the Late Robert Burns*, issued in Edinburgh, 1797, p. 54.
20. Quoted by Mendilow, pp. 330–331.

The following trifles are not the production of the Poet, who, with all the advantages of learned art, and perhaps amid the elegancies and idlenesses of upper life, looks down for a rural theme, with an eye to Theocritus or Virgil. To the author of this, these and other celebrated names their countrymen are, in their original languages, "A fountain shut up and a book sealed." Unacquainted with the necessary requisites for commencing Poet by rule, he sings the sentiments and manners, he felt and saw in himself and his rustic compeers around him, in his and their native language.[21]

Burns went on to quote Shenstone and drop a word of praise for his "divine Elegies." But as though to identify the pastoral tradition in which he wished to take his place, Burns paid his handsomest tribute to the genius of two Scottish predecessors, Allan Ramsay, whose *Gentle Shepherd* and *Ever Green* were about the earliest eighteenth-century collections to adapt the pastoral to modern life, and Robert Fergusson, who furnished the model for "The Cotter's Saturday Night" and some other poems. Though he kept these masters "in his eye," Burns said, "rather with a view to kindle at their flame than for servile imitation," he drew unashamedly upon their themes, their meters, and their style. Later, in a little "Sketch" published in 1800 by his first editor under the title "Poem on Pastoral Poetry,"[22] Burns singled Ramsay out from hundreds of "nameless wretches" who had tried and failed at the craft of "Shepherd-sang," calling him the only modern poet who could match the genius of Theocritus:

> Thou paints auld Nature to the nines,
> In thy sweet Caledonian lines;
> Nae gowden stream thro' myrtles twines
>   Where Philomel,
> While nightly breezes sweep the vines,
>   Her griefs will tell!
>
>   . . .
>
> In gowany glens thy burnie strays,
> Where bonie lasses bleach their claes;
> Or trots by hazelly shaws and braes

21. Reprinted in Robert Burns, *The Poems and Songs of Robert Burns*, ed. James Kinsley, 3 vols. (Oxford: Oxford University Press, Clarendon Press, 1968), III, 971–972.

22. See Burns, *Poems and Songs*, III, 1145.

Wi' hawthorns gray,
Where blackbirds join the shepherd's lays,
    At close o' day.

Wordsworth's poetic tributes to Burns are in the same vein, praising Burns essentially as a poet of nature. One stanza of the poem written (or started) at Burns's graveside alludes to the kind of lyric that Wordsworth was imitating (probably "To a Mountain-Daisy"):

Fresh as the flower, whose modest worth
He sang, his genius "glinted" forth,
Rose like a star that touching earth,
    For so it seems,
Doth glorify its humble birth
    With matchless beams.

(PW, III, 65)

Lyrics of this sort would have helped Wordsworth to think of Burns as a nature poet, but the tradition of the Idyllium in which Wordsworth placed some of Burns's work embraced more than nature poetry. In one of the notes he dictated to Isabella Fenwick, Wordsworth talked about Burns as a nature poet but remarked how rarely the appearances of nature took on any prominence in Burns's poetry, despite his warm allusion to the privilege of describing "fair Nature's face." The reason for this fact was perfectly intelligible to Wordsworth, who would have put a good deal of his own nature poetry into the same class. "Whether he [Burns] speaks of rivers, hills, and woods, it is not so much on account of the properties with which they are absolutely endowed, as relatively to local patriotic remembrances and associations, or as they are ministerial to personal feelings, especially those of love, whether happy or otherwise" (Grosart, III, 154). As the Idyllium described not only external nature but "characters, manners, and sentiments" or these "in conjunction with the appearances of nature," so did Wordsworth celebrate nature not only for her own sake, as he might have done in "the hour of thoughtless youth," but for the human passions "incorporated" with her "beautiful and permanent forms"—nature colored, as it were, by man's mortality.

Among the various strains of pastoral in Burns's poems, the elegiac strain was one of the most pervasive and distinctive, and it was this strain that Wordsworth followed as much as any other when he paid Burns the tribute of imitation. Wordsworth's elegiac voice can be heard in his earliest poems, mingled sometimes with the lugubrious Gothic mode from which he later freed himself, but it rises to extraordinary brilliance in some of the lyrics he wrote in Germany in 1799, about the time he was discussing Theocritus and Burns with Coleridge. Scattered elements of the Lucy poems have been turned up in scattered lyrics of Burns.

> Again the silent wheels of time
> Their annual rounds have driv'n,[23]

must have reminded many readers of Lucy, "Roll'd round in earth's diurnal course," and other examples could be cited. More striking is Burns's homely variant of the pastoral elegy, commemorating "Captain" Matthew Henderson (*Poems and Songs*, I, 438–442). In "The Ruined Cottage" Wordsworth described one pattern of the elegy as he would have learned it from Moschus and Bion—not to speak of Milton:

> The Poets, in their elegies and songs
> Lamenting the departed, call the groves,
> They call upon the hills and streams to mourn,
> And senseless rocks.[24]

Burns's procession of mourners included these and the other conventional figures—flowers, the seasons, the sun and the moon.

> Thee, Matthew, Nature's sel shall mourn,
> By Wood and wild.

But he added some mourners that Sicily had never seen:

> Mourn, ye wee songsters o' the wood;
> Ye grouse that crap the heather bud;

23. "To Miss L-----," *Poems and Songs*, I, 319.
24. I quote from Jonathan Wordsworth's text, *The Music of Humanity* (London: Thomas Nelson and Sons, 1969), p. 35.

Ye curlews, calling thro' a clud;
       Ye whistling plover;
          . . .

Mourn, sooty coots, and speckled teals;
Ye fisher herons, watching eels;
Ye duck and drake, wi' airy wheels
      Circling the lake;
Ye bitterns, till the quagmire reels,
      Rair for his sake!

Mourn, clamouring craiks at close o' day,
'Mang fields o' flowering claver gay;

and so on. When Wordsworth wrote his elegies for his own
Matthew, the village schoolmaster, he picked up and extended
this pattern, developing almost a parody of the classical procession, to include the whole range of rustic society:

Mourn, Shepherd, near thy old grey stone,
Thou Angler by the silent flood,
And mourn when thou art all alone
Thou woodman in the lonesome wood.

Mourn sick man sitting in the shade
When summer suns have warmed the earth,

and so on, through reapers, the mower, the milkmaid, little
girls, "ruddy damsels past sixteen," brothers, mothers, old
women, and "sheep-curs, a mirth-loving corps!" (*PW*, IV, 453–
454).

It is a pity that the Matthew elegies have aroused less interest
and delight than the Lucy poems, for they are no less brilliant.
The fault lies partly in the history of their publication, which
has been disorderly. Three of them Wordsworth put into the
volume of 1800, but some others he left in manuscript for
years. He extracted and printed a fourth poem, revised and
truncated, in 1842. The manuscript drafts from which he
worked, containing two additional poems, were finally published by de Selincourt and Miss Darbishire in 1947 in the
notes to *PW*, IV (451–455). But even then two stanzas were
missed. Written into the notebook which contains the "ballad
Michael," used in Germany and later, these lines deserve to be
set with the other members of the scattered group:

Carved, Matthew, with a master's skill
Thy name is on the hawthorn tree
'Twill live, & yet it seemed that still
I owed another [song *deleted*] verse to thee
I sate upon thy favorite stool
And this my last memorial song
We sang together in the school
I and thy little tuneful throng

These rhymes so homely in attire
With learned ears may ill agree
But chaunted by thy orphan quire
They made a touching melody
Thus did I sing, thy little brood
All followed me with voice and hand
Moved both by what they understood
And what they did not understand.

One other elegy in the volume of 1800 comes straight from Burns. To close his elegy on Matthew Henderson Burns had placed an "Epitaph" in ballad quatrains, addressed to the person who might happen by Matthew's grave. He had already used this form for the final poem in his Kilmarnock volume, "A Bard's Epitaph," and Wordsworth used it for "The Poet's Epitaph," the elegy he wrote in Germany, he said, while he was walking in cold so intense that "the people of the house used to say rather unfeelingly, that they expected I should be frozen to death some night" (Grosart, III, 160). He seems to have celebrated his own imagined death at Goslar just as, according to Coleridge, he may have celebrated the imagined death of his sister in the Lucy poems. "The Poet's Epitaph," published in the 1800 *Lyrical Ballads*, has a satiric vigor that Wordsworth rarely achieved, owing to his resolve to avoid satire. Some of this vigor is visible elsewhere in Burns, if not in "A Bard's Epitaph," but perhaps the most striking similarity between these epitaphs is in the image of the poet set forth in them. Burns's stanza,

Is there a Bard of rustic song,
Who, noteless, steals the crouds among
That weekly this area throng,
                    O, pass not by!

> But with a frater-feeling strong,
> > Here, heave a sigh,[25]

is answered by Wordsworth a little discursively:

> But who is He, with modest looks
> And clad in homely russet brown?
> He murmurs near the running brooks
> A music sweeter than their own.
>
> > . . .
>
> The outward shews of sky and earth,
> Of hill and valley, he has view'd;
> And impulses of deeper birth
> Have come to him in solitude.
>
> In common things that round us lie
> Some random truths he can impart . . .

Both images point up clearly the tradition of pastoral singer in which the poet desired to place himself.

The elegiac voice does not, of course, coincide perfectly with the pastoral voice, and a study of Wordsworth's place in the pastoral tradition ought to glance at other influences upon him besides the major influence of Burns. In later years Wordsworth identified from time to time various poems he had admired when he was learning his craft, and his editors have traced their influence and that of other poems he did not name. It is remarkable how many of these poems fall under Wordsworth's own definition of the Idyllium. Some of them were no more than what Wordsworth called "loco-descriptive" and what we sometimes call "topographical" or "landscape" poems, like "Lewesdon Hill" by William Crowe, or Dyer's "Grongar Hill." Other poems he imitated were more loosely pastoral, like Beattie's "Minstrel," the *Seasons* of Thomson, Collins's "Ode to Evening," or Cowper's *Task*.

The influence of all these poems was largely felt on the verse Wordsworth wrote before 1797.[26] More important for *Lyrical Ballads* were, for example, the poems of John Lang-

25. *Poems and Songs*, I, 247.

26. De Selincourt's notes to *An Evening Walk* and *Descriptive Sketches*, *PW*, I, 318–329, offer a particularly rich catalogue of eighteenth-century influences.

horne, echoed repeatedly by Wordsworth from his earliest writings onward. In 1837 Wordsworth talked of Langhorne as "one of the poets who has not had justice done him" (*HCR*, II, 517), and it was Langhorne's "Country Justice" along with Shenstone's "Schoolmistress" that Wordsworth praised in the same year for having brought the muse down to the level of common life, "to which it comes nearer than Goldsmith, and upon which it looks with a tender and enlightened humanity —and with a charitable, (and being so) philosophical and poetical construction that is too rarely found in the works of Crabbe" (*LY*, II, 829). (Wordsworth never found it possible to praise Crabbe's pictures of rustic life.) "The Oak and the Broom, A Pastoral" in the 1800 volume, while it follows the major lines of Spenser's "February" eclogue in the *Shepherd's Calendar*, is a direct imitation of one or more of Langhorne's "Fables of Flora" (they appear in Anderson's *British Poets*, Vol. XI). The important difference is that Wordsworth prefaced his tale with a characteristic stanza to convert it from a classical, or neoclassical, or even Spenserian pastoral, into a Wordsworthian pastoral:

> His simple truths did Andrew glean
> Beside the babbling rills;
> A careful student he had been
> Among the woods and hills.
> One winter's night when through the Trees
> The wind was thundering, on his knees
> His youngest born did Andrew hold:
> And while the rest, a ruddy quire,
> Were seated round their blazing fire,
> This Tale the Shepherd told.

Other thematic and verbal parallels with Wordsworthian pastoral can be found in Anderson's *British Poets*, the volumes from which Wordsworth said he formed his first acquaintance with Chaucer, Daniel, Drayton, and other English classics.[27] One could move outward to minor English voices not in Anderson—poets like Edward Williams, whose *Poems, Lyrical & Pastoral* (1794) included "Lyrical Pastorals," a "Pastoral Bal-

27. See the Fenwick note to "Yarrow Visited," *PW*, III, 450–451.

lad," "Pastoral Songs," and simple "Pastorals" in profusion, or like Charlotte Smith, whom Wordsworth thought "a lady to whom English verse is under greater obligations than are likely to be either acknowledged or remembered," owing to her having written "with true feeling for rural nature, at a time when nature was not much regarded by English Poets; for in point of time her earlier writings preceded, I believe, those of Cowper and Burns" (*PW*, IV, 403).

But instead of putting together a catalogue of these influences and others, it may be enough to remark simply how they help to set Wordsworth off once more from the ubiquitous and indefatigable Southey, whose experimental eclogues fall over the same years as Wordsworth's, frequently, as has been observed, treating the same subjects in roughly the same manner. For Southey's inspiration was German, not English. After William Taylor introduced him to the Idyls of Voss and Gessner, Southey resolved to write some English equivalents, "sketching features peculiar to England," as he informed Taylor on 24 July 1798. "Like the Germans," he added, "I would aim at something of domestic interest."[28] In a prefatory note to the Eclogues he published in 1799, Southey declared the pastoral tradition to be a dull and undistinguished one, despite some illustrious names: "Pastoral writers, 'more silly than their sheep' have like their sheep gone on in the same track one after another." He had found no pastorals to interest him save Gay's, before he became aware they were burlesques.

Since Southey knew no German in 1799, he had to depend on Taylor's translations of Voss and Gessner, and it is fair to suspect that his reading of *Lyrical Ballads* may have helped to teach him what a domestic tale could be. Wordsworth himself may have known of Gessner, but he evidently knew nothing of Voss until 1799, when Coleridge, who had translated parts of "Luise" some three years earlier (see his letter to John Thelwall, 17 December 1796; *STCL*, I, 283n) mentioned Voss in one of the letters from Germany.[29] The catalogues of homely

28. J. W. Robberds, *Memoir of ... William Taylor*, 2 vols. (London, 1843), I, 213.
29. See Wordsworth's reply, 27 February 1799; *EY*, 255.

pleasures in "Luise" may have left some mark on "Michael," and there were doubtless other German strains in Wordsworth's pastorals, but the central lines of influence remained vigorously English—or at any rate, British.

Despite all the influences upon Wordsworth, important as they were, we should understand that in 1798 and 1800 and even later he was attempting to create a distinctive—we need not say original—kind of pastoral, suited to his own talents and answering his own purposes. There are, to be sure, difficulties in defining and limiting this pastoral. They arise not only from the looseness with which the pastoral (the idyl, the eclogue, the bucolic) was commonly defined in the eighteenth century, but from Wordsworth's strategy of founding his entire poetic revolution upon studies of "low and rustic life" (alternatively "common life" or "rural life"). As we have seen, some very different poems in the volume of 1800 carry the subtitle of Pastoral. It would not be fantastical to think, further, of poems in what we have learned to call the "descriptive-meditative" pattern as pastoral poems: the way in which the landscape delineated in the descriptive parts, at the opening and close of the poem, enters into the solution of a mental problem in the meditative part illustrates perfectly how the mind of man is fitted to the external world, and nature to the mind. "Tintern Abbey" opens (neatly) with an evocation of "these pastoral farms / Green to the very door," and closes with "these steep woods and lofty cliffs / And this green pastoral landscape."

At the other extreme, an interesting case might be made for the *Excursion* as a pastoral poem, an Idyllium. In one portion of the *Recluse*, "Home at Grasmere," Wordsworth called for a pastoral poetry that improved upon classical tradition:

> is there not
> An art, a music, and a strain of words
> That shall be life, the acknowledged voice of life,
> Shall speak of what is done among the fields,
> Done truly there, or felt, of solid good
> And real evil, yet be sweet withal,
> More grateful, more harmonious than the breath,

The idle breath of softest pipe attuned
To pastoral fancies?

(*PW*, V, 327)

Without exerting too much ingenuity the *Excursion* could be
looked upon as just this sort of pastoral. Wordsworth's earliest
surviving statements about the *Recluse*, March 1798 (*EY*, 212),
declared that his object was "to give pictures of Nature, Man,
and Society," and he might have intended to echo the meaning
of "little picture" for the Greek *idyl*. ("Michael" was intended
"to give a picture of a man"; "The Brothers" and "Michael"
together were "to draw a picture of the domestic affections.")
The Pedlar, later the Wanderer, had like Wordsworth himself
drawn his understanding of human nature from rustic people
—an experience that Wordsworth described in language which
has been noticed to echo the Preface to *Lyrical Ballads* (see
PW, V, 412):

> much did he see of men,
> Their manners, their enjoyments, and pursuits,
> Their passions and their feelings; chiefly those
> Essential and eternal in the heart,
> That, 'mid the simpler forms of rural life,
> Exist more simple in their elements,
> And speak a plainer language.

(*Excursion*, I, 341–347; *PW*, V, 20)

After the *Excursion* was published Wordsworth reminded Mrs.
Clarkson (January 1815) that "my conversations almost all
take place out of Doors, and all with grand objects of nature
surrounding the speakers for the express purpose of their
being alluded to in illustration of the subjects treated of" (*MY*,
II, 191).

Other reasons for regarding the *Excursion* as a pastoral poem,
a form of the Idyllium, could readily be devised, and some of
them would seem persuasive. But argument of this sort is
quasi-fanciful, and need not be sustained beyond the point
where it helps us understand how hard it is to draw the limits
of Wordsworth's pastoral mode, the mode of the Idyllium.
From the slightest elegiac lyrics to the grandest philosophical
blank verse, pastoral as Wordsworth defined it lies across an

extraordinary range of his writings and incorporates the central doctrines of his poetic creed.[30]

At the heart of the mode in 1800 was "Michael," and to "Michael" we ought in the end to return. Wordsworth probably gave in the poem itself the cleanest and simplest definition of pastoral as he understood it in 1800, when he described the story as

> the first,
> The earliest of those tales[31] that spake to me
> Of Shepherds, dwellers in the vallies, men
> Whom I already lov'd, not verily
> For their own sakes, but for the fields and hills
> Where was their occupation and abode.

He enlarged the definition in a letter he wrote within a few weeks after completing "Michael." Presenting the volumes of 1800 to Charles James Fox *(EY,* 312–315), he singled out "Michael" and "The Brothers" as the poems which carried the social message he wished to implant in the minds of his readers. The word that rings through the letter like a refrain and distinguishes the class of poems to which "Michael" and "The Brothers" belong is the word "domestic." The most calamitous social development of the age, Wordsworth feared, was "rapid decay of the domestic affections," loosening of the "bonds of domestic feeling," the slow disappearance of the spirit of "independent domestic life." To help check this development Wordsworth attempted in "The Brothers" and "Michael" to portray "the domestic affections" as he knew they existed still among small landowners in the north of England. There is, he explained, a reason why the "domestic affections" in people of this sort will be particularly strong. "Their little tract of land serves as a kind of permanent rallying point for their domestic feelings, as a tablet upon which they are written which

30. Herbert Lindenberger, *On Wordsworth's Prelude* (Princeton: Princeton University Press, 1963), sees Wordsworth clearly as one of "the great pastoral poets" and Book VIII as the *Prelude's* pastoral book ("Sincere Pastoral," pp. 243–252). He goes even further (p. 243) to suggest that "the whole of *The Prelude,* since it claims the primacy of Nature over Art and Society, can be viewed as a version of pastoral."

31. They became "domestic tales" in the edition of 1827.

makes them objects of memory in a thousand instances when they would otherwise be forgotten. It is a fountain fitted to the nature of social man from which supplies of affection, as pure as his heart was intended for, are daily drawn." By exhibiting these domestic affections running strongly through simple rustic people Wordsworth hoped that his poems might achieve their psychological and social purpose—"that they may excite profitable sympathies in many kind and good hearts, and may in some small degree enlarge our feelings of reverence for our species, and our knowledge of human nature." Fox's crisp reply must, incidentally, have been disheartening: "I am no great friend to blank verse for subjects which are to be treated of with simplicity" (Grosart, II, 205).

It is probably needless to remark that the ideal of pastoral poetry here delineated is a distinctively Wordsworthian ideal. If we needed any confirmation of this truth we could find it in Coleridge's (customary) dissent. It was not that Coleridge had a pastoral ideal of his own to advance against that of Wordsworth, but only that his interest ran to other matters. It is illuminating to set alongside Wordsworth's letter to Fox the parallel letter which Coleridge wrote (over Wordsworth's signature) to send to Bishop Wilberforce. Coleridge dictated this letter—which remained unpublished until 1956—to Dorothy and sent a copy of it to Poole, along with a copy of Wordsworth's letter to Fox.[32] Inviting Poole to compare the two letters, Wordsworth's and his own, Coleridge promised that they contained "a good view of our notions & motives poetical & political." We cannot be sure how much Coleridge may have been trying to speak with Wordsworth's voice—his letter restates some important ideas in the 1800 Preface—but Wordsworth's political motives do stand out in contrast to Coleridge's poetical concerns. Coleridge, moreover, moves to a level of discourse not often reached by his partner and touches revealingly on several of the issues that divided them.

The heart of his letter is an extended, rather diffuse account of the way poetic diction becomes corrupted. The account is

32. These matters are summarized, and Coleridge's letter is printed, by Griggs, *STCL*, II, 664–667.

founded on an equation: action is to the affections as language is to things.

> I composed the accompanying poems under the persuasion, that all which is usually included under the name of action bears the same pro[por]tion (in respect of worth) to the affections, as a language to the thing sign[ified]. When the material forms or intellectual ideas which should be employed to [rep]resent the internal state of feeling, are made to claim attention for their own sake, then commences Lip-worship, or superstition, or disputatiousness, in religion; a passion for gaudy ornament & violent stimulants in morals; & in our literature bombast and vicious refinements, an aversion to the common conversational language of our Countrymen, with an extravagant preference given to *Wit* by some, and to outrageous *incident* by others . . .

Coleridge goes on to define the excellence of "our elder Poets" as a kind of directness and immediacy now lost in an age when readers take snobbish pride in comprehending a difficult style. The nearest equivalent passage in Wordsworth's critical writings is the early paragraphs of the 1802 "Appendix" on poetic diction, which may have been composed in response to some of Coleridge's ideas. To judge from the Appendix Coleridge did reasonably well in 1801 at expressing his partner's beliefs, though later in his letter he opened up disagreements. These poems, he went on (on Wordsworth's behalf), were not written for praise or profit. Had they been, he said, "I should have held out to myself other subjects than the affections which walk 'in silence and in a veil' and other rules of poetic diction than the determination to prefer passion to imagery, & (except when the contrary was chosen for dramatic purposes) to express what I meant to express with all possible regard to precision and propriety but with very little attention to what is called *dignity*."

This rather awkward justification of Wordsworth's language must have strained Coleridge's powers of ventriloquism, and it is hard to see how it could have pleased Wordsworth much. While ruling out "personifications of abstract ideas," Wordsworth had nowhere suggested that he preferred passion to imagery (unless Coleridge was perversely overreading the 1800 "Thorn" note); "dignity" was a word he had used in the

1798 Advertisement (not in the 1800 Preface) but in a neutral sense (expressing concern that readers of taste might find some of his expressions lacking in "dignity").

But the relevant thing about Coleridge's letter is the absence of anything that matches the central theme of Wordsworth's letter, that is, a concern with the nature and function of pastoral. In the introduction to the sonnets included in his 1797 *Poems* Coleridge seemed to define something like the Idyllium: "those sonnets appear to me the most exquisite in which moral Sentiments, Affections, or Feelings are deduced from, and associated with, the scenery of Nature." But he did not write any poems that could be called pastorals, unless one thinks of two or three early experiments, or perhaps "The Brook," which Wordsworth once said he thought was to have been "a rural Poem," prefixed with a little epitaph from Burns.[33] Nor did Coleridge in his critical writing give this genre any special praise, or betray any special interest in it—except where he spoke of "Michael" and of "The Brothers," "that model of English pastoral which I have never yet read with unclouded eye" (*BL*, II, 62n). The portrayal of "manners" he always thought an unworthy aim: "the Poet who chooses transitory manners, ought to content himself with transitory Praise."[34] More Augustan than Wordsworth in this respect, as in so many others, he seems to have looked upon the pastoral as a low or unimportant form. For a complex of reasons, most of them sufficiently clear, he appears never to have shared his partner's view that the poetic reform inaugurated in *Lyrical Ballads* was in some degree founded upon a reform of the pastoral mode—that a "lyrical ballad" was a "pastoral ballad" in many of its essential particulars.

For Wordsworth a form like the "pastoral ballad" must have seemed the ideal way of combining the two traditions of eighteenth-century poetry which he most desired to preserve and revitalize: the pastoral, with its truth to nature, and the

33. In the Fenwick note to "The River Duddon"; *PW*, III, 503.
34. Coleridge's marginal note on Ben Jonson; Roberta F. Brinkley, *Coleridge on the Seventeenth Century* (Durham, N.C.: Duke University Press, 1955), p. 641.

ballad, with its authentic voice of passion and its truth to the
elementary feelings of the human heart.[35] Both the pastoral
of classical tradition and the ballad as Wordsworth developed
it were dramatic forms. By combining them he was able to cut
through the illusioned view of life that neo-classic decorum
had required, to look steadily at his subject, to keep his reader
"in the company of flesh and blood." The combination must
have looked for a time ideally suited to his major poetic aims:
"to chuse incidents and situations from common life, and to
relate or describe them . . . in a selection of language really
used by men; and, at the same time, to throw over them a certain colouring of imagination, whereby ordinary things should
be presented to the mind in an unusual way."[36]

But only for a time. Rather ironically, the specific form
which he filtered out in 1800 and called a "pastoral ballad"—
the form, that is, in which "Michael" may originally have been
cast—had a fairly narrow range and purpose, owing largely to
its jocular qualities. Wordsworth would have known that in the
earlier eighteenth-century controversies over the pastoral the
"pastoral ballad" figured as a device of ridicule. In a *Guardian*
essay, for instance (no. 40; 27 April 1713), Pope had pretended
to admire a "Pastoral Ballad" (taken, he said, from an old
manuscript, and "the most beautiful example of this kind" that
he had ever found) written in grotesque and vulgar Somerset-
shire dialect. Swift wrote a pastoral ballad-dialogue in which
he presented coarse rustics in order to satirize the genre.[37]
Hence it is probably fitting that Wordsworth's own form of
the pastoral ballad should have been in some sense a burlesque.
The stanza of the "ballad Michael" he had used in "Ruth"; as
Mary Moorman points out (I, 54), he would have found it in
several poems of Elizabeth Carter, whom he professed to
admire (see Grosart, III, 426–427). But he evidently added the

35. Wordsworth may have observed that Percy connected the two
traditions in the *Reliques*. The connections are discussed by Keith Stew-
art, "The Ballad and the *Genres* in the Eighteenth Century," *ELH*, 24
(June 1957), 120–137.

36. As the Preface read in 1802; Owen, 156n.

37. Harold Williams, ed., *The Poems of Jonathan Swift*, 2nd ed., 3 vols.
(Oxford: Oxford University Press, Clarendon Press, 1958), III, 880–882.

anapestic meter in imitation of "Monk" Lewis, who had used it in some of his macabre tales.[38] By adapting the form to a homely and realistic purpose, carried out with jocular buoyancy, Wordsworth would have been accomplishing the sort of parody he had earlier managed by adapting the form of Bürger's ballads of terror to "The Idiot Boy."

For all its narrowness, the "pastoral ballad" in the form of poems like the abortive "ballad Michael" represents an important transition in Wordsworth's development, falling midway between the very different lyrical styles of 1798 and 1802. Like poems in the volumes of 1807 it has some of the lyrical elegance, and perhaps the sentiment, that Wordsworth found in Ben Jonson, who strongly influenced the lyrical outburst of 1802. Like the poems of 1798 it is dramatic or semidramatic in form, and the characters whose voices we hear speak the language of common life, though rarely the raw colloquial language of passion heard in the earlier dramatic pieces. Overlying the voices and events of the "ballad Michael" and forming a distinct perspective, just as it does in "The Idiot Boy" and in "Peter Bell," is the poet's own exuberant voice speaking an artificially flavored, jocular language in a rollicking meter.

But this transition passed swiftly. The jocular qualities of Wordsworth's ballad verse, which derive from Theocritus and Cowper and Burns, are important, and too commonly overlooked. But they are qualities that Wordsworth, for better or worse, outgrew as he moved toward the lyric styles of his later years, and the somber philosophical mode of the *Prelude* and the *Excursion*. As much as any other single event, the conversion of the anapestic "ballad Michael" into a muted blank-verse narrative signalizes Wordsworth's movement in 1800 away from his early experimental voices into the main region of his song.

38. The stanza form and meter are identical to those of Lewis's "The Stranger: A Norman Tale," in *Tales of Terror* (Kelso, 1799) and "Osric the Lion" in *Tales of Wonder* (1800). Southey may have served as a conductor. When he published his sentimental ballad "Mary" (in *Poems*, 2nd ed., London, 1797), he remarked that its form—a five-line stanza— was adopted from Lewis's "Alonzo the Brave and Fair Imogine."

CHAPTER 6

Beyond the Ballad

The brief intense revival of Wordsworth's lyrical voice in the spring of 1802 broke a long season of silence. Over the fifteen months that followed the completion of "Michael," Wordsworth finished the revisions to his Preface, and to the accompanying poems, that appeared in 1802; he labored unevenly at *Peter Bell* and "The Pedlar" and did some modernizing of Chaucer; he wrote a little blank verse that went into the *Prelude;* he read, or listened to Dorothy read, Spenser, Chaucer, Milton, Daniel, and Ben Jonson (whose verses were once "too *interesting*" to let him go to sleep).[1] But he seemed unsure of his direction and wrote no more than half a dozen new poems. The work he did accomplish cost him grievously. On 22 May 1801 Dorothy reported to Coleridge (*EY*, 335) that her brother's stomach was "in bad plight," and went on to describe their desperate remedy: "We have put aside all the manuscript poems and it is agreed between us that I am not to give them up to him even if he asks for them."

Possibly fortified by the "new regimen" for the control of his stomach that Dorothy spoke of hopefully nine months later (*EY*, 343), Wordsworth broke silence in the middle of March with a bold return to the manner that distinguished the most experimental and controversial ballads of 1798. The first three poems he wrote ("The Sailor's Mother," 11 and 12 March; "Alice Fell," 12 and 13 March; and the "Beggars," 13 and 14 March) were poems that Coleridge would have found "more delightful" in prose, he later declared sardonically, perhaps in the form of "a moral essay, or pedestrian tour" (*BL*, II, 53). But

1. See Dorothy's *Journal* for 11 February 1802.

the "daring Humbleness of Language & Versification" and the "strict adherence to matter of fact" which so shocked Coleridge (*STCL*, II, 830) marked only a few of the thirty-odd poems that Wordsworth poured out in the next three months in a profusion of lyrical styles. These poems included "The Rainbow," "I wandered lonely as a cloud," and some other fine lyrics, but two great poems stand here above all others: the "Intimations" ode (or the first four stanzas of it) and "Resolution and Independence," both published in 1807. By tracing ways in which these two poems are connected with *Lyrical Ballads* we can follow important developments in Wordsworth's poetic strategies and once again find revealing complications in his relationship with Coleridge.

On 13 October 1800 there appeared in the *Morning Post* a singularly Gothic poem of seven stanzas (fifty-one lines) entitled "The Voice from the Side of Etna; or, The Mad Monk. An Ode in Mrs. Ratcliff's manner." Sent in by Coleridge, who had been supplying material irregularly for nearly three years, the poem is essentially a "complaint," spoken by a wretched man, a "Hermit" or a "Monk," who has murdered his "Rosa," the girl he loved. Distracted by grief, he begs for relief from the accusing signs of his own guilt, which he sees everywhere about him in nature.

> Why must the rock, and margin of the flood,
>   Why must the hills so many flow'rets bear,
> Whose colours to a wounded woman's blood
>   Such sad resemblance wear?
>
>   . . .
>
> It is the stormy clouds above,
>   That flash so red a gleam
>   On yonder downward trickling stream;
> 'Tis not the blood of her I love.

The complaint is supposed to have been overheard on the wooded side of Mount Etna by the poet, who finds it "In melody most like an old Sicilian song." The idyls of Theocritus had occasionally evoked "deep-wooded Etna," but we are perhaps expected to think of something like Bion's idyl on the death of Adonis, in which Aphrodite watches "the crimson flood fast trickling flow" from her dying lover (in the translation given in Anderson's *British Poets*, Vol. XIII) and weeps tears which, along with the drops of blood, turn into flowers.

But it is another feature of the "Mad Monk" that has drawn the attention of modern readers to this uncelebrated ode—the startling anticipation, or echo (stanza 2), of the opening lines of Wordsworth's "Intimations" ode:

> There was a time when earth, and sea, and skies,
>   The bright green vale and forest's dark recess,
> When all things lay before my eyes
>   In steady loveliness.
> But now I feel on earth's uneasy scene
>   Such motions as will never cease!
>   I only ask for peace—
> Then wherefore must I know, that such a time has been!
>   "Mad Monk," stanza 2 (1800)

> There was a time when meadow, grove, and stream,
> The earth, and every common sight
>   To me did seem
>   Apparell'd in celestial light,
> The glory and the freshness of a dream.
> It is not now as it has been of yore;—
>   Turn whereso'er I may,
>   By night or day,
> The things which I have seen I now can see no more.
>   "Intimations" ode, stanza 1 (1802, pub. 1807)

It has been generally believed that the first four stanzas of the "Intimations" ode were written in 1802, begun perhaps on 27 March when Dorothy noted in her Journal: "William composed part of an ode." When the similarity between its opening stanza and stanza 2 of the "Mad Monk" was noticed, it was thought to betray another of Wordsworth's many debts to his more innovative partner.[2] For the "Mad Monk" had been

---

2. H. W. Garrod seems to have been the first to advance this belief, in *Wordsworth: Lectures and Essays* (Oxford: Oxford University Press, Clarendon Press, 1923), p. 131n.

printed in 1804 over Coleridge's name in *The Wild Wreath*,[3] a collection of verses edited by the daughter of Mary Robinson, who had been a friend of Coleridge's. Although Coleridge never acknowledged the poem, it has since 1880 been included in his poetical works (see *STCPW*, I, 347–349).

Yet an interesting case can be made for Wordsworth's authorship of this poem, at least in an underlying form. If the case were to be thought plausible, verbal echoes between the "Mad Monk" and the "Intimations" ode might be understood as owing to Wordsworth's having picked up and altered at the beginning of his ode not some published lines of Coleridge's but some lines of his own which he had written and discarded two years earlier—exactly as he did at the beginning of another "Ode," "Tintern Abbey," which echoes these lines written in 1796 or 1797:

> Yet once again do I behold the forms
> Of these huge mountains, and yet once again,
> Standing beneath these elms, I hear thy voice,
> Beloved Derwent, that peculiar voice
> Heard in the stillness of the evening air,
> Half-heard and half-created.[4]

To make the case for the "Mad Monk" as a collaborative poem, originally Wordsworth's, one has to begin with the circumstances surrounding the poem's appearance in the *Morning Post*, and these cannot be understood without looking back to Coleridge's earliest association with that paper, in the palmy days of the *annus mirabilis*.

The facts of this association as they involve Wordsworth were straightened out in 1962 by Robert Woof in a fine, comprehensive article in *Studies in Bibliography*.[5] Between the time when Coleridge formed his agreement with Daniel Stuart to furnish verses and notes for a guinea a week (toward the end of 1797) and the end of 1800, he seems to have given to the *Morning Post* twelve poems that were Wordsworth's in whole

3. Edited by Mary Elizabeth Robinson (London), pp. 141–144.
4. First published in 1949, *PW*, V, 340; see *Chronology*, 27.
5. Robert Woof, "Wordsworth's Poetry and Stuart's Newspapers: 1797–1803," *SB*, 15 (1962), 149–189.

or in part (I do not include the "Mad Monk" in this count). Two of these poems, "The Convict" and "Lewti," were printed in the 1798 *Lyrical Ballads* ("Lewti," of course, was almost immediately canceled; "The Convict" was dropped in 1800); another appeared in the 1807 volumes, where it was titled "The Seven Sisters, or The Solitude of Binnorie"; a fourth, "The Farmer of Tilsbury Vale," which Wordsworth may have sent in himself, appeared in the collection of 1815, along with "The Seven Sisters" (Wordsworth never acknowledged or republished any of the other *Morning Post* poems).

Manuscript drafts of most of these poems survive in notebooks which Wordsworth used at Racedown. It is reasonable to suppose that Wordsworth gave Coleridge the notebooks to look over, or even to plunder (leaves have been cut out of some of them), though some of Wordsworth's later denials are puzzling. "I am quite certain," he avowed to Daniel Stuart in 1838, that except for "The Farmer of Tilsbury Vale" and some political sonnets (which appeared at the time of the invasion terror in 1802 and 1803) "nothing of mine ever appeared in the Morning Post"; indeed that save for these poems and a few letters on political subjects, "not a word of mine ever appeared, sent by myself at least, or as far as I know, by any other Persons, in any Newspaper, Review, Magazine, or Public Journal whatsoever" (*LY*, II, 941–942). Did Wordsworth remember the poems he sent off himself and forget the ones that Coleridge sent? Did he know about the poems Coleridge sent but consider them to be Coleridge's and not his own? We cannot be sure. It is impossible, at any rate, to suppose that he knew nothing about the appearance of these poems, for it must have been the publication of "Lewti" in the *Morning Post*, 13 April 1798, that required its cancellation from the volume of 1798.

How much Coleridge altered or expanded the poems when he sent them in is hard to establish. Perhaps most puzzling of all, though potentially the most revealing, is the first poem, "The Convict," printed on 14 December 1797. For when this poem showed up the following year in *Lyrical Ballads*, it contained readings found neither in the manuscripts nor in the *Morning Post*. In the opening stanzas, for example, nearly every phrase which had been altered for the *Morning Post* was realtered for the *Lyrical Ballads*. Dove Cottage MS. 2 has three trials at the poem's opening lines, which set a background of beneficent nature for the description of misery to follow:

> When extending his radiance the sun from the West
> Diffuses thought tenderest charm
> And the labourer   but an hour from his rest
> Lifts his mattock with   arm
>
>> Notebook (a)

> When extending his beams the mild sun in the west
> Diffuses that exquisite charm
> Which mellows each thought and illumines the breast
> With tender benevolence warm
>
>> Notebook (b)

> When extending his beams the mild sun from the west
> Diffuses that soft mellowing charm
> Which felt through all nature illumines the breast
> With tender benevolence warm.
>
>> Notebook (c)

The published versions of this stanza are as follows:

> The Sun was dilating his orb in the West;
>   And the still Season's mellowing charm,
> Diffus'd thro' all Nature, was felt in the breast,
>   And the breast became kindly and warm.[6]
>
>> *Morning Post* (1797)

> The glory of evening was spread through the west;
>   —On the slope of a mountain I stood
> While the joy that precedes the calm season of rest
>   Rang loud through the meadow and wood.
>
>> *Lyrical Ballads* (1798)

The second stanza of the poem has a similar history. The earliest version survives in the notebook in two drafts and a fair copy which was converted into a second version.

6. Woof prints the MS and *Morning Post* versions but does not comment on the *Lyrical Ballads* variants.

> When the labourer just ending the task of the day
> More chearily presses his spade
> Then feeling the price of existence I stray
> To the cell where the convict is laid
>
>   Notebook (a)

The first three lines are crossed out and rewritten, altering the stanza to read:

> And must we then part from these objects so fair
> In the pain of my spirit I said
> Nor impelled by the thought was I slow to repair
> To the cell where the convict is laid
>
>   Notebook (b)

Only two lines of the revised draft were altered for the *Morning Post*, but both were altered again for *Lyrical Ballads*:

> And must I then part from these objects so fair?
>   In the pain of my spirit I said:
> But, subduing the thought, I made haste to repair
>   To the Cell where the CONVICT is laid.
>
>   *Morning Post* (1797)

> 'And must we then part from a dwelling so fair?'
>   In the pain of my spirit I said,
> And with a deep sadness I turned, to repair
>   To the cell where the convict is laid.
>
>   *Lyrical Ballads* (1798)

If we take the manuscript versions to be Wordsworth's (they are in his hand), the *Morning Post* versions to be Coleridge's (doubtless he sent them in), and the *Lyrical Ballads* versions again to be Wordsworth's (the likeliest possibility), it would appear that Wordsworth discarded his own drafts wherever he found that Coleridge had rejected them. We are, of course, unsure whether "The Convict" was looked upon as a collaborative poem, either at its inception or at some later stage. But John Wordsworth seemed to think it was his brother's in 1801,[7] and

7. He spoke of it to Mary Hutchinson, 9–10 March; see Carl Ketcham, ed., *The Letters of John Wordsworth* (Ithaca: Cornell University Press), p. 104.

years later Wordsworth quoted a stanza of it to Isabella Fenwick (*PW*, II, 474), referring to it as a "discarded poem." Moreover, the bitter indictments of social injustice that lay at the poem's heart—prudently dropped from both printed versions —help to confirm that it was originally and basically Wordsworth's poems.

Coleridge himself clearly felt that he had taken over the poem called "Lewti," for he first contributed it to *Lyrical Ballads* then gave it to Southey for the *Annual Anthology* (1800) —in his own copy Southey marked the poem "W. Wordsworth when a boy, corrected by S. T. C."[8]—and at last printed it in his own collection, *Sibylline Leaves*. He worked over the poem so extensively as to stamp his own style upon it, changing Wordsworth's river Winander to the more exotic Tamaha, substituting first Sara then Lewti for Wordsworth's Mary, and more than doubling the number of lines. These changes persuaded the redoubtable John Livingston Lowes—whose judgment, painful and sobering to review today, should be required reading for attribution scholars—that "the poem itself, in rhythm, diction, mood, and imaginative quality is as unmistakably Coleridge's as it is unmistakably not Wordsworth's."[9] A brief specimen may show, however, how much of Wordsworth remained underneath the surface. One paragraph from the Dove Cottage notebook (MS. 2),

> I saw the white waves oer and oer
> Break against a curved shore
> Now disappearing from the sight
> Now twinkling regular and white
> Her mouth Her smiling mouth can show
> As white and regular a row,

stretched out in Coleridge's *Morning Post* version, became:

> I saw the white waves, o'er and o'er,
> Break against the distant shore.
> All at once upon the sight,

8. See Kenneth Curry, "The Contributors to *The Annual Anthology*," *PBSA*, 42 (1948), 50–65.

9. *The Road to Xanadu* (Boston and New York: Houghton Mifflin, 1927), p. 516.

> All at once they broke in light:
> I heard no murmur of their roar,
> Nor ever I beheld them flowing,
> Neither coming, neither going;
> But only saw them, o'er and o'er,
> Break against the curved shore;
> Now disappearing from the sight,
> Now twinkling regular and white,
> And Lewti's smiling mouth can shew
> As white and regular a row.

The longest and in some ways the most interesting poem Coleridge sent in that spring, "The Old Man of the Alps"—it appeared on 8 March—carries the same signature as "Lewti." Mr. Woof has conjectured intelligently that the pseudonyms which Coleridge signed to the poems may indicate the degree of his participation in them, but conjecture about the way the poem was put together must otherwise rest on the sandy ground of internal evidence, for it survives only as a transcript. Coleridge was at first ready to acknowledge ownership of it— though he kept no copy—for when he was preparing to publish all his "small poems" in 1802 he seems to have asked Francis Wrangham to copy the text from the *Morning Post* and mail it to him so that he could send it to the printer (it is Wrangham's transcript which survives at Dove Cottage).[10] But he must have changed his mind, for the poem never showed up in any collection either partner made.

"The Old Man of the Alps" is "a tale of woe" recited by an aged father to a passer-by. The setting of the tale, while Alpine and not Sicilian, is rather like the setting of the "Mad Monk":

> Beside the torrent and beneath a wood,
> High in these Alps my summer cottage stood.[11]

Shattered by grief at the news of her lover's death, the old man's daughter goes mad and ceases to take delight in the pleasant sights and sounds of nature, hungering only for

10. Wrangham's letter of 5 April 1802 is quoted by Woof, "Wordsworth's Poetry," p. 168.
11. Text from *STCPW*, I, 248–251.

> the deep moan that spoke the tempest near;
> Or sighs which chasms of icy vales outbreathe,
> Sent from the dark, imprison'd floods beneath.

After telling at last of her tragic drowning, the old man pauses, and the poem closes abruptly with a six-line prayer uttered by the poet. The prayer, at least, must have been Coleridge's. How much else was his it is impossible to say, but the strong affinities the poem shows with Wordsworth's early tales of domestic grief—the sort sketched briefly, for example, in *An Evening Walk*—make it seem plausible that Coleridge here built, as he did in "Lewti," upon a text that was substantially his partner's.

To these tangled textual problems that lay in the background of the "Mad Monk's" appearance in the *Morning Post* must be added the tangled personal troubles that Coleridge had got himself into by 1800. Chronic financial distress had begun to build up for him after his return from Germany in 1799. To supplement the Wedgwood annuity of £150, much of which he drew and spent in advance, Coleridge had gone to London to work on the *Morning Post* in November, writing verse and political essays. Having accepted advance payments for his labor, which proved fearfully taxing, Coleridge was obliged to stay at it through March 1800. When he did get away from London, he left behind him unfulfilled promises, periodically renewed, to provide Stuart with a second part of his brilliant character of Pitt and a character of Napoleon.[12] Meanwhile he had undertaken for Longman first a translation of Schiller, then an account of his tour of the north of England, and had drawn advance payments for both. He completed part of the Schiller (at the cost of much agony) before the year was out, but the tour of the north evidently became a tour of Germany, to be published as a series of letters, then hung fire endlessly. Ultimately, Wordsworth offered to help by turning over to Coleridge his own German journal (to be used without his name), but by March 1801 the venture was abandoned and

12. The first part of "Pitt" appeared in the *Morning Post* on 19 March 1800. Stuart later reported that "for ten or twelve years afterwards, whenever Coleridge required a favour from me, he promised Bonaparte" (*Gentleman's Magazine*, n.s. 9 [May 1838], p. 488).

Wordsworth assumed his partner's debt to Longman for the advances paid months earlier (see *STCL,* I, 654, and *EY,* 321). Another advance of £25, paid by Richard Phillips, a bookseller, for a piece of work which Coleridge declared contemptuously might have taken him a fortnight to complete *(STCL,* II, 661) had to be repaid suddenly in January 1801 under a threat of lawsuit. And throughout this period Coleridge was struggling to clear himself of what he considered to be a moral obligation by laying out his "great work," the life of Lessing.

Haunted by these and other painfully drawn-out harassments, Coleridge arrived at Grasmere at the end of June 1800, where he stayed about a month before settling at Keswick. Having agreed to join Wordsworth in preparing a new edition of *Lyrical Ballads,* he busied himself with revising and copying poems, preparing instructions to the printer, and straining to finish "Christabel." He had furnished nothing of his own to the *Morning Post* since leaving London. On August 10, however, he received from his old Stowey neighbor, Thomas Poole, in response to an invitation issued eight months earlier, two long letters on agricultural problems, for publication in the *Morning Post* (see *STCL,* I, 617–618). Before he could write these up for submission, Coleridge had to yield to pressing demands from Phillips and was evidently able to send nothing that month to the paper except a ten-line scrap of his Schiller translation (it appeared on 6 September). One gathers that he had little else on hand to send, for he had written only scraps of verse all year. It was not before the end of September, probably, that he tossed off his satire of Sir James Mackintosh (published, with omissions, in the *Morning Post* on 4 December). In November he did write "The Stranger Minstrel" for Mrs. Mary Robinson ("The Snow-drop,"[13] dated October by Griggs, *STCL,* I, 639–642, belongs to 1798), but the promised contributions to *Lyrical Ballads,* for the category of "Poems on the Naming of Places," looked for hopefully by the Wordsworths as late as mid-October, never materialized.

Meanwhile (on 14 September) Coleridge's son Derwent had

13. These three poems may be found in *STCPW,* I, 350–358.

come into the world, bringing fresh anxiety to his father by threatening to expire within a few weeks of his birth. "Hour after hour," Coleridge wrote in his notebooks (entry 813), the baby "made a noise exactly like the Creeking of a door which is being shut very slowly to prevent its creeking." The birth, with its attendant distress, coincided with a fresh financial crisis which Coleridge met by a typical series of maneuvers. *"Forced"* to pay an old Cambridge debt of £8, he wrote on 16 September to Godwin, asking for the loan of £10 until 1 October, at which time he expected, he said, to "have claim to as much money as I shall want" (*STCL*, I, 621–622). Godwin at once obliged, and on 22 September Coleridge again promised repayment by the end of the month. His plan for raising the money soon became clear. On 28 September he sent Stuart an essay on agriculture together with one (or possibly two) copied straight out of Poole's letters, declaring to Stuart: "I have written five more Essays of the same length on this subject" (*STCL*, I, 626). The next day he seems to have mailed off one or two more essays from Poole's letters, then about 30 September (*STCL*, I, 627) explained that he was "prevented by Mrs. Coleridge's distress concerning our Infant from transcribing the fifth Essay." He went on to detail the contents of the (probably unwritten) fifth, sixth, and seventh essays, and added optimistically: "You may [th]en republish PITT, to which I shall lead—then you shall have a second part of PITT, & Bonaparte." Toward the end of the letter Coleridge offered, at what psychological cost we can only guess, "to recommence my old occupation, binding myself down to send you six columns a week." He closed by asking Stuart to send £10 for him to Godwin: "Before this week has passed I trust I shall have gone a good way towards earning it.—"

But Coleridge did not manage to earn it in the way he expected. He did, apparently, write one of the promised essays (published in the *Morning Post* 14 October) but seems not to have finished the others (nor, of course, the Pitt, nor the Bonapart). On 4 October, after sitting up all night "writing Essays for the newspaper," as he told the Wordsworths (see Dorothy's *Journal*, 4 October), Coleridge left his family and walked down to Grasmere, called there "peremptorily," he wrote Stuart, by Wordsworth's illness (*STCL*, I, 628)—though Dorothy's journal says nothing of any illness of William's until the afternoon of the fifth. He must have found his friends in a mood that contrasted uncomfortably with his own, for a week or so previously they had met the old leech-gatherer on the road—the meeting later to be commemorated in "Resolution and Independence."[14] On 4 and 5 October the partners read and talked about "Christabel," on the sixth they resolved not to print it, and on the seventh Coleridge walked back alone to Keswick.

What the dropping of "Christabel" meant to Coleridge came out only very slowly as the months and years rolled by. Within the week (9 October) he explained evenly to Davy that the poem was "so much admired by Wordsworth, that he thought it indelicate to print two Volumes with *his name* in which so much of another man's was included—& which was of more consequence—the poem was in direct opposition to the very purpose for which the Lyrical Ballads were published" (*STCL*, I, 631). But Wordsworth's admiration for "Christabel" was mixed, as some of Coleridge's later remarks reveal, and his rejection of it, together with Coleridge's inability to finish it, must have helped to give Coleridge the keenest sense of frustration and defeat he had yet experienced. Some of this feeling Coleridge betrayed in a notebook entry of 30 October (no. 834): "He knew not what to do—something, he felt, must be done—he rose, drew his writing-desk suddenly before him —sate down, took the pen—& found that he knew not what to do."

Whatever the case, when Coleridge walked back to Keswick on 7 October he was reaching a critical stage in his fortunes. Not only were his hopes for "Christabel" checked, together with his creative powers, but his health was beginning to break decisively. Some later comments place this melancholy event in September or October of 1800. "For the last four months," Coleridge wrote Poole on 6 January 1801, "I have not had a

---

14. See Dorothy's *Journal* for 3 October, in which she seems to speak of a meeting that took place 26 September.

fortnight of continuous health" (*STCL*, II, 661). On 17 May he reported that his illness had run through "the whole Fall" of the previous year (*STCL*, II, 730). "Nine dreary months—" he complained on 5 July, "and oh me! have I had even a fortnight's full & continuous health?" (*STCL*, II, 740). The same month Wordsworth told Poole that their friend "has been confined to his *bed* one may say, the half of the last ten months" (*EY*, 339). Doubtless connected with the physical breakdown, if not always in ways we can be sure of now, were the failure of Coleridge's marriage and the beginning of his *habitual* use of opium, both of which events Griggs traces to the autumn and winter of 1800 (*STCL*, II, 731n).

It is hardly to be wondered at that Coleridge abandoned the essays he was supposed to write and fixed upon another means of meeting his obligations to the *Morning Post*. The night of his return to Keswick, 7 October 1800, he wrote Stuart a dispirited letter in which he described "the accidental constitution of my intellect—in which my taste in judging is far, far more perfect than my power to execute—& I do nothing, but almost instantly it's defects & sillinesses come upon my mind, and haunt me, till I am completely disgusted with my performance, & wish myself a Tanner, or a Printer, or any thing but an Author" (*STCL*, I, 629). Promising once more to supply the long-promised essays, and voicing grief at "poor Mrs. Robinson's illness," Coleridge added laconically: "I shall fill up these Blanks with a few Poems—." Stuart cut the letter up to send it directly to his printer, and only one of the poems survives on it (the manuscript is in the British Museum). It is a lyric, probably in its origins a Lucy poem, which Wordsworth had written in Germany and sent to Coleridge. Coleridge probably supplied the title, "Alcaeus to Sappho," intended as a compliment to Mrs. Robinson, who was "Sappho" to *Morning Post* readers. The other poems in the letter can be identified by looking through the *Morning Post* for the period following the letter's dispatch and arrival in London. "Alcaeus to Sappho" was not printed until 24 November, but on 13 October appeared the "Mad Monk," on 14 October Wordsworth's "Solitude of Binnorie," and on 21 October Wordsworth's "Inscription for a Seat by a Road

Side . . ."

How much Coleridge altered these particular poems is again
quite uncertain. The clearest case ought to be that of the "Solitude of Binnorie" ("The Seven Sisters"), a ballad with Scottish and German antecedents, which tells of seven girls who
to escape pursuit plunge into the sea at a spot now marked
by "Seven little Islands green and bare."

> Each like a tall maid's grave there are
>   Seven mossy heaps hard by;
> The fishers say, those sisters fair
> By faeries were all buried there,
>   And there together lie!

(Morning Post version)

The ballad might be called a curse poem, closer to "Hart-leap
Well" than to "The Thorn," but not very close to either, owing
to the lilting, impersonal manner of its telling. An elaborate
prefatory note to the poem in the *Morning Post*, which recorded a debt, almost certainly reflects Coleridge's gallantry
toward a friend (though it is enigmatically signed "M.H."):
"It would be unpardonable in the author of the following
lines, if he omitted to acknowledge that the metre (with exception of the burthen) is borrowed from 'The Haunted Beach of
Mrs. Robinson.' " But the textual differences between the *Morning Post* version and the version Wordsworth published in
1807 can be accounted for in (at least) two ways: they may
represent revisions made by Coleridge in 1800, or revisions
made by Wordsworth in 1807. Miss Carol Landon, who first
studied the *Morning Post* version,[15] declared for the latter
alternative on the grounds that the 1807 version showed some
clear improvements over the 1800; she finds "no evidence of
Coleridge's hand either before or after the poem's publication
in the *Morning Post*." (One could object that evidence of this
sort, elusive to begin with, may well have been masked by
whatever revisions Wordsworth did make in 1807, but without the underlying manuscript the case remains speculative.)

15. Carol Landon, "Wordsworth, Coleridge, and the *Morning Post*:
An Early Version of 'The Seven Sisters,' " *RES*, n.s. 11 (November 1960),
392–402.

Equally unsure is the case of "Inscription for a Seat by a Road Side," first written in couplets at Windy Brow in 1794 (Coleridge archly signed it "VENTIFRONS" for the *Morning Post*) then rewritten in blank verse in 1797.[16] Drafts of the blank-verse version are scattered through Dove Cottage MS. 11. The opening lines, following the convention of the "Inscription," invite the traveler to pause and think of the afflicted or of the wanderers who have found a momentary repose at the roadside seat. One version mentions

> The houseless, homeless, vagrants of the earth
> Or that poor man the rustic artisan.

These creatures show up in what appears to be the final draft in the notebook. But the *Morning Post* version dropped them in favor of

> The foot-worn soldier and his family
> . . . wife and babe, and boy, perchance,
> Garb'd like his father, and already bound
> To his poor father's trade!

We cannot be sure where the soldier came from, but the other people in the notebook sound more like Wordsworth than like Coleridge, and, as de Selincourt declared *(PW*, I, 372), the "rather obvious piety" at the close of the *Morning Post* version is more like Coleridge than like Wordsworth:

> yea, sleep
> The sleep of death, and dream of blissful worlds,
> Then wake in Heav'n, and find the dream all true!

If we conclude that Coleridge simply touched up and padded out his partner's poem when he sent it to Stuart, we can find support in a fascinating reference to this poem in Coleridge's notebooks (probably jotted down some time in October, 1800; *STCNB*, entry 830) which may now seem freshly meaningful: "The Sopha of Sods . . . poem hid in a tin box—stooping from sublime Thoughts to reckon how many Lines the poem would make."

16. See *Chronology*, 25, 27, and *PW*, I, 300–302 and 372.

Despite the lines that Coleridge may have added to one or another of these poems, despite the alterations he may have made, despite all the textual uncertainties, it is reasonable to suppose that here, as with the poems published two years earlier, the underlying material was Wordsworth's. What the circumstances taken all together suggest is simply this: driven by financial (and psychological) necessity, Coleridge, having run out of Poole's prose, proceeded to furnish the *Morning Post* with Wordsworth's poems, copied with perfunctory revisions from manuscripts in his possession, the "Mad Monk" among them.

The presence of the "Mad Monk" among these poems brings us up against the plain fact which connects the poem to Coleridge—its publication over his name in 1804. The circumstances that surrounded this publication are far from clear, but some conjectures can be made from the facts we do know. When Mary Robinson's daughter set about preparing a volume of poetical tributes to her mother, she wrote Coleridge to ask for a contribution. On 27 December 1802 Coleridge replied (*STCL*, II, 903–906), declining in the most positive terms to be associated with some of the other names proposed as contributors —specifically "Peter Pindar," Tom Moore, and "Monk" Lewis. He also alluded to an earlier work edited by Miss Robinson, her mother's posthumous *Memoirs* (1801), in which his poem "The Stranger Minstrel" had been printed without his knowledge or consent: "I understood that an excessively silly copy of Verses, which I had absolutely forgotten the very writing of, disgraced me & the volumes." Coleridge had sent "The Stranger Minstrel" in "a private Letter" to Mrs. Robinson, and he sorrowfully pronounced its publication "subversive of all social confidence."

Actually, "The Stranger Minstrel" was one of several pieces that Coleridge had sent to Mrs. Robinson between 1798 and 1800 as part of an active exchange of compliments and verse. He evidently let her read *Osorio*, for instance, and he certainly showed her "Kubla Khan," for in her ode "To the Poet Coleridge" (dated October 1800 and signed "Sappho" in the posthumous edition of her *Memoirs*[17]) she quotes phrases from it, calling it the "NEW PARADISE," which may have been its first title. It seems likely that Coleridge also sent her at one time or another the "Mad Monk." On any other assumption the poem's appearance in *The Wild Wreath* after Coleridge had refused a contribution is difficult to account for. The version which Miss Robinson printed differs in a number of readings from the version printed in the *Morning Post* and is four lines shorter. She may have been able to find a copy among her mother's papers, and disregarding Coleridge's indignation she may have printed it exactly as she had printed "The Stranger Minstrel" —that is, without Coleridge's knowledge or consent.

Is it conceivable that Coleridge would have sent off a poem of Wordsworth's in a private letter? Just as conceivable, one might answer, as that he should have sent it off to a public newspaper. The point is that the "Mad Monk" shows affinities to poems of Mrs. Robinson's, as though composed in answer to them. Her "Anselmo, the Hermit of the Alps," for instance, is spoken largely by a solitary man (he lives "deep in a forest's silent shade") who mourns for his "gentle Rosa." "The Murdered Maid" presents a hermit who follows a track of "ruby drops" on the snow to find his loved one dead.[18] Other like resemblances might be cited. In the end they explain why Coleridge would have sent the "Mad Monk" to Mrs. Robinson, but they do not prove anything about the authorship of the poem. For one thing, Coleridge could easily have added "Rosa" to the "Mad Monk" as he added "Lewti" to Wordsworth's poem. For another, affinities between the "Mad Monk" and Mrs. Robinson's poems could just as well be marks of Wordsworth's obligations as of Coleridge's, for Wordsworth may have borrowed more freely than we have hitherto realized from this now forgotten poetess whom Coleridge is certain to have praised to him.

Actually, Wordsworth need scarcely have borrowed from

---

17. *Memoirs of the late Mrs. Robinson, written by herself,* ed. M. E. Robinson, 4 vols. (London, 1801), IV, 145–149.

18. Miss Landon, "Wordsworth. . . ," pp. 396–397, notes these affinities. See also Robert Woof, "Wordsworth's Poetry," pp. 174–175.

Mrs. Robinson. Poems about hermits and monks were entirely conventional, as a glance at contemporary magazines and miscellanies will show. Hermits, for that matter, abound in Wordsworth, as Lane Cooper noticed as long ago as 1909,[19] from *Descriptive Sketches* through *Peter Bell* and "Tintern Abbey" to the *Prelude* and the *Excursion*. One might cite in particular the ending of the story of Vaudracour and Julia (*Prelude*, IX), where the stricken lover secludes himself in his isolated lodge "Deep in a Forest," and among "those solitary shades" wastes out his days, "an imbecile mind" (in the Fenwick notes Wordsworth converted him into a "monk"; *PW*, II, 478). Or one might cite "The Somnambulist" of 1828, a late ballad loosely reminiscent of the "Mad Monk." It is the tale of a knight who loses his Emma by sending her plunging into a torrent in a clumsy effort to awaken her from sleep. Overcome with remorse,

> Within the dell he built a cell
>   And there was Sorrow's guest;
> In hermit's weeds repose he found,
>   From vain temptation free;
> Beside the torrent dwelling—bound
> By one deep heart-controlling sound,
>   And awed to piety.
>
>   (*PW*, IV, 54)

If on the whole external evidence for the authorship of the "Mad Monk" is inconclusive, internal evidence can be found to point with surprising insistence to Wordsworth. We have, I think mistakenly, come to believe that Wordsworth developed an interest in the ode form, in which two or three of his greatest poems were cast, relatively late. To hold this view is to accept a narrower concept of the ode than Wordsworth probably had. His early experiments with passionate lyrical utterance sometimes verged upon the ode, and even such a poem as "Tintern Abbey" was a mixed type. "I have not ventured to call this Poem an Ode," Wordsworth said in his

---

19. "The 'Forest Hermit' in Coleridge and Wordsworth," *MLN*, 24, 33–36.

1800 note, "but it was written with a hope that in the transitions, and the impassioned music of the versification, would be found the principal requisites of that species of composition."

Most interesting of all these experiments is a poem that Wordsworth published in the 1800 *Lyrical Ballads*, " 'Tis said, that some have died for love." It would be helpful to know something more than we do know about this poem's composition. Little is offered us by Wordsworth or by his editors. If the Fenwick note to three of the Lucy poems is thought to be disappointingly terse ("These poems were written in Germany, 1799"; Grosart, III, 23), the note to " 'Tis said" is exasperating: it reads simply "1800." De Selincourt omits even an entry for the poem in his notes; Dowden said nothing about it; Knight detected a resemblance to Burns's "The Banks o' Doon," in which the poet, who has lost his loved one, tells how painful the sounds and sights of nature have become:

> Ye banks and braes o' bonie Doon,
>   How can ye bloom sae fresh and fair;
> How can ye chant, ye little birds,
>   And I sae weary fu' o' care!
> Thou'll break my heart, thou warbling bird,
>   That wantons thro' the flowering thorn . . .[20]

Mark Reed has identified stubs of leaves in Dove Cottage MS. 16 which contained " 'Tis said," along with "The Farmer of Tilsbury Vale" and "Song for the Wandering Jew." Calling it "plainly a Grasmere poem," Reed notes that it was sent to the printer for the 1800 volume in a letter postmarked 16 August (*Chronology*, 326).

If Burns influenced " 'Tis said," he also influenced the "Mad Monk," for the resemblance between these two poems is altogether striking. " 'Tis said" is about the same length as the "Mad Monk" (fifty-two lines, instead of fifty-one) and like the "Mad Monk" is made up mainly of eight-line stanzas, each containing one alexandrine, with the other lines varying from

20. W. A. Knight's note is in Vol. II, p. 180, of his *Poetical Works of William Wordsworth* (London, 1896). I quote the "B" version of Burns's poem, found in Kinsley's edition of the *Poems and Songs*, II, 575–576.

three to five feet in length. The only difference is that the variation and the rhyme scheme are regular in the pertinent stanzas of " 'Tis said," irregular in the "Mad Monk."[21]

More striking even than resemblances of form are the thematic and tonal resemblances between these poems. Like the "Mad Monk" " 'Tis said" is essentially a complaint uttered by a wretched man who dwells alone, not "on Etna's side" but "Upon Helvellyn's side." Having lost his loved one (not Rosa but Barbara), he begs distractedly, like the speaker in the "Mad Monk," for relief from the torment inflicted on him by objects in nature: clouds, the sky, leaves, a thrush, the Eglantine, a mountain stream. One stanza (which might almost have come from the "Mad Monk") will suffice to show the pattern:

> Roll back, sweet rill! back to thy mountain bounds,
> And there for ever be thy waters chain'd!
> For thou dost haunt the air with sounds
> That cannot be sustain'd;
> If still beneath that pine-tree's ragged bough
> Headlong yon waterfall must come,
> Oh let it then be dumb!—
> Be any thing, sweet rill, but that which thou art now."

The poet who overhears the complaint is deeply affected by it, just as in the "Mad Monk," though here he voices his response at greater length, turning finally to address his own loved one (in blank verse):

> Ah gentle Love! if ever thought was thine
> To store up kindred hours for me, thy face
> Turn from me, gentle Love! nor let me walk
> Within the sound of Emma's voice, or know
> Such happiness as I have known to-day.

The Longman manuscript of *Lyrical Ballads* 1800, Vol. II, in the Yale University Library, reveals that Emma's name was added in a revision of the poem's closing lines. There is no counterpart to her in the "Mad Monk," but the shadow of

21. It might be observed that an eight-line stanza containing a single alexandrine was later used for odes by both Coleridge ("Ode to Tranquillity," *STCPW*, I, 360–361) and Wordsworth ("Ode to Duty," *PW*, IV, 83–86). Gray's "Ode, to Adversity" doubtless served both poets as a model.

Lucy does fall across that poem. One stanza, spoken by the mournful voice, appears to recapitulate a poem of 1799 (published in 1800), "Strange fits of passion I have known":

> Last night, as o'er the sloping turf I trod,
>> The smooth green turf to me a vision gave:
>>> Beneath my eyes I saw the sod,
>>> The roof of Rosa's grave.

If we were to meet these four lines "running wild in the deserts of Arabia," as Coleridge once put it, would we not scream out, as he did, "Wordsworth!" *(STCL,* I, 453)? Concordance tests, if they were thought to be needed, would support us. The word "turf," never used by Coleridge (if we leave the "Mad Monk" itself out of the counts) occurs sixty times in the Wordsworth concordance; Coleridge used "trod" six times, to Wordsworth's forty-six. Tests made elsewhere in the poem show an equally startling bias. Coleridge never used "plot" to mean a piece of ground; Wordsworth used it fifteen times. Coleridge used "margin" only once (he preferred "marge"); Wordsworth used it thirty-four times. Coleridge never used "chestnut" ("a fine shewy tree and its wood excellent but that, alas! it dies away at the *heart* first—poor me!" he later wrote in his notebooks; entry 2914; October-November 1806); Wordsworth used it seven times (including plurals and compounds). Instances of this sort could be multiplied impressively.

In fact, so striking and so abundant is this kind of evidence that it has aroused suspicion. David Erdman has put the case that only intentional parody of Wordsworth's style could account for these verbal echoes and clusters of characteristic words.[22] That such evidence can be ambivalent, once the pos-

22. In his reply to my case for Wordsworth's authorship, "Who Wrote *The Mad Monk?" BNYPL,* 64 (April 1960), 224–237. Woof in his *SB* article, "Wordsworth's Poetry and Stuart's Newspapers," expresses partial agreement with Erdman. He thinks (p. 174) that Coleridge wrote the poem in parodic imitation not of Wordsworth but "of the kind of writing that Wordsworth and Coleridge attacked" in the 1800 Preface. The result is "what one might call a gothic pastoral elegy" (p. 176). As for the resemblance to " 'Tis said," Woof feels that may only imply "a lazy borrowing."

sibility of parody is raised, is indeed a fascinating notion: the more quintessentially Wordsworthian a passage is, in its vocabulary, tone, and style, the greater the likelihood that Coleridge wrote it! (One can only pray that this argument will not fall into the hands of the anti-Stratfordians.)

In writing up poems for the *Morning Post* Coleridge may very well have added some lines or stanzas of his own with burlesque intentions. He was capable of writing parodies, though most of those he had written were plainly marked. And he was capable of mocking Wordsworth. But there is a large objection to be raised here. If Coleridge made the "Mad Monk" into a parody, whatever it was to begin with, it must have been one sort of parody he defined contemptuously in the *Biographia:* (I, 55n): "an attempt to ridicule a silly and childish poem, by writing another still sillier and still more childish." And the poems of Wordsworth's that Coleridge would have had to think silly and childish—all then unpublished—were poems that we know he admired. They include a hypothetical early version of part of the "Intimations" ode and two Lucy poems turned in for the volume of 1800: "Strange fits of passion" and " 'Tis said, that some have died for love."

Burlesque of the first two pieces would have been incidental, and we probably need to consider only the third, which comes closest to the "Mad Monk." Could Coleridge have thought this poem silly and childish? The kind of analysis Erdman brought to bear on the "Mad Monk" might make quite a few of Wordsworth's poems look silly. The Gothic strain runs strong through the early verse and well into the 1800's, and its excesses can seem absurd. To take an example, if nobody in all of Wordsworth ever struck a wound, as Erdman observes in showing that the "Mad Monk" is a "travesty," nobody ever made his moan, either—except in " 'Tis said, that some have died for love." And what an absurd moan this is, complete with melodramatic gestures ("my hand is on my heart") and bold aggressive cries directed at insensate objects ("move thou cottage from behind that oak"). Can we be expected to take seriously the moan of a man who chases a harmless bird about? You there, "thou Thrush,"

Into yon row of willows flit,
Upon that alder sit;
Or sing another song, or chuse another tree.

Yet whatever strains of absurdity Coleridge may have found in this poem in 1800—and this is the point—he gave an extravagantly high opinion of it in 1817. Summing up Wordsworth's virtues in Chapter XXII of the *Biographia* (II, 123), Coleridge listed, fifth, "a meditative pathos, a union of deep and subtle thought with sensibility; a sympathy with man as man . . . Here the man and the poet lose and find themselves in each other, the one as glorified, the latter as substantiated. In this mild and philosophic pathos, Wordsworth appears to me without a compeer." The first poem he then cited as illustrating this high virtue was " 'Tis said, that some have died for love."

The "Mad Monk," if we take it to be essentially Wordsworth's poem, may be thought to illustrate this virtue to a lesser degree, mainly because it is less finished, more melodramatic. But it remains no less Wordsworthian, as the reader's sensibilities ought to confirm without the aid of thematic parallels or vocabulary counts. On the whole, it is impossible to imagine that the "Mad Monk" can be all Coleridge's and not at all Wordsworth's. The textual histories of the poems in whose company it turned up in the *Morning Post* suggest that it was a Wordsworth poem in its origins, touched up by Coleridge for one purpose or another.[23]

And here a final speculation, fragile but teasing, might be offered. The letter of 27 February 1799 in which Wordsworth sent Coleridge the poem Coleridge mailed to Stuart on 7 October

---

23. What Coleridge could have meant by identifying its manner with Mrs. Radcliffe's when he sent it to the *Morning Post* is hard to guess. Perhaps he took this means of labeling the poem a parody, as Erdman suggested, by emphasizing its Gothic qualities (in 1810 Coleridge offered Wordsworth the recipe for "a Romance in Mrs. Radcliffe's style"— *STCL*, III, 294), though no reader could be expected to know what it was a parody of, the pertinent poems of Wordsworth's being unpublished. Perhaps he meant something more subtle which now escapes us. Wordsworth, we might observe, had already written in Mrs. Radcliffe's manner: *The Borderers* owes something to her *Romance of the Forest*, and it was Mrs. Radcliffe who developed what has been called the explained supernatural, of the sort Wordsworth used in *Peter Bell*.

1800 under the title "Alcaeus to Sappho" contained another poem, now lost (see *EY*, 256n). But surely Coleridge in his urgent need would have sent this poem along to Stuart, too. If he did, and if Stuart printed it, the poem would have had to be the "Mad Monk" in its original form. Wordsworth alluded to his poem as "One day the darling of my heart," and this would then have had to be the opening line of a preamble or frame to the tale of the mad hermit. " 'Tis said, that some have died for love" has an analogous frame, the little epilogue spoken by the poet to his "Emma":

> Ah, gentle Love! if ever thought was thine
> To store up kindred hours for me, thy face
> Turn from me, gentle Love.

But one can press the speculation no further.

Hardly less teasing and rather more important are the "Mad Monk's" connections with Wordsworth's "Intimations" ode. Here the possibilities are clear and limited. One, widely accepted, is that at the very opening of his great ode Wordsworth echoed some lines of a poem which Coleridge had written two years earlier and published in a newspaper. A second is that Wordsworth used lines he had drafted some years earlier but which had meanwhile been publicly burlesqued by Coleridge. A third possibility is the simplest: that Wordsworth echoed some lines of a poem he had himself written, then discarded because he had worked up a more finished treatment of its theme.

There are sound reasons for thinking this possibility the likeliest. It is scarcely conceivable that Wordsworth's sensitivities would have allowed him to use lines of his own which he knew had been burlesqued; it is hard to believe that he would have imitated lines that Coleridge wrote. The partners in *Lyrical Ballads* were, we know, capable of echoing each other's work. Coleridge even picked up in "Dejection" one of the phrases shared by the "Mad Monk" and the "Intimations" ode: "There was a time when, though my path was rough." But we have no examples of imitation or parody that approximate the extended parallels here of form and language. The easiest thing to believe is that these parallels reveal the poet responsible for them not in the act of echoing another's work, but in the act of revising his own.

This conclusion, moreover, harmonizes with what we know about Wordsworth's poetic development. To put it very simply, the pertinent lines in the "Mad Monk" are spoken by a distracted lover for whom the "steady loveliness" of nature has vanished; their function is to reveal the passion and terror that color the speaker's mind—to follow, as it were, the fluxes and refluxes of his imagination. Here is the experimental technique of the early lyrical ballads. In " 'Tis said," which might be looked upon as a transition poem, similar lines are spoken by a bereaved lover, but here their function is to heighten for us the emotional fears and the affections of the poet, who steps into focus at the end of the poem. In the final stage, that represented in the "Intimations" ode, the lines are heard once more, this time in the poet's own voice. Their function is simply to express an experience of loss, and through it a deep personal feeling. Here is the mature technique of the *Prelude* and other philosophical verse. Excessively neat though it may seem, this progression accurately and strikingly recapitulates the growth of Wordsworth's poetic strategy.

The other great poem from the spring of 1802 is connected in rather different ways with some of the *Lyrical Ballads*, and tracing the connections may again help us to see the movement of Wordsworth's poetic strategy. In looking at the antecedents of "Resolution and Independence" we can follow the slow growth of a poetic idea through several trials and partial expressions, culminating in a major poem.

The incident at Grasmere in which the poem has been thought to take its origin—the meeting on a road with the old leech-gatherer—has long been identified in Dorothy's journal. As Dorothy observed him he was "an old man almost double," wearing a coat thrown over his shoulders like a cloak; of his ten children, she noted, all but one, a sailor, were dead. We have a general sense of the tradition that links this solitary old man with other solitary figures that appear to Wordsworth, some of them in certain "spots of time," to chasten or inform his sensibilities. The "Old Cumberland Beggar" presents in the figure of an aged wanderer "a silent monitor," though one incapable of providing either "fortitude" or "circumspection"; he only keeps the mind disposed to "virtue and true goodness." The encounter with the discharged soldier, taken into the *Prelude*, Book IV, opens like "Resolution and Independence" with a description of nature, featuring the glittering surface of the road and the peaceful sound of flowing water; the soldier's "stately air of mild indifference" and his ghastly calm seem to produce a "strange half-absence" in what he says; in the *Prelude* the meeting leaves the poet subdued, "with quiet heart."

But beyond these parallels, it should be remembered that "Resolution and Independence" is a refinement and development of at least two earlier efforts to treat the same theme in terms of the same events, and in something like the same language. The first of these efforts appeared in the *Lyrical Ballads* of 1800, number IV among "Poems on the Naming of Places." Composed in October 1800, about two weeks after the meeting on the road with the leech-gatherer, this poem commemorates a meeting of the same sort a month earlier on the shore of Grasmere lake. Although Wordsworth testified in his Fenwick note that "the fact occurred strictly as recorded" (*PW*, II, 488), Dorothy made no record of it in her journal, and one suspects that the two meetings were telescoped in Wordsworth's imagination, for they come out much alike in the telling. The poet in the company of two friends (Dorothy and Coleridge) was walking by the lake in "vacant mood" one "calm September morning," "delighted" to hear "the busy mirth" of reapers in the fields,

> when suddenly,
> Through a thin veil of glittering haze, we saw
> Before us on a point of jutting land
> The tall and upright figure of a Man
> Attir'd in peasant's garb, who stood alone
> Angling beside the margin of the lake.

The three friends at once rashly cry out at the idleness of anyone who can thus waste a day at harvest time. But upon approaching him they see

> a man worn down
> By sickness, gaunt and lean, with sunken cheeks
> And wasted limbs, his legs so long and lean
> That for my single self I look'd at them,
> Forgetful of the body they sustain'd.—

Too weak for the labor of harvesting, the man was trying to
extract a living from "the dead unfeeling lake." Subdued and
chastened, the three friends soon found

> The happy idleness of that sweet morn,
> With all its lovely images, was chang'd
> To serious musings and to self-reproach.

As the final lines of the poem report, they name the spot
"POINT RASH-JUDGEMENT" to commemorate the "admonish-
ment" they all received.

After the volume of 1800 was published, and the interval
of more than a year during which Wordsworth's creative energies lay virtually inactive, he touched peripherally on the theme
of "Resolution and Independence" at the very start of the lyric
outburst of 1802, by commemorating another encounter on the
road, of uncertain date. In her journal Dorothy called the poem
"The Singing Bird"; later it became "The Sailor's Mother." The
setting this time was a foggy wet morning, and the figure the
solitary poet meets is a woman wrapped in a cloak, a woman,
"Not old, though something past her prime," with "A Roman
Matron's gait." Bemused at first by her dignity and strength,
the poet shortly awakens from his "lofty thoughts" and proceeds to question the figure before him, as he questioned the
leech-gatherer. (My readings are from DC MS. 41.)

> With the first word I had to spare
> I said to her, "Beneath your cloak
> What is it you are carrying there?"

Her reply (she has a cage and bird that belonged to her dead son) is cast in some of the plainest colloquial speech that Wordsworth ever used in verse, and the poem ends flatly without any comment by the poet; the impression her words make upon his mind must be inferred by the reader.

At this stage in Wordsworth's development of this theme, Coleridge played a decisive role. In April 1802 he sent Wordsworth some poems, one of them trivial, another deeply serious. The trivial poem was "The Mad Moon in a Passion," accurately characterized by Robert Woof as "a slight, joking, familiar piece of verse arising out of Wordsworth's and Coleridge's habits of poeticizing."[24] Wordsworth's response to it took shape in "The Tinker" (*PW*, IV, 366–367). The serious poem was, of course, the "Dejection" ode in an early form, itself a response to the portion of Wordsworth's "Intimations" ode composed on 27 March. The relations between "Dejection" and Wordsworth's two great poems of 1802 are very important, but they have been widely and sensitively discussed, most recently by William Heath,[25] and there is no need to rehearse these discussions here. What is pertinent is that shortly after reading "Dejection" Wordsworth turned to the composition of "Resolution and Independence," drawing upon his memory of the incident eighteen months in the past and upon treatments of the theme he had already essayed.

Coleridge may have shown at this time some of the sardonic hostility he later expressed to the diction and management of "The Sailor's Mother." But the language of "Resolution and Independence" in its earliest version was hardly less colloquial than that of "The Sailor's Mother." Scraps of this version are found in the Longman manuscripts of the 1807 volumes (in the British Museum) and in a notebook that belonged to Sara Hutchinson (now DC MS. 41); these were printed for the

24. "A Coleridge-Wordsworth Manuscript and 'Sara Hutchinson's Poets,'" *SB*, 19 (1966), 226–231. George Whalley first published the poem, "A soliloquy of the full Moon, She being in a Mad Passion," in *Coleridge and Sara Hutchinson* (London: Routledge and Kegan Paul, 1955), pp. 5–7.

25. *Wordsworth and Coleridge: A Study of Their Literary Relationships in 1801–1802* (Oxford: Oxford University Press, Clarendon Press, 1970), pp. 69–107.

first time by Miss Darbishire in 1952 (*PW*, II, 539–541). One
stanza later deleted made the leech-gatherer oddly resemble
the Sailor's mother with her birdcage under her cloak:

> He wore a Cloak, the same as women wear
> As one whose blood did needful comfort lack:
> His face look'd pale as if it had grown fair
> And, furthermore, he had upon his back
> Beneath his cloak, a round and bulky Pack;
> A load of wool or raiment, as might seem,
> That on his shoulders lay as if it clave to him.

Another deleted stanza illustrates the plainness of the old man's
discourse, and his Wordsworthian particularity:

> Feeble I am in health these hills to climb
> Yet I procure a living of my own
> This is my summer work, in winter time
> I go with godly Books from Town to Town.
> Now I am seeking Leeches up & down
> From house to house I go, from Barn to Barn
> All over Cartmell Fells & up to Blellan Tarn.

Other scraps survive only in Wordsworth's comment on the
version, made in response to Sara Hutchinson's criticisms about
a month after he composed it. Although he revised the poem
almost at once, in response to the criticisms, dropping nearly
all the lines spoken directly by the leech-gatherer, he failed to
move far enough for Coleridge, who later found the poem dis-
figured by that characteristically Wordsworthian fault, "INCON-
STANCY of the *style*" (*BL*, II, 97).

Coleridge's criticisms were only echoes of the running disagreement over dramatic technique. What is important here
is the revelation of Wordsworth's artistic growth afforded by
the contrasts between "Resolution and Independence" and its
forerunners. For in "Resolution and Independence" Wordsworth adapted his earlier experiments to a style and verse form
used for a similar experiment by Chatterton, "the marvellous
Boy," and achieved at last the total design he seems to have
been forming.

Wordsworth's intentions are best revealed in his own explicit commentary, the letter to Mary and Sara Hutchinson of

14 June 1802 (*EY*, 364–367). "Resolution and Independence" opened, like "Point Rash-Judgement" and "The Sailor's Mother," in the "descriptive-meditative" convention, with an evocation of nature. After a night of wind and rain "the sun is rising calm and bright," birds sing in the woods, "And all the air is fill'd with pleasant noise of waters." But the commentary makes it clear that here nature is more than a frame, more than an instrument for softening the sensibilities. The experience of the poem is rooted in the working of nature on the mind. Moreover, the experience becomes, like Coleridge's in "Dejection," a deeply personal one, for the first time involving the poet in his role as poet.

I describe myself as having been exalted to the highest pitch of delight by the joyousness and beauty of Nature and then as depressed, even in the midst of those beautiful objects, to the lowest dejection and despair. A young Poet in the midst of the happiness of Nature is described as overwhelmed by the thought of the miserable reverses which have befallen the happiest of all men, viz Poets—I think of this till I am so deeply impressed by it, that I consider the manner in which I was rescued from my dejection and despair almost as an interposition of Providence. "Now whether it was by peculiar grace A leading from above"—

Wordsworth then takes some pains to set forth the meaning of this last phrase—to explain how by heightening the stature of the old man, removing him almost to another world, he had tried to communicate the supernatural feeling that enveloped his mind (he quotes from the early version of the poem an occasional phrase he later deleted).

A person reading this Poem with feelings like mine will have been awed and controuled, expecting almost something spiritual or supernatural—What is brought forward? "A lonely place, a Pond" "by which an old man *was*, far from all house or home"—not stood, not sat, but "*was*"—the figure presented in the most naked simplicity possible. This feeling of spirituality or supernaturalness is again referred to as being strong in my mind in this passage—"*How came he here* thought I or what can he be doing?" I then describe him, whether ill or well is not for me to judge with perfect confidence, but this I can *confidently* affirm, that, though I believe God has given me a strong imagination, I cannot conceive a figure more impressive than that of an old Man like this, the survivor of a Wife and ten children, travelling alone among the mountains and all lonely places, carrying with him his own fortitude, and the necessities which an unjust state of society has entailed upon him.

Wordsworth concluded his defense of the poem by justifying the plainness of the leech-gatherer's utterance on the grounds of dramatic propriety. "It is in the character of the old man to tell his story in a manner which an *impatient* reader must necessarily feel as tedious."

But there is a difference here from the kind of defense he had made of "The Thorn" two years earlier, as there is a difference in the two poems. The reader of "Resolution and Independence" has to be patient enough, one supposes, to sense the feelings of the old man, but more important—in fact, fundamental here to the esthetic experience—he has to "read with the feelings of the Author." For only if he does this will he receive the kind of pleasure the poem was intended to give— the pleasure of contemplating "the fortitude, independence, persevering spirit, and the general moral dignity of this old man's character." The difference points up the crucial shift in Wordsworth's poetic tactics. In "The Thorn" he had made a tree "impressive" by showing the reader the effect it had on a superstitious imagination; in "Resolution and Independence" he had made a man "impressive" by revealing directly the response his own imagination had made, and inviting the reader to share it. The center of this poem lies in the delineation not of a character's feelings but of the poet's own feelings, the ebb and flow, the fluxes and refluxes of conflicting emotions brought finally to a triumph over anxiety and despair.

When Wordsworth learned that he had failed in his aim in "The Thorn," he wrote a lengthy explanation but left the poem (for a time) as it was. When he learned that "Resolution and Independence" had failed for one or two of his readers, he revised the poem with no sense of betraying his principles. Persuaded, evidently by Sara, that naked simplicity was not enough to make his old man impressive, Wordsworth added a stanza in which he tried to achieve this aim by the use of imagery drawn from nature. This tactic was a new one in

Wordsworth's treatment of the theme. The old Cumberland beggar had been laconically described as "solitary" and "aged." The discharged Soldier, "tall / And lank, and upright," with arms "long & lean," loomed up both "ghostly" and "ghastly," but the most memorable phrases in the sketch present him as "a desolation, a simplicity."[26] The old fisherman in "Point Rash-Judgement" was "tall and upright," "gaunt and lean," but nothing more. The sailor's mother, though compared to "a mountain storm," is, by the device of a single image ("A Roman Matron's gait"), made to loom almost out of time, casting a momentary trance on the poet's imagination—but the image, of course, was drawn from history, not from nature.

The importance Wordsworth attached to the images he drew from three realms of nature to represent the leech-gatherer (a stone, a sea-beast, a cloud) is revealed in a brief comment he made in the 1815 Preface. These images, he said, illustrate the imagination's various powers. "The stone is endowed with something of the power of life to approximate it to the sea-beast; and the sea-beast stripped of some of its vital qualities to assimilate it to the stone; which intermediate image is thus treated for the purpose of bringing the original image, that of the stone, to a nearer resemblance to the figure and condition of the aged Man" (*PW*, II, 438). There is a loss as well as a gain in Wordsworth's releasing the active powers of his imagination for this assignment, instead of keeping them muted by implication and understatement, but no reader of "Resolution and Independence" is likely to feel regretful.

As a consequence of Wordsworth's revisions, the explications of "Resolution and Independence" become redundant; the poem's design stands forth in ample clarity. They help, however, to strengthen our awareness of design, of the artist's control shaping his poem to his ultimate esthetic purpose. Dorothy's simple postscript has the same effect. Reproving Sara Hutchinson for her imperceptiveness, she reminded her to look always for the real point or tendency of William's poems, "and above all never think that he writes for no reason but merely because a thing happened" (*EY*, 367).

26. I quote from the original version established by Beth Darlington, "Two Early Texts," *BWS*, pp. 425–448.

The history of "Resolution and Independence" loosely recapitulates the major steps in Wordsworth's artistic growth from 1797 through his great decade. A central turn took place in the summer of 1802, when in deference to Sara Hutchinson's criticisms and probably Coleridge's, he gave up the use of accidental circumstances and bald narrative detail that had distinguished his earlier experiments. But as we have noticed, the change in Wordsworth's manner in 1802 involved more than diction. The poems he wrote in the spring, except for a few he stubbornly cast in the early experimental style, are centered on the poet's own imaginative activity and illustrate the uses of nature that mark the mature Wordsworthian manner. Perhaps the best general comparison of the *Lyrical Ballads* with the lyrical pieces of 1802 and later remains Helen Darbishire's astute, sensitive introduction to her edition of the 1807 *Poems in Two Volumes*, written in 1914. "The language," she observed, "is no longer 'the language spoken by men' but the richly reminiscent language of the poets." Setting "Lucy Gray" (in which Wordsworth had tried, he said, "to exhibit poetically complete solitude") alongside "The Solitary Reaper," Miss Darbishire pointed to the significant difference: "In *Lucy Gray*, the concept of solitude is given objectively in the incidents and issue of the story, in *The Solitary Reaper* subjectively through the poet's vision of the scene."[27] Moreover, the later poem exhibits "the magic of poetry that accepts tradition, not of that which defies it," and this remark applies widely to the poems which Wordsworth wrote in the tradition of Jonson, Daniel, and other poets he read in his set of Anderson's *British Poets* in the silent year of 1801 and afterward.

The story of *Lyrical Ballads* does not stop at 1802, with the publication of the third edition, incorporating Wordsworth's last major revisions, for in later years Wordsworth turned back from time to time to the mode of his experimental poems. These ventures were rarely sustained, and seem to have been made with less and less assurance, but a few of them show revealing

27. I quote from Miss Darbishire's revised edition, *Poems in Two Volumes* (Oxford: Oxford University Press, Clarendon Press, 1952), pp. xliii–xliv.

affinities with earlier poems, along with revealing differences.

One such venture was "The Waggoner," the first long poem Wordsworth undertook after bringing the *Prelude* to completion. He wrote the poem the way he had written "The Idiot Boy," rapidly, *con amore*, "under a lively impulse of feeling,"[28] in a space of about two weeks at the beginning of 1806. He evidently meant to issue it with *Peter Bell*, which he regarded as a companion piece ("The Waggoner" being a poem of the Fancy, *Peter Bell* a poem of the Imagination). But checked by the "timid scruples" he names in a revision of the closing lines (see *PW*, II, 203–204), he held the poem unpublished for some thirteen years. When it did appear it had, like *Peter Bell*, been much revised, and only the first two manuscripts of 1806 give a true reflection of the poem we ought to think of as a late lyrical ballad.

Like *Peter Bell*, "The Waggoner" is a narrative framed by extended remarks made by the poet, remarks to which Wordsworth attached large importance. "The opening descriptive lines," he said later, were intended "to put his reader into the state of mind in which he wished it [the poem] to be read" (Grosart, III, 429–430). These lines are less dramatic than the prologue and frame lines of *Peter Bell*, but they show an equivalent plainness and a similar meditative play of the poet's fancy:

> At last this loitering day of June
> This long, long day is going out
> The Night-hawk is singing his frog-like tune
> Twirling his Watchman's rattle about
> That [?solitary] Bird
> Is all that can be heard
> In silence deeper far, than that of deepest noon.
>
> · · ·
>
> In the sky and on the hill
> Every thing is hush'd and still

28. See his letter to Hans Busk, 6 July 1819; *MY*, II, 547. The quotation is from Wordsworth's autograph note on one of the two earliest manuscripts of "The Waggoner," Ashley MS. 4637 in the British Museum, quoted by permission of the Trustees of the British Museum. All quotations from the poem's text are from the other early manuscript, DC MS. 56.

> The clouds shew here and there a spot
> Of a star that twinkles not
> The air is like a Lion's den
> Close and hot, and now and then
> Comes a tired and sultry breeze
> With a haunting, and a panting
> Like the stifling of disease.

This leisurely account of the weather was apparently meant to set up a contrast with the thunderstorm that shortly bursts, leading to the scene of drunken revelry in the poem's second canto. Wordsworth once again was trying to follow patterns set by Burns. He admired the delicate moral sympathy, mingled with gusto, with which Burns could portray drunkenness, in "Death and Doctor Hornbook" and other poems (see *HCR*, I, 88–89). In particular he liked Burns's contrast in "Tam o'Shanter" between the "anger of the tempest" and the roaring joyful confusion inside the tavern.[29] The tempest Wordsworth managed about in the way Burns had:

> total darkness came anon
> And he and everything was gone
> The rain rush'd down, the road was batter'd
> As with the weight of billows shatter'd

followed by:

> peals of thunder clap on clap
> With now and then a dismal flash
> And somewhere as it [seems] a crash
> Among the rocks with weight of rain.

Compare Burns's:

> The rattling showers rose on the blast;
> The speedy gleams the darkness swallow'd;
> Loud, deep, and lang, the thunder bellow'd.

Followed by:

> The doubling storm roars thro' the woods;
> The lightnings flash from pole to pole;
> Near and more near the thunders roll.[30]

29. "A Letter to a Friend of Robert Burns," Grosart, II, 13–14.
30. Burns, *Poems and Songs*, II, 559–560.

But the other side of the contrast Wordsworth managed less
well. Talking to Crabb Robinson he had singled out fourteen
lines of "Tam o'Shanter," beginning

> The night drave on wi' sangs and clatter;
> And ay the ale was growing better.

These lines Wordsworth evidently meant to imitate when he
presented the Waggoner and the Sailor drinking at the "Cherry
Tree":

> What bustling jostling high and low
> A universal overflow
> What tankards foaming from the tap
> What store of Cakes in every lap
> What thumping stumping overhead
>   . . .
> As if it heard the fiddle's call
> The pewter clatters on the wall
> The very bacon shews its feeling
> Swinging from the smoky ceiling.

While there are glimpses here of Wordsworth's old, mock-
heroic ballad style, comparison with Burns is disappointing.
The fault lies not simply in "The Waggoner's" diffuseness, as
compared to Burns's intensity (though for some readers that
may be reason enough to make the poem fail), but in Wordsworth's handling of the tactic he admired most of Burns, his
assumption, that is, of a poetic self and his projection of that
self as a dramatic personage into the narrative. For the poetic
speaker of "The Waggoner" is not at all like the poetic speaker
of "Tam o'Shanter." The story of Tam is told as though by a
man who shares the language, the superstitions, and the ambivalent moral attitudes of a Scottish villager; the story of Benjamin is told by "a simple water-drinking Bard" who stands
above the events and recites them in the self-conscious diction
of a story-teller. Where Burns's moral condemnation is pungent
and forthright, dramatically appropriate—

> Ah, *Tam!* Ah, *Tam!* thou'll get thy fairin!
> In hell they'll roast thee like a herrin!—

Wordsworth's sympathy is flat, rather sanctimonious, and entirely personal. In this regard, the differences between "The Waggoner" and *Peter Bell* in its earlier forms reveal a slackening in Wordsworth's control of his dramatic identity.

The long, self-conscious epilogue to "the Waggoner" brings once more into view a principle Wordsworth had cherished from the beginning of his concentration on the ballad. After completing the narrative of Benjamin, the poet turns to his listener, anticipating an objection:

> A poor Castastrophy say you
> Adventure never worth a song
> Be free to think so for I too
> Have thought so many times and long.

He goes on to answer the objection by giving an account of the poem's origins:

> But what I have and what I miss
> I sing of these it makes my bliss
> Nor is it I who play the part
> But a shy spirit in my heart
> That comes and goes, will sometimes leap
> From hiding-places ten years deep.

This account reminds us of one way of distinguishing Wordsworth's poems from "the popular Poetry of the day," by showing how "the feeling therein developed gives importance to the action and situation and not the action and situation to the feeling." In "The Waggoner," as in his earlier semidramatic poems, Wordsworth distinctively alters traditional notions of a ballad's purpose—to tell a story, relate an adventure, bring a narrative through its catastrophe to a moral summing-up. Resolved to avoid "gross and violent stimulants," Wordsworth denied any place to gaudy incident, or catastrophe, or "moving accident" at the center of a lyrical ballad. Some of the most characteristic and innovative ballads record events hardly worthy of recording, adventures hardly worth a song. "Simon Lee," to which Wordsworth pointed in the 1800 Preface when he offered some illustrations of the way his poems worked, provides a parallel to "The Waggoner," and illustrates the principle:

> My gentle reader, I perceive
> How patiently you've waited,
> And I'm afraid that you expect
> Some tale will be related.

The expectation is met with a disarming, low-keyed invitation to respond to the poem's quiet event in the way the poet had responded:

> O reader! had you in your mind
> Such stores as silent thought can bring,
> O gentle reader! you would find
> A tale in every thing.
> What more I have to say is short,
> I hope you'll kindly take it;
> It is no tale; but should you think,
> Perhaps a tale you'll make it.

The principle by which the traditional shape of the ballad was altered found its fullest illustration in the next long poem that Wordsworth completed after finishing "The Waggoner." Properly called the last lyrical ballad, "The White Doe" followed the plot of a ballad of Percy's,[31] but Wordsworth's version centered not on the physical events described but on the internal movements of imagination and feeling in the minds and hearts of the characters. In later years Wordsworth took pains to make this crucial difference clear. "The true action of the poem was spiritual," he said in 1836 of the work which he considered "in conception, the highest work he had ever produced" (Grosart, III, 430). The Fenwick note refuted comparison with poems and ballads of Scott's, thought to be similar. "Sir Walter pursued the customary and very natural course of conducting an action, presenting various turns of fortune, to some outstanding point on which the mind might rest as a termination or catastrophe. The course I attempted to pursue is entirely different" (*PW*, III, 543).

31. "The Rising in the North"; see *PW*, III, 538–542.

Wordsworth's attempt to pursue his course, to follow the principle by which the action of a ballad was internalized, spiritualized, like all the other innovative tactics of *Lyrical Ballads* brought him into conflict with Coleridge, who argued (rather querulously this time) from more conservative views. The conflict probably arose from the affinities between "The White Doe" and "Christabel." The preface Wordsworth wrote and intended to publish with his poem does not survive, but Coleridge told Bryon in 1815 that in it Wordsworth admitted "that the peculiar metre and mode of narration he had imitated from the Christabel" (*STCL*, IV, 603). What Coleridge meant by the mode of narration is not clear, but some of "The White Doe's" other features make it look in many ways like Wordsworth's answer to the supernatural themes and medieval apparatus of "Christabel." De Selincourt justly summarized their affinities to each other (and to Scott's "Lay of the Last Minstrel"): each "is a tale of feudal times, having as its heroine a lady of high birth surrounded by warring hates and the violence of battle, to which her innocence and beauty afford a striking contrast; each has a setting of northern landscape and medieval architecture, and each is in part bathed in the romantic atmosphere of moonlight."[32] It would not be hard to find even closer echoes of "Christabel," like these lines from an early manuscript of "The White Doe," later dropped (*PW*, III, 553):

> But list the dog, the household guard,
> Repeats a faint uneasy howl;
> And from the distant crags are heard
> The hootings of the riotous owl.

Coleridge's opinion of "The White Doe" was doubtless swayed by these affinities, and the poem reawakened a number of the old controversies between Wordsworth and himself. When Wordsworth finished it in January 1808, he intended to

32. Kathleen Coburn has enumerated other parallels between these two poems "of the Gothic romance genre, based on the commonplace Gothic materials": "Coleridge and Wordsworth and 'the Supernatural,' " *UTQ*, 25 (January 1956), 121–130.

have it published immediately. But moved perhaps by the
mixed reception of his 1807 volumes and by old habits of de-
pendency, he resolved to send the manuscript to Coleridge,
who was in London. Almost at once word came that Coleridge
had fallen alarmingly ill, and Wordsworth hurried there, expecting after consultation to see his poem through the press.
But Coleridge must have raised objections which the partners
were unable to resolve. After Wordsworth had gone back to
Grasmere, leaving Coleridge as "plenipotentiary" to handle
details of publication,[33] Coleridge talked of revising the poem,
and Dorothy, who was anxious to see the poem published and
disheartened by her brother's ebbing resolve, was obliged to
beg Coleridge "simply [to] mention the passages, to which
you object, without attempting to alter them" (*MY*, I, 230). In
due time Coleridge spelled out his objections in a letter to
Wordsworth that seems to have caused Wordsworth to with-
draw his manuscript and stop publication.[34]

Since the version of the poem that Coleridge saw no longer
survives, we cannot be sure just what his objections were. As
it now stands, and almost certainly in its original shape, "The
White Doe" has the superficial form of some of the curse
poems the partners had written in 1797 and 1798. It begins at
the scene of a tragic event, and describes the relics of the event
now visible: a ruined priory, a chapel, a graveyard, and a
ghostly animal that haunts one of the graves therein:

> It was a solitary mound:
> Which two spears' length of level ground
> Did from all other graves divide
> As if in some respect of pride
> Or sorrow that retains her mood,
> Still shy of human brotherhood
> Or guilt that humbly would express
> A penitential loneliness.[35]

33. So Coleridge told Longman on 23 May; *STCL*, III, 115.

34. Coleridge's letter can be read in de Selincourt's notes (*PW*, III,
545–547), together with a full account of the exasperations and mis-
understandings that arose from the incident; the full text is in *STCL*,
III, 107–115.

35. These lines appear in *PW*, III, 288, but I quote them from the
earliest MS, DC MS. 61.

After moving back through time and recounting the story, the poem ends where it began (*PW*, III, 340):

> by that single grave,
> That one sequestered hillock green.

But "The White Doe" is quite unlike the other ballad poems and curse poems, as Dorothy seemed to recognize when she wonderingly pronounced it upon its conclusion to be "very different from any other poem that my Brother has written" (*MY*, I, 187). The difference lay not simply in the style but in the management of the poem's events. Here Wordsworth moves as far as possible from a straightforward ballad recital. Dropping even the machinery of an observer or narrator, he places the center of the poem inside the sensibilities of the participants.

Coleridge would have understood that his partner's purpose was to internalize, to spiritualize, the "catastrophe" of the poem. Wordsworth must have explained this intention in discourse, and when he got back to Grasmere he spelled it out in a letter to Coleridge, refuting some criticisms made by Lamb and Hazlitt (who had seen the manuscript in London). He had told Lamb, he said (*MY*, I, 217–219), that "the main catastrophe was not a material but an intellectual one," that the "principle of action" of the characters was "throughout imaginative." Hence Lamb's notion "as to the principal characters doing nothing" was ridiculous, said Wordsworth. No true poet need feel obliged to provide external incidents, he continued, moving to an eloquent defense of the poetic ideal he had tried to achieve:

If he is to be a Dramatist, let him crowd his scene with gross and visible action; but if a narrative Poet, if the Poet is to be predominant over the Dramatist,—then let him see if there are no victories in the world of spirit, no changes, no commotions, no revolutions there, no fluxes and refluxes of the thoughts which may be made interesting by modest combinations with the stiller actions of the bodily frame, or with the gentler movements and milder appearances of society and social intercourse, or the still more mild and gentle solicitations of irrational and inanimate nature.

Coleridge would in earlier years have had some sympathy

with this poetic ideal, especially as it distinguished the poet from the dramatist, for his own supernatural poems had partially exemplified it. But in those years it was Wordsworth who had raised the pertinent objections, and the remarkable thing about Coleridge's criticism of "The White Doe" is the way in which it turns these very objections back upon Wordsworth. When "The Ancient Mariner" was still largely unwritten, Wordsworth, finding the proposed sequence of events too dreamlike, had suggested some incidents to provide logical connections—notably, the shooting of the albatross. When the poem was published he found among its "great defects" (in the severe note he published in 1800) the fact that "the events having no necessary connection do not produce each other," and that, moreover, the central character "does not act, but is continually acted upon." Eight years later Coleridge in his turn suggested delicately that "if there were any serious defect" in "The White Doe," "it consisted in a disproportion of the Accidents to the spiritual Incidents, and closely connected with this, if it be not indeed the same,—that Emily is indeed talked of, and once appears; but neither speaks nor acts in all the first 3 fourths of the Poem" (*STCL*, III, 107–108). To remedy this defect Coleridge "conceived two little Incidents" which, he felt, would with a little abridgment, "bring to a finer Balance the *Business* with the *Action* of the Tale."

As for the meter of "The White Doe," avowedly modeled on that of "Christabel," Coleridge again pointed back at Wordsworth charges Wordsworth himself had made. He dropped the preface when he gave the poem to Longman, he said, because he feared that the mention of any obligations might cause unwelcome talk (we should not be misled by Coleridge's complaint to Byron, that he had "not learnt with what motive Wordsworth omitted the original a[d]vertisement"; *STCL*, IV, 603). He then went on to raise some doubts.

The metre being—as you observed of your poem in general, rather dramatic than lyric, i.e., not such an arrangement of syllables, not such a metre, as acts a priori and with complete self-subsistence (as the simply anapestic in its smoothest form, or the praise of Bacchus in Dryden's Ode) but depending for it's beauty always, and often even for it's metrical existence, on the *sense* and *passion*—I have something like the same suspicion that you entertained concerning Xtable, how far this would or would not be an obstacle to its popularity.

Though he must have been conscious of the ironies in these remarks, Wordsworth would have been touched, too, in a sensitive spot by the appeal to reputation, and after an interval he rewrote the poem in an effort to meet Coleridge's objections. Coleridge may thus have helped to improve "The White Doe," at the cost of slowing its publication, but he also acted out once more the role he seems to have played through the years of *Lyrical Ballads*. Holding, that is, to a stubbornly conservative position, he disapproved—discriminatingly but unrelentingly—of his partner's innovative ventures into fresh modes and techniques, and ultimately checked their development.

Epilogue

No account of the Wordsworth-Coleridge partnership and of the poetry it nurtured could close without some notice of the Christmas at Coleorton in 1806—Coleridge's first Christmas in England after his return from Malta. He joined the Wordsworth household on 21 December with his son Hartley. "I think I never was more happy in my life," wrote Dorothy to Lady Beaumont, "than when we had had him an hour by the fireside; for his looks were much more like his own old self, and, though we only talked of common things, and of our Friends, we perceived that he was contented in his mind" (*MY*, I, 121). By that fireside in the evenings after Christmas Wordsworth read the *Prelude* aloud to the little circle which held "all, whom I deepliest love, in one room all," as Coleridge put it in his moving response to this experience, the ode "To William Wordsworth."[1] The lines in which Coleridge described those readings are some of the tenderest he ever wrote:

> Eve following eve,
> Dear tranquil Time, when the sweet sense of Home
> Becomes most sweet! hours for their own sake hail'd,
> And more desir'd, more precious, for thy song!
> In silence list'ning, like a devout Child,
> My soul lay passive; by thy various strain
> Driven as in surges now, beneath the stars,
> With momentary Stars of my own Birth,
> Fair constellated Foam still darting off
> Into the darkness! now a tranquil Sea
> Outspread and bright, yet swelling to the Moon!

Other less tranquil lines of Coleridge's response would have been evoked by the recollections and the prophecies that closed the *Prelude*. After recalling the summer "on Quantock's grassy Hills," the season "wherein we first / Together wanton'd in wild Poesy" (XIII, 393, 413–414), Wordsworth talked of the hopes he cherished for a future partnership in which he and

---

1. Quoted from the original version, given to Wordsworth; *STCPW*, II, 1083–1084.

Coleridge ("Restored to us in renovated health") would be "joint-labourers" in the work of redeeming modern men, fallen into idolatry and servitude:

> Prophets of Nature, we to them will speak
> A lasting inspiration, sanctified
> By reason and by truth; what we have loved,
> Others will love; and we may teach them how;
> Instruct them how the mind of man becomes
> A thousand times more beautiful than the earth
> On which he dwells.

Wordsworth's vision of the *Recluse* here revealed may have given Coleridge some delight, but his talk of Coleridge's regeneration could only have given pain. Setting forth his own vision of Wordsworth now securely lodged among "the truly Great" in "the Choir / Of ever-enduring Men," Coleridge told how Wordsworth's "faithful Hopes" of him only stirred old frustrations:

> O Friend! too well thou know'st, of what sad years
> The long suppression had benumb'd my soul,
>
> . . .
>
> Sense of pass'd Youth, and Manhood come in vain;
> And Genius given, and knowledge won in vain;
> And all, which I had cull'd in Wood-walks wild,
> And all, which patient Toil had rear'd, and all,
> Commune with Thee had open'd out, but Flowers
> Strew'd on my Corse, and borne upon my Bier,
> In the same Coffin, for the self-same Grave!

Coleridge's melancholy response, though itself a splendid brief revival of his poetic power, seemed to put out of question any renewal of creative partnership. Yet some renewal of shared endeavor and joint strategy did follow over the next three years, as Wordsworth finished the poems for his 1807 volumes and wrote "The White Doe," a little of the *Recluse*, and three or four prose essays, while Coleridge put *The Friend* together. We have already reviewed some of the conflicts and some of the critical writing provoked by this renewed collaboration. Its best poetic fruits were two blank-verse addresses, Coleridge's the poem with which it began, the lines "To W. Wordsworth," Wordsworth's a meditation evoked by his unhappy visit to Coleridge in London in the spring of 1808. The two poets had gone to a gallery together, and Wordsworth had twice heard Coleridge lecture on Shakespeare at the Royal Institution, but his time was spent, he said, "confined chiefly to Mr. Coleridge's sick room" (*MY*, II, 659), where they talked about "The White Doe" and other matters. He set out to return to Grasmere early Sunday morning, 3 April, "in a very thoughtful and melancholy state of mind" (*MY*, I, 209), torn by prophetic anxieties about his partner.

> Press'd with conflicting thoughts of love and fear
> I parted from thee, Friend, and took my way
> Through the great City.

In twenty powerful lines Wordsworth tells how his spirits were steadied (not restored) by a "visionary scene": the empty, winding streets whitened by a fresh snowfall, and looming up above, "pure, silent, solemn, beautiful,"

> The huge majestic Temple of St. Paul
> In awful sequestration, through a veil,
> Through its own sacred veil of falling snow.

Wordsworth left these lines unpublished, but they deserve the place Mrs. Moorman has given them (II, 125), beside his other spots of time.[2]

With the expiration of *The Friend* some two years later, the renewed partnership faded, to come to an end in the shattering estrangement of 1810. From this time onward Coleridge was too sorely hurt to give his open trust, Wordsworth too exasperated and embittered to require it. Yet Wordsworth remained as sensitive as ever to Coleridge's critical opinions. When he learned in 1815 that Coleridge was going to publish his lines of tribute, Wordsworth wrote to beg him not to:[3] "the commendation would be injurious to us both" (*MY*, II, 238). At the same time he asked peremptorily why Coleridge

2. They can now be read in *PW*, IV, 374–375, and Moorman, II, 126.
3. Coleridge went ahead with publication in *Sibylline Leaves* (1817) but revised the poem extensively and changed the title to "To a Gentleman . . ."

had been disappointed in the *Excursion:* "Pray point out to me
the most striking instances where I have failed." Coleridge's
polite and thoughtful reply (*STCL*, IV, 571–576), which we
have already glanced at, is prefaced by a reminiscence of the
conversations that took place at Racedown, Alfoxden, Grasmere, and elsewhere. He was disquieted, he said, at having
to write,

knowing how poor a substitute must Letters be for a vivâ voce examination of a Work with it's Author, Line by Line. It is most un-
comfortable from many, many Causes, to express anything but
sympathy, and gratulation to an absent friend, to whom for the
more substantial Third of a Life we have been habituated to look
up: especially, where our Love, tho' increased by many and different
influences, yet begun and throve and knit it's Joints in the perception of his Superiority. It is not in *written words*, but by the hundred modifications that Looks make, and Tone, and denial of the
FULL sense of the very words used, that one can reconcile the
struggle between sincerity and diffidence.

Coleridge went on to explain his disappointment by gently
reminding Wordsworth what his expectations were, and promised a fuller statement in the preface to his own poems he was
then writing. Two or three months later, when the preface
turned into a draft of the *Biographia* (owing partly to this exchange with Wordsworth), Coleridge accomplished brilliantly
what he knew he alone could do, that is, make a just and search-
ing appraisal of Wordsworth's defects and virtues, a "true
philosophical Critique" (*STCL*, IV, 620).

Wordsworth's reaction to the critique took two forms. Coleridge had not expected to "please or satisfy" his partner, and
he was right. Wordsworth expressed disapproval at once, telling
Crabb Robinson (*HCR*, I, 213) that the *Biographia* as a whole
had "given him no pleasure" and that he was "not satisfied"
with the evaluation of his poems ("the praise is extravagant and
the censure inconsiderate"). Nothing is more melancholy to
read than Robinson's account of a dinner party that took place
a few weeks later (*HCR*, I, 214–215), where the two poets appear to have acted out a grotesque parody of their old relationship:

Coleridge spoke of painting in that style of mysticism which is now his habit of feeling. Wordsworth met this by dry, unfeeling contradiction. The manner of Coleridge towards Wordsworth was most respectful, but Wordsworth towards Coleridge was cold and scornful. Coleridge declared that painting was not an art which could operate on the vulgar, and Wordsworth declared this opinion to be degrading to the art. Coleridge illustrated his assertions by reference to Raphael's Madonnas. Wordsworth could not think that a field for high intellect lay within such a subject as a mother and child, and when Coleridge talked of the divinity of those works, Wordsworth asked whether he thought he should have discerned those beauties if he had [not] known that Raphael was the artist; and when Coleridge said that was an unkind question, Wordsworth made no apology.[4]

The other way in which Wordsworth reacted to the *Biographia,* besides signaling cold disapproval, was to take meticulous note of Coleridge's criticisms and, as we have seen, to revise his poems to meet them. These revisions appeared in the volumes of 1820, but even afterward Wordsworth remained unwaveringly responsive to Coleridge's poetic judgment, however much it clashed against his own. In 1824 he sent Coleridge for critical appraisal his partly completed translation of Virgil. By this time Coleridge had become pretty well convinced that his partner's poetic faculties had declined. His thoughtful remarks on the Virgil exhibit delicacy and a sure critical sense. He had spent three days going through the first book of the translation, he wrote to Wordsworth, but he was troubled by

4. It is mainly Crabb Robinson on whom we rely for accounts of Wordsworth's attitudes toward Coleridge in the years that followed the estrangement, and we ought perhaps to allow for bias in these reports. Robinson had views of his own on poetry and on human nature and behavior. Yet we should not underrate the shrewdness and the insight of this remarkable observer. No literary man himself but an indefatigable reader and friend of literary men, Robinson formed acquaintances with nearly all the Romantic writers. He followed their works as they appeared, heard Hazlitt lecture, "listened with rapture to the dreamy monologues of Coleridge" and "relished the wit and pathos of Charles Lamb" (*HCR,* II, 775), visited Landor and Blake, traveled with Wordsworth and Southey, talked to Goethe about Byron, and lived long enough to greet new novels by Dickens and Thackeray, to dine with Emerson and go to breakfast parties with Browning ("the crazy poet, but a sensible man in prose conversation"—*HCR,* II, 642) and Tennyson ("who looks like a bandit of genius"—II, 591). Robinson's self-effacing, rather laconic reports have always the ring of authenticity.

an inability to strike the proper distance, and by his perception of Wordsworth's characteristic unevenness.

I am haunted by the apprehension that I am not feeling or thinking in the same spirit with you, at one time, and at another *too much* in the spirit of your writings. Since Milton, I know of no poet with so many *felicities* and unforgettable lines and stanzas as you. And to read, therefore, page after page without a single *brilliant* note, depresses me, and I grow peevish with you for having wasted your time on a work *so* much below you that you cannot *stoop* and *take.* (*STCL*, V, 353)

In the notes he made detailing comments on the translation (the MS is in the Wordsworth Library at Dove Cottage) Coleridge was freer and more direct. He found the task of translating Virgil scarcely possible at all, and Wordsworth's qualifications for it relatively weak. For these reasons, and more particularly because Wordsworth's reputation as a "Regenerator" of the English language would be tarnished by the Augustan diction of his translation, Coleridge flatly dissuaded publication. "For to *you* I dare not be insincere," he went on, softening his charge, "—tho' I conjecture, from some of your original Poems (of the more recent, I mean) that our tastes & judgements differ a shade or two more than formerly—& I am unfeignedly disposed to believe, that the long habits of minute discrimination have over-subtilized my perceptions." We do not know whether these notes were sent to Wordsworth, but the letter would have been enough. Wordsworth stopped work and left in manuscript what he had finished.[5]

The long, quiet epilogue to the partnership was brightened by a tour that Wordsworth and Coleridge impulsively made together through Belgium, Germany, and Holland in 1828, accompanied by Wordsworth's daughter Dora. Observers of the two poets on their travels remarked on the contrast in their appearance and manners—Coleridge dressed in black like a clergyman, "placid and benevolent," talking ceaselessly; Wordsworth dressed coarsely like a Westmorland farmer, bustling and practical, enthusiastically playing the role of

5. A portion of one book did appear in the *Philological Museum* in 1832.

tourist.[6] But observers also commented on their compatibility, their evident mutual respect.

The respect appears to have survived to the end. Wordsworth visited Coleridge several times in the winter of 1830–31 at Highgate and held "long conversations" with him (*LY*, II, 546). What they talked about we cannot know, but Coleridge's last recorded comments on his partner show most of the old admiration, along with the old regrets. The disagreement about dramatic method seems to have stayed at the front of his mind. "Can dialogues in verse be defended?" he asked in 1832, while speaking of Wordsworth, and promptly answered: "I cannot but think that a great philosophical poet ought always to teach the reader himself as from himself." Prose, he conjectured, may be a different matter, but in any case he had "no admiration for the practice of ventriloquizing through another man's mouth." Wordsworth, he continued, with "more of the genius of a great philosophical poet than any man I ever knew, or, as I believe, has existed in England since Milton," should never have dropped the contemplative manner. "His proper title is, *Spectator ab extra*."[7] Seven months later Coleridge seemed almost to forget that Wordsworth had ever held any other title—indeed, that there had ever been a difference between them about dramatic method. Wordsworth and Goethe shared, he said, an "utter non-sympathy with the subjects of their poetry. They are always, both of them, spectators *ab extra*,—feeling *for*, but never *with*, their characters."[8]

This confident and singularly forgetful pronouncement, uttered by an old man looking back over the years to events and persons and issues of his youth, forms a fittingly ironic close to this partnership. For Wordsworth was consistently critical of Goethe on about the same grounds as Coleridge's. He did not use the term "ventriloquism," but he appears to have had something like it in mind when he talked to Lady Richard-

6. See Moorman, II, 435–436.
7. "Table Talk," in Thomas Raysor, *Coleridge's Miscellaneous Criticism* (London: Constable and Co., 1936) pp. 411–412.
8. *Ibid.*, p. 415.

son in 1841 (Grosart, III, 435–436). (He also had in mind something like the notions of negative capability and the egotistical sublime.[9]) Believing Goethe overrated, Wordsworth could not rank him high in either class of great poets, those like Homer and Shakespeare, "whose universal minds are able to reach every variety of thought and feeling without bringing their own individuality before the reader," or those like Spenser and Milton, "whom you can trace individually in all they write." Goethe aimed to be in the first class, Wordsworth believed, but failed. "You find the man himself, the artificial man, where he should not be found." Goethe remained, in short, the *spectator ab extra*, incapable of dramatic self-projection, of disguising his own distinctive voice, of subsuming his own identity in the universal—like Wordsworth himself, in Coleridge's summary judgment.

Wordsworth's final words on Coleridge, uttered to Barron Field and other friends, were sympathetic and discriminating. When he learned of Coleridge's death in 1834, he confessed that even during their long separation "his mind has been habitually present with me, with an accompanying feeling that he was still in the flesh" (*LY*, II, 710). To another friend[10] he described Coleridge as "the most *wonderful* man" that he had ever known, and pronounced a judicious summary of his talents and accomplishments, citing the originality and seminal power of his thinking, while regretting the addiction to metaphysics: had he given his energies to poetry, "he might have done more permanently to enrich the literature, and to influence the thought of the nation, than any man of the age."

But these were private words. The last he published, and

9. These notions may have circulated for years before Keats gave them names and (later) a kind of authority. In January 1811 Lamb told Crabb Robinson that he thought Wordsworth somewhat narrow and rigid: "He does not, like Shakespeare, become everything he pleases, but forces the reader to submit to his individual feelings" (*HCR*, I, 17). Late that year, Coleridge made the same distinction between Shakespeare and Milton: "Shakespeare became all things well into which he infused himself, while all forms, all things became Milton" (Thomas Raysor, *Coleridge: Shakespearean Criticism*, 2nd ed., 2 vols. [London: J. M. Dent; New York: E. P. Dutton, 1960], II, 66–67).

10. R. P. Graves; Grosart, III, 469.

the last poetry that Coleridge directly inspired, were the lines put into the magnificent elegiac quatrains Wordsworth wrote almost *ex tempore* upon the death of James Hogg.

> The mighty Minstrel breathes no longer,
> 'Mid mouldering ruins low he lies;
> And death upon the braes of Yarrow,
> Has closed the Shepherd-poet's eyes:
>
> Nor has the rolling year twice measured,
> From sign to sign, its stedfast course,
> Since every mortal power of Coleridge
> Was frozen at its marvellous source;
>
> The 'rapt One, of the godlike forehead,
> The heaven-eyed creature sleeps in earth:
> And Lamb, the frolic and the gentle,
> Has vanished from his lonely hearth.
>
> Like clouds that rake the mountain-summits,
> Or waves that own no curbing hand,
> How fast has brother followed brother,
> From sunshine to the sunless land!

These lines, and the moving reflection on his own mortality which follows them, not grandly philosophical but ballad-like in their simplicity and power, make up Wordsworth's finest summary tribute to his partner in the great ballad-experiments undertaken nearly forty years earlier.

Index

Index

Omitted from this index are place names, names of fictional characters, and abbreviations for frequently cited standard editions (Grosart and Owen). The names of Wordsworth and Coleridge, titles like *Lyrical Ballads* and Dove Cottage Manuscripts, and terms like "poetic diction" and "dramatic" are not routinely indexed, lest the index engulf the book. But all works by Wordsworth and Coleridge *are* indexed (even a few unwritten ones), as are common terms or concepts of special interest.